Fallen Rook P

CW00796964

Scottish Broadsword
and
British Singlestick

Part of the Academy of Historical Arts Study Guide series.

Author:
Keith Farrell

Editor:
Daria Izdebska

1st Edition
20th October 2014
ISBN 978-0-9926735-1-2
Published by Fallen Rook Publishing

The Academy of Historical Arts and Fallen Rook Publishing are divisions within Triquetra Services (Scotland), a charitable organisation registered in Scotland: registration number SC042086.

Version and Copyright Information

Version: 1ˢᵗ Edition
Date: 20ᵗʰ October 2014
Copyright © Keith Farrell, 2014
ISBN 978-0-9926735-1-2

Note about Illustrations

Daria Izdebska designed the book cover, and Ben Kerr prepared the scanned illustrations from Roworth's 1798 treatise.

Publisher

This book has been published by Fallen Rook Publishing, a division of Triquetra Services (Scotland), which is a charity registered in Scotland with number SC042086; published in Glasgow, United Kingdom, in October 2014.

Table of Contents

Dedication:

To Daria, my dearest friend,
and my constant inspiration.

Acknowledgements

Various people have helped me immensely both with this book and with my general skills and direction in life.

Firstly, I would not have discovered an enjoyment for the Scottish broadsword if Paul Macdonald had not introduced me to it back in 2009. Since then, I have continued to work with it and have become fascinated by the weapon, its history and its culture.

Much of my work recreating the Scottish broadsword systems has been in cooperation with Ben Kerr, and I am grateful for the ideas, discussions, insights and training opportunities over the years. Thanks are also due for Ben's preparation of the scanned illustrations from the Roworth treatise.

Finally, I would like to thank Daria Izdebska for helping me improve my scholarship and my writing skills. She put up with me and gave me support throughout the process, for which I am immensely grateful, and she is responsible for both the delightful front cover and several thorough rounds of edits. My sincere thanks for all the help both directly and indirectly connected with this project!

Keith Farrell
4th August 2014

Foreword: why this book has been written

In August of 2013, my co-instructor Alex Bourdas and I published our first study guide, for German longsword. The original intention was to create a brief but comprehensive study guide for use within the Academy of Historical Arts, but the scope of the project ballooned and became more ambitious. The book became popular outwith the Academy and has become a standard textbook in some other schools as well.

In the Academy of Historical Arts, at least in Glasgow, our two main disciplines are the German longsword and the Scottish broadsword. Since we now have a study guide for the longsword, I thought it would be useful to have a book for the broadsword as well, so that students of that discipline would have a textbook to which to refer to help guide their studies.

This is not intended to be a book about the Jacobites or Highland clans. There is a wealth of literature already written about these aspects of history. There is less literature about historical Scottish swordsmanship, which is the subject of this work.

The structure of this book is quite different to that of the longsword study guide, since the nature of the discipline is very different. Students of the broadsword are lucky to have a choice of many manuals with clear instructions written in English, unlike the sources for Liechtenauer's longsword! However, there is often a lot of misunderstanding and misconception around the contexts of society and martial culture with regard to the Scots and the Highlanders in particular, so this seemed like an important aspect to address in this book.

My hope is that readers will find this book helpful, regardless of knowledge or experience with the broadsword. Maybe there will be some new information about the masters, or the discipline; perhaps some new information about the context that surrounds the broadsword. Perhaps a student will even be inspired to read further and produce his or her own research on the subject.

In terms of singlestick, this is a discipline we have practised for years in the Academy, without a huge amount of evidence to support our implementation of the practice. At the HEMAC Glasgow 2014 event, I ran a workshop exploring different singlestick methods and styles from across the centuries in the British Isles, which was a resounding success. I was asked to turn my lesson plan into an article, but I decided to do a proper job of exploring the subject and include it within this book.

Singlestick is often misunderstood; or at least, people tend to understand only a small part of the overall tradition. Hopefully this book will provide a useful reference for students, and I hope that I have managed to bring together much of the research on the subject and present it in a clear and readable fashion. I would not be surprised if I am missing some information on the subject, because there has not been much written literature produced about singlestick compared with other disciplines, but hopefully my readers will forgive any omissions on my part and instead take the opportunity to write something themselves to help improve the scope and availability of written material on the subject.

It is my intention that this book will be useful for students both within and outwith the Academy, and that it will help to inspire people to read further into the issue. In some areas, I had to cut short my explanations, to remain within the scope of this book. There were all kinds of paths that would have been fascinating to explore further! Perhaps over the next few years, others may choose to build upon the foundations set out here to produce better, more extensive scholarly works. I would be very happy if people could build upon my work and develop further literature to aid new students of these fascinating disciplines of broadsword and singlestick.

Sincerely,

Keith Farrell
Senior Instructor
Academy of Historical Arts
Triquetra Services (Scotland)
Registered Charity (SC042086)

Chapter 1: 17th - 19th Century Scotland

The Highlanders have become romanticised characters from history, cutting a dashing figure in the imagination with their kilt, broadsword and targe. However, such romantic ideals do not often match the realities of history. This chapter will provide information about the Scots in the 16th, 17th and 18th centuries, looking at their ways of fighting, along with relevant contextual information for the study of Scottish swordsmanship. Hopefully, readers will be inspired to emulate these feats of greatness and skill.

It is important to understand the contexts of society and martial culture at the time of the sources that we study, otherwise we run the risk of creating new misconceptions in our battle against older, more pervasive misconceptions.[1] Scottish history has the benefit of being entertaining as well as educational, so hopefully this part of the book will remain interesting and engaging while laying the appropriate foundations for understanding later chapters.

1.1   Scottish Royalty and the Jacobite Uprisings

To be able to understand the rest of this book, it will be helpful to have a rough idea of some key points in Scottish history. This section will provide a summary of some key events, showing how the country developed through the 16th, 17th and 18th centuries, and illustrating its changing relationships with England and France.

Even within Scotland itself, people from different areas and regions treated each other with hostility. The Highlanders and the Lowlanders regarded each other with suspicion, although much of the nobility tended to take the Lowland point of view. From 1567-1625, the monarch of Scotland was James VI. He did not travel far within his domains, and did not make the effort to visit the Highlands or islands. In fact, he viewed the Highlanders as

---

[1] Matt Galas. "The Notion of Martial Culture." Brian Price. *Teaching & Interpreting Historical Swordsmanship*. Highland Village: Chivalry Bookshelf, 2005. Page 18.

savages. He tried to impose a Lowland education upon the Highland nobles,[2] and his policies were designed to "extirpate all traces of Gaelic culture from Scotland."[3] This only helped to keep the two parts of the country culturally separate, rather than bringing them together and strengthening the internal bonds of the nation.

Queen Elizabeth I of England died on the 24th of March 1603 without an immediate heir. James VI of Scotland was the next closest relative, so he assumed the throne of England in April that year. Both kingdoms remained separate countries; although James had united the crowns and wanted to bring together the kingdoms into a single country called *Magna Britannica* (Great Britain),[4] there was no parliamentary union for another century.[5] Nonetheless, James took for himself the title of "King of Great Britain, France and Ireland" in 1604.[6]

When James VI died in 1625, he was succeeded by his son Charles I. Like his father, Charles made his court in England, and ruled Scotland by corresponding with the Scottish Parliament.[7] However, unlike his father, Charles did not understand his Scottish subjects very well, and his meddling style of government upset many of the people holding different forms of authority in Scotland, including the Church.[8]

These disagreements between the Scottish people and their king caused many Scots to sign the National Covenant in 1638 in an attempt to protect their right to practise their religion without royal interference. This led to the Bishops Wars from 1639-1641, which in turn sparked off the Wars of the Three Kingdoms: a set of civil wars against the rule of Charles I in each of the kingdoms

---

[2] Richard Oram. *The Kings and Queens of Scotland*. Stroud: Tempus Publishing, 2004. Page 228.
[3] Magnus Magnusson. *Scotland: the Story of a Nation*. London: HarperCollins, 2000. Page 406.
[4] Ibid. Page 401.
[5] Richard Oram, 2004. Pages 228-229.
[6] Magnus Magnusson, 2000. Page 401.
[7] Richard Oram, 2004. Pages 230 & 237.
[8] Ibid. Page 237.

of Scotland, England and Ireland, spanning a period of several years from 1644-1651.

The leader of the rebel forces in the English Civil War was of course the infamous Parliamentarian, Oliver Cromwell. The history of the English Civil War is worthy of its own study; suffice it to say here that Cromwell won the war, captured Charles I, had the king executed, and established England as a republic.

Although the Scots had fought a civil war over their disagreements with the policies of Charles I, they were unhappy about the execution of their king by a foreign state. Although Charles was king of both countries, the nations were not united in any other way, and the Scots did not approve of the fact that the English Parliament put the king of Scotland to death without any diplomatic proceedings.

 Prince Charles, the king's son, had escaped to France in 1644. The Scottish Parliament therefore named Prince Charles as their new king, Charles II, as soon as they heard that his father had been killed.[9]

In 1650, Charles II returned to Scotland, and signed the National Covenant. The support shown to the king by the Scottish Parliament upset the English Parliament, who took offence at the perceived Scottish defiance of their new republic. The English parliament dispatched Cromwell and his New Model Army to punish the Scottish Parliament. On the 3rd of September 1650, the English force met the Scottish army at the Battle of Dunbar, where Cromwell won a crushing victory. Cromwell then marched upon Edinburgh and established military occupation of Scotland that lasted until 1660.[10]

As Cromwell pushed further north into Scotland, Charles II put together a small army and invaded south into England. However, Cromwell hastened south and brought Charles II to battle at Worcester on the 3rd of September 1651. Exactly a year after his

---

[9] Ibid. Page 241.
[10] Ibid. Page 242.

major victory at Dunbar, Cromwell crushed another Scottish army, and forced Charles II to flee to France.[11]

In 1653, Cromwell dissolved the English Parliament, and on the 16th of December 1653, he became Lord Protector of England, Ireland and Scotland, effectively uniting the kingdoms under his rule. He died from ill health on the 3rd of September 1658.[12]

His son, Richard Cromwell, succeeded as Lord Protector – but was a weak ruler, and was forced to resign in 1659.[13] The Protectorate was over, and royalty was re-established. In 1660, Charles II was restored as king of England and Scotland. Over the next twenty years, Charles governed Scotland and tried to bring the Church more under his control. This led to another round of war with the Covenanters in 1679.[14] Charles put down the Covenanters, but he was no longer a popular monarch. He died in February 1685.

His younger brother James succeeded him, becoming James VII of Scotland and II of England. However, in the spring of 1685, he faced separate uprisings against him in both Scotland and England. James put down both rebellions and had the leaders executed.[15] However, his Catholicism was not popular in Scotland or in England. In November 1688, the Protestant Prince William of Orange invaded England, and James fled from London. The English Parliament decided that James had effectively abdicated in favour of William. Before the end of the year, the Scottish Parliament had made a similar decision, and so James VII and II was no longer king.[16] In 1689, the Scottish Parliament announced that William would become William II, king of Scotland. In England, he became William III.[17]

---

[11] Ibid. Page 243.

[12] Peter Gaunt. *Oliver Cromwell*. Oxford: Wiley-Blackwell, 1996. Page 204.

[13] James Rees Jones. *Country and Court: England 1658–1714*. London: Edward Arnold, 1978. Pages 113-120.

[14] Richard Oram, 2004. Page 244.

[15] Ibid. Pages 248-249.

[16] Ibid. Page 249.

[17] Ibid. Page 251.

Those who supported James and his right to the throne were known as the Jacobites. The first Jacobite uprising in Scotland against William took place in 1689, led by the Viscount Dundee. The royal army put down the uprising and William tried to rein in the Highland clans, leading to the infamous Massacre of Glencoe in 1692.[18]

In an attempt to placate the Scottish nation after this massacre, in 1695 William allowed the Scots to set up the Company of Scotland to pursue foreign trade. This development allowed Scotland to trade with England's colonies, something hitherto forbidden by England's Navigation Acts.[19]

This also allowed Scotland to attempt its disastrous Darien Scheme: the establishment of a colony on the Isthmus of Panama, to control trade flowing between the Atlantic and the Pacific. For this venture, the Company raised between £220,000 and £400,000, a sum which has been described as "a quarter"[20] or perhaps even "half the total available capital in Scotland."[21]

However, in 1699 the colony failed for the first time due to problems such as disease and attacks by the Spanish. Scotland sent a second expedition, which failed in 1700. Thus, Scotland's economy took a major blow. William's poor handling of this affair (such as not allowing English colonies to provide support for the failing Scottish colony, to avoid antagonising Spain) meant that many Scots who lost their money on the venture were even less happy with their king.[22] In 1700, William and the English House of Lords proposed a closer union between England and Scotland, but the House of Commons rejected the notion.[23]

In 1701, James VII died in France, and his son Prince James was declared by the French king to be "King James VIII and III of

---

[18] Ibid. Pages 252-253.
[19] Ibid. Page 253.
[20] Magnus Magnusson, 2000. Page 528.
[21] John Prebble. *The Darien Disaster*. New York: Holt, Rinehart and Winston, 1968. Page 56.
[22] Richard Oram, 2004. Page 254.
[23] Magnus Magnusson, 2000. Page 532.

Great Britain",[24] encouraging the Jacobite supporters in Scotland. The English Parliament did not want to see another Catholic James on the throne, so in 1701 they passed the Act of Settlement to ensure that the succession of the English and Irish crowns after William would go first to his sister-in-law Anne and then to the Protestant house of Hanover, rather than to James.

William died in 1702 and was succeeded by Anne, who ruled until 1714. She was "concerned with the stability of her realms",[25] and believed that Scotland was "of immense importance to English security".[26] As far as she was concerned, uniting the Parliaments of the two countries was a critical step to ensure that her kingdoms remained safe, secure and stable.[27]

However, the Scottish Parliament passed the Act of Security in 1703, stating that after Anne's death, the crown of Scotland would not go to the successor of the crown of England, unless the Scottish Parliament agreed that it was in the best interests of Scotland. Effectively, Scotland was preparing to place the Catholic prince James on the throne, with French backing. This, along with other provocations, made the English Parliament worry about their continued security.[28]

The English Parliament responded in 1705 with the Alien Act, described as "An Act for the effectual securing of the kingdom of England from the apparent dangers that may arise from several Acts lately passed by the Parliament of Scotland."[29] It threatened economic sanctions unless the Scottish Parliament sent representatives to negotiate an "Incorporating Union" between the two countries.[30] These representatives were duly nominated, along with representatives of the English Parliament, and between them they negotiated the Articles of Union.

---

[24] Ibid. Page 533.
[25] Ibid. Page 540.
[26] Ibid. Page 539.
[27] Ibid. Page 540.
[28] Ibid. Pages 541-542.
[29] Ibid. Page 543.
[30] Ibid.

From the 3rd of October 1706 until the 16th of January 1707, the Scottish Parliament debated these Articles to decide whether or not to accept them. On the 16th of January, the final vote was held, and the Treaty of Union was ratified. The English Parliament ratified the Treaty on the 19th of March, and so the Treaty and Act of Union came into force on the 1st of May 1707.[31]

Many people of Scotland were not very happy about this. In 1713, the House of Commons levied a tax on malt in Scotland, in contravention of the Act of Union. The Earl of Seafield, the Duke of Argyll and the Earl of Mar put forward a Resolution to the House of Lords demanding the repeal of the Act of Union, which was defeated by a tiny majority of only four votes. The nobility of both Scotland and England were unhappy with the state of affairs. All of this led to a growing resentment in Scotland, and a growing support of the Jacobite cause.[32]

In 1708, Louis XIV of France hatched a plan with Prince James with a French contingent of 5000 soldiers, and a fleet to bring him and the troops to Scotland. The intention was that James would then raise an army of those Scots who were loyal to his cause. The French fleet set sail, but the Royal Navy did not allow the landing to take place, and so the French admiral returned the fleet to France. The 1708 uprising never quite managed to begin.[33]

In 1714, Queen Anne died, and her successor George, Elector of Hanover, landed in England to claim his crown. Across the whole of Britain, people resented that the crown was to be taken by a German.

In September 1715, there was a brief and unsuccessful Jacobite uprising in the West Counties of England. In October and November, another small uprising of English Jacobites took place in northern England, but this was also unsuccessful. [34] It is interesting to see that these two uprisings, entirely independent of the larger and better known Scottish uprising that same year,

---

[31] Ibid. Page 553.
[32] Ibid. Page 557.
[33] Ibid. Pages 559-560.
[34] Ibid. Page 563.

were rebellions by English supporters of the Jacobite cause. Not all Jacobites were Scottish.

In the same month, the Earl of Mar raised the flag of "King James" at Braemar, gathering Highland nobles and fighting men to the standard. This force laid siege to Perth and took it in the name of King James. At the same time, there was an uprising of Jacobite supporters in the western Highlands, although their initial engagements with government forces were unsuccessful. The two Jacobite groups joined forces in late October.[35]

This combined force numbered more than 10,000 men, and was a significant fighting force. Magnus Magnusson makes the important note that this army was "by no means an exclusively Highland army: nearly half of its strength consisted of units from the lowlands of the north-east. It was in an important sense a national army, intent on fighting for liberty, breaking the Union with England and restoring the Stewart dynasty to the throne of Scotland."[36]

At the Battle of Sheriffmuir on the 13th of November 1715, a government army under the Duke of Argyll met the Jacobite army and prevented it from advancing any further. Although the battle was more or less a draw, afterwards the Jacobite campaign lost much of its momentum. Prince James landed in Scotland on the 22nd of December. In January, he set up court in Perth for three weeks, but then retreated to Montrose where he took a ship to Flanders. The 1715 uprising was also a failed attempt to re-establish the Stewart monarchy in Scotland.[37]

In 1716, Parliament passed a Disarming Act, making it illegal for anyone to possess "Broad Sword or Target, Poignard, Whinger or Durk, Side Pistol, Gun, or other warlike Weapon".[38] However, this Act was not very well enforced, so the Jacobites retained weapons that were in good condition, only handing in those that were in too

---

[35] Ibid.
[36] Ibid.
[37] Ibid. Pages 565-566.
[38] John Gibson. *Traditional Gaelic Bagpiping, 1745-1945*. Montreal: McGill-Queen's University Press, 1998. Page 26.

poor condition for further use. The Act was even beneficial to those it was supposed to inhibit: since the government provided compensation for weapons handed in by the Highlanders, some Jacobites imported large numbers of scrap weapons from the continent and handed them in to the government, making a large profit from the compensation![39]

In 1719, another uprising took place, this time supported by Spain instead of France. The intention was to make two landings in Britain: one main invasion of England, and a diversionary landing in the north of Scotland. The main invasion fleet suffered disaster from the weather in the English Channel, and never made it to Britain. However, the smaller fleet carrying the diversionary force managed to land on the Isle of Lewis, where local Jacobites joined the Spanish troops.[40]

They crossed to the mainland, establishing their headquarters in Eileen Donan castle. It was here that they received news of the failure of the main invasion fleet. There was disagreement in the Jacobite ranks: some wanted to embark onto the Spanish ships and leave Scotland, others wanted to remain. George Keith, the Earl Marischal of Scotland, sent away the Spanish ships to quell any arguments against remaining.[41]

A Royal Navy squadron bombarded Eileen Donan, destroying the castle. The government also dispatched a sizeable land force of infantry, cavalry and artillery from Inverness. On the 10th of June, this government force encountered the Jacobite and Spanish troops at Glen Shiel. By the end of the day, the government forces had won the field and caused the Jacobites and Spanish to withdraw. The following day, the Spanish surrendered, while the Jacobites melted back into the Highlands. Thus the 1719 uprising also ended in failure.[42]

---

[39] William Taylor. *The Military Roads in Scotland*. Isle of Colonsay: House of Lochar, 1996. Page 18.
[40] Magnus Magnusson, 2000. Pages 571-572.
[41] Ibid. Pages 572-573.
[42] Ibid. Pages 573-574.

In 1725, General Wade arrived in the Highlands, with the task of upholding the law, improving order, and further pacifying the Highland clans. He undertook several building projects to improve military facilities, but one of his greatest contributions to Scottish infrastructure was the huge system of roads that he built.

He raised six Highland Companies, to be a police force in the Highlands. These became the Black Watch, which later became the 42nd Regiment of Foot in the British Army. He also enforced the 1725 Disarming Act, a stronger version of the 1716 legislation, although this new Act was just as ineffective as the previous one.

In 1727, the Hanoverian king George I was succeeded by his son, now George II. Around the 1730s, Scotland was beginning to prosper from the economic benefits of the Union. Jacobite support seemed to be dwindling.[43]

On the 23rd of December 1743, Prince James, the so-called "James VIII and III", formally appointed his son Charles (the "Bonnie Prince Charlie") as Prince Regent. France had been planning an invasion of Britain for early the following year, intending to land in England and collect English Jacobite supporters to bolster their numbers. There was also to be a diversionary landing in Scotland. However, in typical fashion, the main French fleet ran into stormy weather, and the invasion failed before it even made contact with the Royal Navy. The 1744 invasion was called off.[44]

Prince Charles had sailed with the French fleet, but had returned to France after the storm. He tried to convince the French to mount another invasion, but Louis XV refused. Therefore, Charles organised a new invasion on his own initiative, raising funds for the expedition, and trying to rally supporters. He sailed for Scotland on the 5th of July 1745. En route, his two ships encountered a British warship: in the ensuing engagement, the main transport ship carrying most of the mercenaries and military equipment was badly damaged, and had to return to France.

---

[43] Ibid. Page 584.
[44] Ibid. Page 585.

Charles continued with a single ship, landing at Eriskay on the 23[45]rd of July.[45]

Initially the Highland lords were unwilling to pledge their support to this poorly equipped and relatively unsupported uprising. However, once Charles travelled to the mainland, his following gradually increased. He raised his standard at Glenfinnan on the 12th of August, and from there, he and his force travelled south.[46]

On the 17th of September, the Jacobite force occupied Edinburgh. Just four days later, the government army engaged the Jacobites at the Battle of Prestonpans. The battle lasted merely ten minutes and was disastrous for the government.[47]

Although matters seemed to be going well for the Jacobites, their force was still very small, numbering less than 2000 men. Comparatively, the north of the country was strongly supportive of the government, raising a further 20 Highland Companies for the British Army. Parts of the lowlands were also staunchly against the Jacobite cause, with Glasgow and Ayrshire showing particular hostility to the Prince.[48]

The Jacobites went to great lengths to recruit more chieftains to their cause, and by the end of October, their force numbers more than 5000 infantry, and at least 500 cavalry. Artillery was sent from France to support the Jacobites. Further French support was promised, with plans laid to invade England in December 1745. The British government prepared for full-scale war.[49]

In November, the Jacobites marched south into England, occupying Carlisle and other towns, finally reaching Derby. They intended to gather support from English Jacobites in Lancashire and Manchester, but little such support was forthcoming. On the 4th of December, the Jacobites held a council of war in Derby, to discuss their strategy. Lord George Murray and most of the other

---

[45] Ibid. Page 586.
[46] Ibid. Pages 589-590.
[47] Ibid. Page 594.
[48] Ibid. Page 597.
[49] Ibid. Pages 598-599.

high-ranking officers urged the Prince to retreat and avoid destruction at the hands of the government armies that were closing upon their position. Murray managed to convince the Prince to withdraw, but Charles was furious, and decided not to take any further advice from his most able advisors. On the 6th of December, the Jacobite army withdraw back towards Scotland, crossing the border on the 20th.[50]

Upon their return to Scotland, Charles found that the government had consolidated and improved its military position in Scotland, retaking Edinburgh, and strengthening its various garrisons. However, the Jacobite garrison in Perth had also grown in size, as news of the Prince's march southwards had reached the Highlands. This brought another 4000 men into the Prince's forces.[51]

The Prince gathered his forces and marched towards Stirling. On the 17th of January 1746, part of his army came into contact with government forces of General Hawley at Falkirk Muir. The Jacobites won the battle, although their leaders did not pursue the advantage, and this lost the Jacobites the initiative that they needed for the rest of their campaign. Meanwhile, the Prince was descending into alcoholism, and he was losing his ability to make coherent decisions.[52]

On the 30th of January, the Duke of Cumberland arrived in Edinburgh to relieve General Hawley of command. The Jacobites returned to Perth after failing to take Stirling Castle, then decided to move north to Inverness. Cumberland's forces pursued the Jacobites. The forces came together at the field of Culloden, just outside Inverness.

On the 16th of April 1746, the Battle of Culloden was fought. It was disastrous for the Jacobites, and the Prince's army was completely routed from the field. The 1745 uprising had failed, like each uprising before it. The Prince's hopes of regaining the

---

[50] Ibid. Pages 603-605.
[51] Ibid. Page 607.
[52] Ibid. Pages 608-609.

throne of Scotland were shattered: he fled to Skye, and then to France, and he died a broken man in 1788.[53]

In 1746, a new disarming law called the Act of Proscription came into being, although it was not enforced until 1747. It was more severe than the Act that followed the 1715 uprising. Rather than banning specified weapons, like the 1716 Act, it simply banned all "Arms and warlike Weapons", although specified groups of people were allowed to continue to possess and bear arms.[54] It also took measures to ban common items of Highland dress, such as the plaid and kilt.[55] The Act was modified and extended in 1747 and 1748 – although neither of these additions, nor the original legislation, outlawed bagpipes, as is commonly assumed to have been the case.[56] The Act of Proscription was eventually repealed in 1782.[57]

After this last Jacobite uprising, some Jacobite sympathies still simmered among the British populace, but Scotland stopped trying to place a Stewart king upon the throne. Rather than working against the government, the country as a whole began to throw itself into the Union and work towards the greater good of the nation.

1.2 The Scottish People

Where possible in the rest of this chapter, I intend to provide excerpts from primary sources where possible to show and illustrate how the Scots and their visitors perceived the country during the time period in question, and shortly afterwards. To accomplish this, I will provide several quoted passages, although I will do my best to keep them concise and relevant!

---

[53] Peter Harrington. *Culloden 1746: The Highland Clans' Last Charge*. London: Osprey, 1991. Page 86.
[54] John Gibson, 1998. Page 26.
[55] Ibid. Pages 27-28.
[56] Ibid. Page 28.
[57] Ibid. Page 30.

A Warlike Society

Before Culloden, the Highlanders were a warlike society and they enjoyed both using and bearing arms. Weapons were carried openly in public, even at the market and at church. This state of affairs was regarded in the Highlands as being entirely normal:

> The habits of the Highlanders were also, at this time, essentially warlike. "The use of arms," to borrow a description from an anonymous writer, "formed their common occupation, and the affairs of war their ordinary pursuit. They appeared on all public occasions, at market, and even at church, with their broadswords and their dirks; and, more recently, when the use of fire-arms became general, they seldom travelled without a musket and pistol."[58]

Even after the disarming Acts were passed by Parliament, some Scots would still go about wearing their blades, and others would take up military service in the Highland Regiments for the opportunity to continue to wear weapons. Major General David Stewart made the following observations:

> In the Highlands, men were accustomed to go continually armed,—a custom which they were most anxious to retain. At the period now under consideration, the carrying of arms was prohibited by penalties; less severe, indeed, than those which were afterwards enacted, but sufficiently galling to a high-spirited and warlike people. Young men, therefore, gladly availed themselves of the privilege of engaging in a profession which relieved them from the sense of degradation and dishonour attached to the idea of being disarmed.

> Hence it became an object of ambition with all the young men of spirit to be admitted, even as privates, into a service which procured them the privilege of wearing arms. [An old gentleman in Athole, a friend of mine, Mr Robertson of Auchleeks, carried this spirit so far, that, disobeying all restrictions against carrying arms, he never laid them aside, and wore his dirk even when sitting in his dining-room, until his death, in his 87th year.] This accounts for the great number of men of respectable families who

---

[58] A.T. Thomson. *Memoirs of the Jacobites of 1715 and 1745.* Vol. 2, London: R. Bentley, 1845. "Rob Roy MacGregor Campbell."

were to be found in the ranks of the Black Watch,—a circumstance which has often excited the surprise of those who were ignorant of the extent to which the motives above mentioned operated.[59]

Across Scotland, people were used to war. Such state of affairs, from small disagreements or armed altercations to larger uprisings and campaigns, was not unusual. Several generations of the same family in Edinburgh could remember one conflict or another, not a single generation without experience of war:

> Sir Walter Scott observes, that the generation of his own time alone can remember Edinburgh in peace, undisturbed by civil commotion. The fathers of that generation remembered the days of 1745—their fathers the disturbances of 1715. The fathers of those who had witnessed the rebellion of 1715 could remember the revolution of 1688.[60]

Since violence and weapons were common in the Highlands, it was to these that people turned for justice when the law would not (or was unable to) help. Samuel Johnson described the "irregular justice" that was present in the Highlands, and noted that after the Act of Proscription and other Acts designed to improve the state of lawfulness in Scotland, thievery had begun to be repressed and that now people could travel through the Highlands "without danger, fear or molestation":

> In the Highlands it was a law, that if a robber was sheltered from justice, any man of the same clan might be taken in his place.

> This was a kind of irregular justice, which, though necessary in savage times, could hardly fail to end in a feud, and a feud once kindled among an idle people with no variety of pursuits to divert their thoughts, burnt on for ages either sullenly glowing in secret mischief, or openly blazing into public violence. Of the effects of this violent judicature, there are not wanting memorials. The cave is now to be seen to which one of the Campbells, who had injured

[59] David Stewart. *Sketches of The Character, Manners and Present State of the Highlanders of Scotland; with details of The Military Service of the Highland Regiments*. Vol. 1, 3rd edition, Edinburgh: Archibald Constable and Co, 1825. Part 3, "Section I – Black Watch."
[60] A.T. Thomson, Vol. 3, 1845. "Lord George Murray."

the Macdonalds, retired with a body of his own clan. The Macdonalds required the offender, and being refused, made a fire at the mouth of the cave, by which he and his adherents were suffocated together.

Mountaineers are warlike, because by their feuds and competitions they consider themselves as surrounded with enemies, and are always prepared to repel incursions, or to make them. Like the Greeks in their unpolished state, described by Thucydides, the Highlanders, till lately, went always armed, and carried their weapons to visits, and to church.

Mountaineers are thievish, because they are poor, and having neither manufactures nor commerce, can grow richer only by robbery.

They regularly plunder their neighbours, for their neighbours are commonly their enemies; and having lost that reverence for property, by which the order of civil life is preserved, soon consider all as enemies, whom they do not reckon as friends, and think themselves licensed to invade whatever they are not obliged to protect.

By a strict administration of the laws, since the laws have been introduced into the Highlands, this disposition to thievery is very much represt. Thirty years ago no herd had ever been conducted through the mountains, without paying tribute in the night, to some of the clans; but cattle are now driven, and passengers travel without danger, fear, or molestation.

Among a warlike people, the quality of highest esteem is personal courage, and with the ostentatious display of courage are closely connected promptitude of offence and quickness of resentment. The Highlanders, before they were disarmed, were so addicted to quarrels, that the boys used to follow any publick procession or ceremony, however festive, or however solemn, in expectation of the battle, which was sure to happen before the company dispersed.[61]

Samuel Johnson travelled through the Highlands in 1773, during which time he observed that certain far-flung parts of the country

---

[61] Samuel Johnson. *A Journey to the Western Islands of Scotland*. London: W. Strahan, 1775. Pages 96-99.

were left undefended by these disarming acts. He spent some time ruminating about the ethics of disarming a nation and concluded that it is not always the right thing to do:

> The last law, by which the Highlanders are deprived of their arms, has operated with efficacy beyond expectation. Of former statutes made with the same design, the execution had been feeble, and the effect inconsiderable. Concealment was undoubtedly practised, and perhaps often with connivance. There was tenderness, or partiality, on one side, and obstinacy on the other. But the law, which followed the victory of Culloden, found the whole nation dejected and intimidated; informations were given without danger, and without fear, and the arms were collected with such rigour, that every house was despoiled of its defence.

> To disarm part of the Highlands, could give no reasonable occasion of complaint. Every government must be allowed the power of taking away the weapon that is lifted against it. But the loyal clans murmured, with some appearance of justice, that after having defended the King, they were forbidden for the future to defend themselves; and that the sword should be forfeited, which had been legally employed. Their case is undoubtedly hard, but in political regulations, good cannot be complete, it can only be predominant.

> Whether by disarming a people thus broken into several tribes, and thus remote from the seat of power, more good than evil has been produced, may deserve inquiry. The supreme power in every community has the right of debarring every individual, and every subordinate society from self-defence, only because the supreme power is able to defend them; and therefore where the governor cannot act, he must trust the subject to act for himself. These Islands might be wasted with fire and sword before their sovereign would know their distress. A gang of robbers, such as has been lately found confederating themselves in the Highlands, might lay a wide region under contribution. The crew of a petty privateer might land on the largest and most wealthy of the Islands, and riot without control in cruelty and waste. It was observed by one of the Chiefs of Skye, that fifty armed men might, without resistance ravage the country. Laws that place the subjects in such a state, contravene the first principles of the compact of authority: they exact obedience, and yield no protection.

It affords a generous and manly pleasure to conceive a little nation gathering its fruits and tending its herds with fearless confidence, though it lies open on every side to invasion, where, in contempt of walls and trenches, every man sleeps securely with his sword beside him; where all on the first approach of hostility came together at the call to battle, as at a summons to a festal show; and committing their cattle to the care of those whom age or nature has disabled, engage the enemy with that competition for hazard and for glory, which operate in men that fight under the eye of those, whose dislike or kindness they have always considered as the greatest evil or the greatest good.

This was, in the beginning of the present century, the state of the Highlands. Every man was a soldier, who partook of national confidence, and interested himself in national honour. To lose this spirit, is to lose what no small advantage will compensate.

It may likewise deserve to be inquired, whether a great nation ought to be totally commercial? whether amidst the uncertainty of human affairs, too much attention to one mode of happiness may not endanger others? whether the pride of riches must not sometimes have recourse to the protection of courage? and whether, if it be necessary to preserve in some part of the empire the military spirit, it can subsist more commodiously in any place, than in remote and unprofitable provinces, where it can commonly do little harm, and whence it may be called forth at any sudden exigence?[62]

Such thoughts from this era in British history are quite fascinating. This passage sounds similar to many modern discussions about the morality of owning weapons for self-defence, but it dates from almost two and a half centuries ago.

Wealth and Sustenance

The Highlands of Scotland were not very rich, compared to other parts of Europe. The people got by and made do with what they had, but it was often a much less comfortable life than was available elsewhere.

---

[62] Samuel Johnson, 1775. Pages 206-211.

Food was not always plentiful, although this depended very much on the region. For example, Donald Macleod wrote about his upbringing and the constant hunger that he suffered on the Isle of Skye:

> The only article of food that he had, either here [Inverness] or in his grand-father's house [on the Isle of Skye], in abundance, was milk and fish. Bread was dealt out with a very sparing hand; the porridge, or rather water-gruel, was greatly too thin; and as to the soup-meagre, made of oatmeal and a small handful of greens, (which, with a little barley-bread was his most common dinner), it did not deserve the name of soup, or broth, so much as that of water tinged with those ingredients. With regard to fish, although even the common people were, on many occasions, plentifully supplied with this delicate food, it was neither found palatable for any great length of time, nor yet nutritious, unless duly seasoned with salt, and mixed, in using it, with something of the mealy or farinaceous kind; articles of provision in which the northern counties of Scotland were, at that time, miserably deficient. So that, on the whole, our hero confesses, that he very seldom had a full and satisfactory meal; or rose from the table without a degree of appetite.[63]

When he apprenticed with stonemasons in Inverness, the situation became even more desperate. He was still undernourished, to the point where he had to leave and seek his fortunes elsewhere in the country because of hunger:

> While Macleod remained in his grandfather's family in the Isle of Skye, scantiness of more solid provision was, in some measure, compensated by liberal supplies of milk: and, now and then, on holidays, they were treated with an egg. But, [here in Inverness] with the stone-cutters he found not one egg, and of milk very little. He felt the pinching pain of want. His situation became unsupportable. Extreme hunger induced him to harbour thoughts of breaking loose from his master, and trying to satisfy the cravings of nature in some other part of the kingdom.[64]

---

[63] William Thomson. *Memoirs of the Life and Gallant Exploits of the Old Highlander, Serjeant Donald Macleod*. 2nd edition, London: Peterborough-House Press, 1791. Pages 13-14.
[64] Ibid. Page 15.

However sometimes food was more available and diets were better. When Samuel Johnson journeyed through the Highlands in 1773, he found that in some places there was plenty to eat and drink. Sometimes he was surprised to be "supplied with so much exotic luxury", theorising that perhaps much of it came from foreign trade.[65] His account is quite different from that of Donald Macleod, although his visit to the Highlands was almost a century later and in the post-Culloden era. His status was also that of a visitor and guest, not of a young apprentice to a craftsman. These changes in date and circumstance may account for the great difference in the provision and availability of supplies.

He describes the kind of bread that the natives made:

> Their native bread is made of oats, or barley. Of oatmeal they spread very thin cakes, coarse and hard, to which unaccustomed palates are not easily reconciled. The barley cakes are thicker and softer; I began to eat them without unwillingness; the blackness of their colour raises some dislike, but the taste is not disagreeable. In most houses there is wheat flower, with which we were sure to be treated, if we staid long enough to have it kneaded and baked. As neither yeast nor leaven are used among them, their bread of every kind is unfermented. They make only cakes, and never mould a loaf.[66]

Apparently in the Hebrides, whisky was an important part of the daily nourishment, and was something that might often be taken before breakfast:

> A man of the Hebrides, for of the women's diet I can give no account, as soon as he appears in the morning, swallows a glass of whisky; yet they are not a drunken race, at least I never was present at much intemperance; but no man is so abstemious as to refuse the morning dram, which they call a skalk.

> The word whisky signifies water, and is applied by way of eminence to strong water, or distilled liquor. The spirit drunk in the North is drawn from barley. I never tasted it, except once for experiment at the inn in Inverary, when I thought it preferable to

---

[65] Samuel Johnson, 1775. Page 125.
[66] Ibid. Pages 122-123.

any English malt brandy. It was strong, but not pungent, and was free from the empyreumatick taste or smell. What was the process I had no opportunity of inquiring, nor do I wish to improve the art of making poison pleasant.

Not long after the dram, may be expected the breakfast, a meal in which the Scots, whether of the lowlands or mountains, must be confessed to excel us. The tea and coffee are accompanied not only with butter, but with honey, conserves, and marmalades. If an epicure could remove by a wish, in quest of sensual gratifications, wherever he had supped he would breakfast in Scotland.[67]

He noticed that in the Western Isles, the traditional dinner was quite similar to the fare to which he was accustomed in England, with only minor differences:

A dinner in the Western Islands differs very little from a dinner in England, except that in the place of tarts, there are always set different preparations of milk. This part of their diet will admit some improvement. Though they have milk, and eggs, and sugar, few of them know how to compound them in a custard. Their gardens afford them no great variety, but they have always some vegetables on the table. Potatoes at least are never wanting, which, though they have not known them long, are now one of the principal parts of their food. They are not of the mealy, but the viscous kind.

Their more elaborate cookery, or made dishes, an Englishman at the first taste is not likely to approve, but the culinary compositions of every country are often such as become grateful to other nations only by degrees; though I have read a French author, who, in the elation of his heart, says, that French cookery pleases all foreigners, but foreign cookery never satisfies a Frenchman.[68]

Finally, he noticed that although the Scots set the table in a fashion with which he was familiar, the adoption of cutlery was only a recent development:

---

[67] Ibid. Pages 123-124.
[68] Ibid. Pages 125-126.

Their suppers are, like their dinners, various and plentiful. The table is always covered with elegant linen. Their plates for common use are often of that kind of manufacture which is called cream coloured, or queen's ware. They use silver on all occasions where it is common in England, nor did I ever find the spoon of horn, but in one house.

The knives are not often either very bright, or very sharp. They are indeed instruments of which the Highlanders have not been long acquainted with the general use. They were not regularly laid on the table, before the prohibition of arms, and the change of dress.

Thirty years ago the Highlander wore his knife as a companion to his dirk or dagger, and when the company sat down to meat, the men who had knives, cut the flesh into small pieces for the women, who with their fingers conveyed it to their mouths.[69]

After the Act of Proscription that disarmed the Highlanders, they resented being deprived of their weapons, but especially so their dirk, as this was such a useful and multifunctional tool.[70]

However, in other areas of Scotland such as the Hebrides, even as a guest, Johnson found very poor quality and quantity of food:

The petty tenants, and labouring peasants, live in miserable cabins, which afford them little more than shelter from the storms. The Boor of Norway is said to make all his own utensils. In the Hebrides, whatever might be their ingenuity, the want of wood leaves them no materials. They are probably content with such accommodations as stones of different forms and sizes can afford them.

Their food is not better than their lodging. They seldom taste the flesh of land animals; for here are no markets. What each man eats is from his own stock. The great effect of money is to break property into small parts. In towns, he that has a shilling may have a piece of meat; but where there is no commerce, no man can eat mutton but by killing a sheep.

---

[69] Ibid. Pages 126-127.
[70] James Logan. *The Scottish Gael*. London: Smith, Elder and Co, 1831. Page 218.

Fish in fair weather they need not want; but, I believe, man never lives long on fish, but by constraint; he will rather feed upon roots and berries.[71]

Although the peasants in places such as the Hebrides were very poor, the Scottish nobles were often rich men, with wealth able to support ridiculous expenditure.

After the 1715 Jacobite uprising, many Jacobite nobles were taken to the Tower of London, whereupon extortion was practised on those nobles who were able to pay. An account of this extortion follows, showing the vast reserves of wealth that some Scottish nobles were able to draw upon to make their lives easier:

> Corruption and extortion gave every advantage to those who could command money enough to purchase luxuries at an enormous cost. (...)
>
> Mr. Forster and a Mr. Anderton, who were allowed to live in the Governor's house, were charged the sum of five pounds a-week for their lodging and diet,—a demand which, more than a century ago, was deemed enormous. (...) Mr. Forster, it must be added, was obliged to pay sixty guineas for his privilege of living in the governor's house and Mr. Anderton to give a bribe of twenty-five guineas for having his irons off. A similar tax was made upon every one who entered, and who could pay, and they were thankful to proffer the sum of twenty guineas, the usual demand, to be free from irons. (...)
>
> Many of the prisoners being men of fortune, their tables were of the most luxurious description; forty shillings was often paid for a dish of peas and beans, and thirty shillings for a dish of fish; and this fare, so unlike that of imprisonment, was accompanied by the richest French wines.[72]

In summary, the working classes generally had a somewhat limited access to wealth and food, although in more prosperous times and places the diet improved. By comparison, the nobles were exceptionally wealthy, and could spend small fortunes to

---

[71] Samuel Johnson, 1775. Pages 234-.235
[72] A.T. Thomson, 1845. "William Gordon, Viscount Kenmure."

ensure their own comfort. It is impossible to make blanket statements about the economy and diet of the entire population of the country due to the variations between region, time period, and walks of life.

Physical Fitness and Athleticism

Before Culloden, the Highlanders excelled in sports and physical activities as well as the practice of arms. After Culloden, they could no longer keep their weapons, but they did maintain their interest in sports. Even taking into account the issue of poor diet, they practised all kinds of physical skills to develop strength and stamina, and could perform impressive feats both in civilian and military life:

> A Highlander's speed of foot was ever proverbial—the young men being trained to the exercise. The old Highland foot-race, Geal-ruith, always included a hurdle leap. Running up the steep breast of a mountain has long been a popular race.[73]

There were many games played and practised in the Highlands with the purpose of building strength, stamina and other healthy qualities. Robert Fittis wrote in his book *Sports and Pastimes of Scotland* that "their pastimes were feats of strength and agility", and that the Highlanders displayed a natural ability for athletics:

> An aptitude for athletics seems inherent in the Highlander. His forefathers were "mighty hunters;" but, in strange contrast, they disliked fish and fishing —a dislike attributable perhaps to the fact that fish had some place in the Celtic mythology. Their pastimes were feats of strength and agility, most of which have descended to the present day. Putting the stone, throwing the hammer, and tossing the caber, are amongst the oldest of the Highland games. Tossing the caber is a difficult feat in which few excel. The caber is the branchless trunk of a young tree, which is balanced perpendicularly in both hands, and then suddenly propelled upwards with a jerk, so as to make it describe a somersault before touching the ground. As to the putting stone, we are

---

[73] Robert Scott Fittis. *Sports and Pastimes of Scotland*. Paisley: Alexander Gardner, 1891. Page 183.

assured that in former times it was the custom to have one of these lying at the gate of every chieftain's house, and on the arrival of a stranger, he was asked as a compliment to throw." Another feat was to raise a stone of 200lb., at least, from the ground, and deposit it upon the top of another, four feet high. The stripling who could accomplish this was thereupon dubbed "a man," and allowed to wear a bonnet: and he attained to the higher dignity of "a pretty man," when he evinced due dexterity in wielding the claymore. Hammer-throwing must have been an every-day recreation at the Highland smiddies or forges.[74]

In addition to these general games and sports, Fittis describes activities with a more evident martial skillset, and relates that King James VI thought that such games were very important for his son to learn:

Tilting at the Ring consisted in mounted competitors galloping singly, spear in hand, towards a ring which was suspended by a spring in a sheath affixed to a transverse beam oil pole, at a slight elevation above their heads, and endeavouring to bring off the ring on point of the spear—three courses in succession being allowed each competitor to accomplish the feat.

James VI., in his *Basilikon*, bids his son "specially use such games on horseback, as may teach you to handle your arms thereon ; such as the tilt, the ring, and low-riding for handling of your sword."

Up to about the end of last century [the 18th century], Tilting at the Ring was a favourite sport of the different Societies of Scottish Chapmen, at their annual gatherings for the election of office-bearers.[75]

It is important to realise that the Scots did not build their fearsome reputation as swordsmen by training solely with the sword, or by studying for years under a fencing master without recourse to other activities. They trained extensively with the sword, before the Act of Prohibition, but they supplemented this training with athletic activities to develop their physicality.

---

[74] Ibid. Page 181.
[75] Ibid. Page 204.

We often have the idea that in previous centuries, people were significantly shorter than people are now. This was not necessarily the case: David Stewart wrote about the standard height of the Scottish soldiers in the British Army, and in fact the average height was not so much different from today. Height (or lack thereof) was no barrier to success, as even the shorter soldiers were able to undertake and achieve heavy and difficult physical tasks:

> The standard height was five feet seven inches for full grown men, and five feet six for growing lads. When companies were complete on parade, none under five feet eight inches were allowed to be in the front rank. The grenadiers were always a body of tall men. But although the standard was nominally kept at the above height, there were men of five feet five in the centre rank, and those undersized men were frequently able to undergo greater fatigues than any other in the corps.[76]

Further examples of impressive physical ability and athleticism can be found in some of the well-known memoirs of Highlanders at war. Donald Macleod tells of one encounter where he was forced to leap across a small river in order to win a fight against an opponent with much greater reach and tactical options:

> The famous battle of the Sheriffmuir, near Dumblane, had lasted upwards of an hour, when a French officer, perceiving that our hero was making great havoc, with his broad sword, wherever he went, had the courage to oppose him; but, in a few minutes, his head was, by a touch of Macleod's hand, severed from his body. A horseman, seeing this, sprung forward on Donald like a tyger. A small water-course was between them, with the aid of which Donald was able to make a stand. But the horseman with his long sword wounded him in the shoulder, and was pressing him sorely, when he leaped forward, across the water-course, and plunged his sword into the horse's belly. The animal fell down, and his rider was immediately hewn in pieces by the enraged Serjeant, who, in the act of stabbing his horse, had been cut in the head by the horsemen's sabre, into the very brain. He bound his head fast

---

[76] David Stewart, 1825. Part 3, "Section VI – Fraser's, Montgomery's, and Royal Highlanders."

with a handkerchief, otherwise, as he says, he verily believed it would have fallen into pieces.[77]

The Battle of Mulroy in 1688 was Donald McBane's first experience of battle, as part of a government regiment. His unit was charged by Highlanders and broke under the onslaught. McBane turned and ran, fleeing for several miles before considering himself safe:

> We drew up in a line of battle as best we could, our Company being on the right. We were no sooner in order but there appears double our number of the Mcdonalds, which made us then to fear the worst, at least for my part. I repeated my former wish [that he had still been spinning tobacco, rather than being a soldier] (I never having seen the like). The Mcdonalds came down the hill upon us without either shoe, stocking, or bonnet on their head. They gave a shout and then the fire began on both sides and continued a hot dispute for an hour. Then they broke in upon us with their sword and target and Lochaber axes, which obliged us to give way. Seeing my Captain sore wounded and a great many more with heads lying cloven on every side, I was sadly affrightened, never having seen the like before. A Highland-man attacked me with sword and targe and cut my wooden-handled bayonet out of the muzzle of my gun. I then clubbed my gun and give him a stroke with it, which made the butt-end to fly off. Seeing the Highlandmen to come fast upon me, I took to my heels and run thirty miles before I looked behind me.[78]

At the Battle of Killiecrankie in 1689, McBane performed an even more impressive feat. In a similar fashion, his regiment was attacked and broken by a Highland charge; again, McBane fled, and this time he tried to take a horse to make his escape rather than running all the way to safety. In hot pursuit was a Highlander who did not allow him to take a horse. McBane had to keep fleeing, pursued by his foes, until he came to the river. It was eighteen feet wide between two rocks;[79] he leapt the entire distance, losing only a single shoe for his trouble:

---

[77] William Thomson, 1791. Pages 40-41.

[78] Mark Rector. *Highland Swordsmanship: Techniques of the Scottish Swordmasters*. Union City: Chivalry Bookshelf, 2001. Page 25.

[79] This distance is not an exaggeration. The Killiecrankie Visitor Centre marks the spot of "The Soldier's Leap", eighteen feet across, which can be visited by tourists. In the visitor centre courtyard, the distance is marked on the ground, so that

At length our enemy made their appearance at the top of a hill. We then gave a shout, daring them, as it were, to advance, which they quickly did to our great loss. When they advanced, we played our cannon for an hour upon them. The sun going down caused the Highlanders to advance on us like mad men, without shoe or stocking, covering themselves from our fire with their targes. At last they cast away their muskets, drew their Broad Swords and advanced furiously upon us, and were in the middle of us before we could fire three shots apiece, broke us and obliged us to retreat. ... I fled to the baggage and took a horse in order to ride the water. There follows me a Highland man with sword and targe in order to take the horse and kill my self. You'd laugh to see how he and I scampered about. I kept always the horse betwixt him and me. At length he drew his pistol and I fled. He fired after me. I went above the pass where I met with another water very deep. It was about eighteen foot over betwixt two rocks, I resolved to jump it, so I laid down my gun and hat and jumped and lost one of my shoes in the jump.[80]

Obviously fear lent him wings, yet he would have been unable to perform such a feat if he did not possess some amount of physical strength and athletic ability. Other examples of physical ability can be found in historical accounts, some of which will now be presented in an examination of duels and single combats undertaken by Scottish swordsmen. Although there may have been some amount of inflation and embellishment in some of these stories, and although we should not trust such tales completely, there is a kernel of truth that we can accept: that Scots did aspire to developing a high level of physical and athletic aptitude, and to having the ability to draw upon these skills in times of need.

The Scottish Character

Johnson clearly believed that the country had become better and more lawful after Culloden (merely 27 years before his visit to the Highlands). He remarked on the general change and improvement

---

children and enthusiastic adults can try to make the same leap themselves, without the risk of falling into the river.
[80] Mark Rector, 2001. Page 26.

of manners among the people and suggested that the Scots were becoming richer and more industrious as well:

> There was perhaps never any change of national manners so quick, so great, and so general, as that which has operated in the Highlands, by the last conquest, and the subsequent laws. We came thither too late to see what we expected, a people of peculiar appearance, and a system of antiquated life. The clans retain little now of their original character, their ferocity of temper is softened, their military ardour is extinguished, their dignity of independence is depressed, their contempt of government subdued, and the reverence for their chiefs abated. Of what they had before the late conquest of their country, there remain only their language and their poverty. Their language is attacked on every side. Schools are erected, in which English only is taught, and there were lately some who thought it reasonable to refuse them a version of the holy scriptures, that they might have no monument of their mother-tongue.
>
> That their poverty is gradually abated, cannot be mentioned among the unpleasing consequences of subjection. They are now acquainted with money, and the possibility of gain will by degrees make them industrious. Such is the effect of the late regulations, that a longer journey than to the Highlands must be taken by him whose curiosity pants for savage virtues and barbarous grandeur.[81]

Several times in his book, he wrote of the civility and manners of the Scots with whom he came into contact. He found that even the lower classes were noteworthy in their disposition and conduct:

> We took two Highlanders to run beside us, partly to shew us the way, and partly to take back from the sea-side the horses, of which they were the owners. One of them was a man of great liveliness and activity, of whom his companion said, that he would tire any horse in Inverness. Both of them were civil and ready-handed. Civility seems part of the national character of Highlanders. Every chieftain is a monarch, and politeness, the natural product of royal government, is diffused from the laird through the whole clan. But they are not commonly dexterous:

---

[81] Samuel Johnson, 1775. Pages 127-129.

their narrowness of life confines them to a few operations, and they are accustomed to endure little wants more than to remove them.[82]

He also remarked on the education and skill with language that he observed in his hosts. Sometimes his hosts were unimpressed when he paid them compliments about their education, as in this anecdote:

> The landlord attended us with great civility, and told us what he could give us to eat and drink. I found some books on a shelf, among which were a volume or more of Prideaux's Connection.
>
> This I mentioned as something unexpected, and perceived that I did not please him. I praised the propriety of his language, and was answered that I need not wonder, for he had learned it by grammar.
>
> By subsequent opportunities of observation, I found that my host's diction had nothing peculiar. Those Highlanders that can speak English, commonly speak it well, with few of the words, and little of the tone by which a Scotchman is distinguished. Their language seems to have been learned in the army or the navy, or by some communication with those who could give them good examples of accent and pronunciation. By their Lowland neighbours they would not willingly be taught; for they have long considered them as a mean and degenerate race. These prejudices are wearing fast away; but so much of them still remains, that when I asked a very learned minister in the islands, which they considered as their most savage clans: "Those," said he, "that live next the Lowlands."[83]

However, while Johnson approved of the general improvements in manners and education of the Scots, and while he believed that these were in no small part due to the disarming of the Highlanders, he also observed that certain far-flung parts of the country were left undefended by these Acts.[84] As a result of the disarming Acts, he found that the common practice of fighting with the traditional weapons had virtually disappeared:

---

[82] Ibid. Pages 59-60.
[83] Ibid. Pages 74-75.
[84] Ibid. Pages 206-211.

After all that has been said of the force and terrour of the Highland sword, I could not find that the art of defence was any part of common education. The gentlemen were perhaps sometimes skilful gladiators, but the common men had no other powers than those of violence and courage.[85]

To summarise this section, the ideal Highlander was religious and moral, physically strong and able, brave and martially skilled. James Grant describes the soldier Farquhar Shaw and his father in the book *Legends of the Black Watch*. These were two men who exemplified several important traits for the Highlanders:

Farquhar was a perfect swordsman, and deadly shot alike with the musket and pistol; and his strength was such, that he had been known to twist a horse-shoe, and drive his skene dhu to the hilt in a pine log; while his activity and power of enduring hunger, thirst, heat, cold and fatigue, became a proverb among the companies of the Watch: for thus had he been reared and trained by his father, a genuine old Celtic gentleman and warrior, whose memory went back to the days when Dundee led the valiant and true to the field of Rinrory, and in whose arms the viscount fell from his horse in the moment of victory, and was borne to the house of Urrard to die. He was a true Highlander of the old school; for an old school has existed in all ages and everywhere, even among the Arabs, the children of Ishmael, in the desert; for they, too, have an olden time to which they look back with regret, as being nobler, better, braver, and purer than the present. Thus, the father of Farquhar Shaw was a grim duinewassal, who never broke bread or saw the sun rise without uncovering his head and invoking the names of "God, the Blessed Mary, and St. Colme of the Isle; "who never sat down to a meal without opening wide his gates, that the poor and needy might enter freely; who never refused the use of his purse and sword to a friend or kinsman, and was never seen unarmed, even in his own dining-room; who never wronged any man; but who never suffered a wrong or affront to pass, without sharp and speedy vengeance; and who, rather than acknowledge the supremacy of the House of Hanover, died sword in hand at the rising in Glensheil.[86]

---

[85] Ibid. Page 265.
[86] James Grant. *Legends of the Black Watch*. London: Routledge, Warne, and Routledge, 1859. "The Story of Farquhar Shaw."

1.3   Duels and Single Combats

There are several accounts of duels and single combats involving Highlanders with broadswords that help to illustrate the level of skill and ability that such individuals achieved. The Highlanders were renowned for their skill at arms and their amazing athleticism, and also their willingness to fight at any provocation! In 1773, during his journey through the Highlands, Samuel Johnson noted this culture of revenge among the Highland people:

> Till the Highlanders lost their ferocity, with their arms, they suffered from each other all that malignity could dictate, or precipitance could act. Every provocation was revenged with blood, and no man that ventured into a numerous company, by whatever occasion brought together, was sure of returning without a wound.[87]

Of course, not all examples of single combats stemmed from personal grudges and revenge. Sometimes the battlefield would give the opportunity for individuals to excel. For example, at the Battle of Culloden, Major Gillies MacBean engaged several of the enemy and distinguished himself nobly by stepping alone into a breach in the wall to prevent government troops from making a flanking attack on his regiment. With his broadsword and targe, he cut down thirteen men, including the Lord Robert Ker.[88] His opponents were armed with swords, muskets and bayonets, and MacBean suffered "several bayonet wounds and musket balls" before he fell, even though a government officer tried to save him out of respect for his bravery.[89] After the battle, mortally wounded in several places, Gillies MacBean crawled six hundred yards from where he was cut down, dragging himself into a barn where he could make himself comfortable on the straw before dying.[90]

John Parker Lawson writes about the official casualty list for Culloden: "according to the official accounts published by the government, the royal army had only 50 men killed, and 259

---

[87] Samuel Johnson, 1775. Pages 211-212.
[88] Peter Harrington, 1991. Page 74.
[89] Ibid.
[90] Ibid. Page 81.

wounded, including 18 officers, of whom four were killed."[91] If all these numbers are correct, then the 13 men killed by Gillies MacBean accounted for a quarter of the total deaths suffered by the government forces – an impressive achievement for a single man.

Such bravery, skill at arms and personal strength are characteristic of tales of the Highland warrior, along with a strict moral code and the desire to right any perceived wrongs. After Culloden, a Scottish officer who served with the government army felt that an English officer had insulted his country. He demanded satisfaction; this duel quickly became a melee, with several officers participating:

> Knowing that there were several deserters from the royal army among the insurgents, the duke [of Cumberland] ordered a strict inspection to be made of the prisoners in order to find them out. No less than thirty-six were recognised, and being brought to a summary trial, were convicted, and suffered the death of traitors. Among these was one Dunbar, who had been a sergeant in Sowle's regiment. He had taken a suit of laced clothes from Major Lockhart at the battle of Falkirk, which being found in his possession, he was dressed in them, and hanged, and his body exposed for forty-eight hours on the gibbet. A young gentleman of the name of Forbes, a relative of Lord Forbes, is also said to have perished on this occasion. He had served as a cadet in an English regiment, but, being from principle attached to the Jacobite interest, had joined the standard of the prince.
>
> An incident occurred after the execution of this unfortunate gentleman, which assumed an alarming appearance, and might have led to serious consequences had the war been continued. Before Forbes was cut down from the gibbet, an English officer, with a morbidness of feeling which seems to have seized the officers as well as the common soldiers of the army, plunged his sword into the body of Forbes, exclaiming, at the same time, that "all his countrymen were traitors and rebels like himself." This exclamation being heard by a Scottish officer who was standing hard by, the offended Scotchman immediately drew his sword, and demanded satisfaction for the insult offered to his country.

---

[91] John Parker Lawson. *Historical Tales of the Wars of Scotland*. Vol. 2, Edinburgh: A. Fullerton, 1839. Page 392.

The Englishman instantly accepted the challenge, and in a short time the combat became general among the officers who happened to be on the spot. The soldiers, seeing their officers engaged, beat to arms of their own accord, and drew up along the streets, the Scotch on one side and the English on the other, and commenced a warm combat with fixed bayonets. Information of this affray having been brought to the Duke of Cumberland, he hastened to the scene of action, and by his persuasions put an end to the combat. He found the Scotch greatly excited by the affront offered them; but he soothed their wounded feelings by complimenting them for their fidelity, their courage, and exemplary conduct.[92]

Culloden was a battle that took place between government troops and rebel forces, with Scottish and English troops on both sides. This anecdote is the only time when battle lines at Culloden drew up by nationality, with Scots fighting against English – where the combatants were all part of the same victorious government army. The battle itself was divided by politics rather than nationality.

In the aftermath of the Battle of Killiecrankie, individual Highlanders harried the retreating government troops. Sometimes they displayed courage and martial prowess by attempting to engage their opponents in a more heroic fashion:

He [General Mackay] then marched his men slowly down the hill, and retired across the Garry with no interruption except from one Highlander, a powerful fellow, who suddenly appeared armed with a Lochaber axe. He knew the General, and was standing in the river to cut him down. As the General was the last who passed the river, having halted on the other side to see whether he was pursued, he stood still, and ordered his servant, who was also a man of great bodily strength, to clear the ford. He immediately went up, and with one blow cut off the Highlander's head, exclaiming in Gaelic – "This is hard work, my father's brother!"[93]

[92] John Keltie. *History of the Scottish Highlands, Highland Clans and Scottish Regiments*. Vol. 1, Edinburgh: A. Fullerton, 1875. "Prince Charles Edward Stuart – Characteristic bravery of the Highlanders and the aftermath."
[93] John Parker Lawson, Vol. 2, 1839. Pages 458-459.

General Mackay was himself a Highlander, and likely his servant was also a Highlander. Therefore the above passage describes an engagement between Highlanders, rather than a Highlander against an Englishman.[94] Another anecdote from the same battle was that a Highland priest harried the fleeing government troops with his broadsword, achieving great success:

> A Highland tradition relates that the latter [Brigadier Balfour] was killed by a Roman Catholic priest named Robert Stewart, nephew of Stewart of Ballechin. This clerical warrior is said to have followed the fugitives in their flight down the river and towards the Pass wielding a huge broadsword, cutting down numbers of them. So fearfully did he exert himself, that at the conclusion of the carnage his hand was so swollen as to make it necessary to cut away the net work of the hilt of the sword before it could be extricated. He cut down Brigadier Balfour for contemptuously refusing to receive quarter from him.[95]

Sometimes it was not the enemy who posed the greatest threat, but rather the individuals who were supposedly on one's own side. Duels and less formal fights could erupt between colleagues at any given time. Around the year 1640, a Major Sommerville was attacked by a Captain Crawford in Edinburgh, and was forced to defend himself in a duel. The men had had disagreements previously, and the Captain decided to resort to violence to resolve the issue:

> The Captain, armed with a long broadsword and a Highland dirk, came up to Major Somerville and said – "If you are a pretty man, draw your sword" – at the same time pulling out his own sword and dagger. (...) We are told that the Major's "honour and preservation gave him no time to consult the convenience or inconvenience he was now under, either as to the present charge or disadvantage of weapons, having only a large cane in his hand, which he usually carried when walking, and the sword which General Ruthven had recently given him. It hung in a shoulder-

---

[94] If this study guide can help people realise that many of the battles were not "Scots versus English", but rather that they were fought between rebel and government forces with Scots and English on both sides, then it will help to correct this unfortunately common misconception that plagues popular history of 17th and 18th century Scotland.

[95] John Parker Lawson, Vol. 2, 1839. Page 461.

belt far back, as the fashion then was, and he was forced to guard two or three strokes with his cane before he got out his sword, which being now drawn, he soon put his adversary on the defensive, by bearing up so close to him, and pressing his thrusts, that the Captain, for all his courage and advantage of weapons, was forced to give way, with difficulty parrying the redoubled thrusts which Somerville made at him.

The combat, for so in effect it was, although accidental, began about the middle of the Lawnmarket. Somerville drives down the Captain, still fighting, near to the goldsmiths' shops, where, fearing to be nailed to the boards, these shops being then all of timber, he resolved a notable blow to revenge all his former efforts. Making, therefore, a feint, having parried Somerville's thrust with his dagger, the Captain suddenly turns his hand, and by a back blow with his broadsword he thought to have *hamshekelled* (hamstringed) him on one if not both of his legs, which Somerville only prevented by nimbly leaping backward, interposing the thick cane in his left hand, which was cut in two by the violence of the blow. And now Providence so ordered it that the Captain, missing his mark, overreached himself so far that he could not recover his sword in time to a fit posture of defence before Somerville, having beaten up the dagger in the Captain's left hand with the remaining part of his own stick, instantly closes with him, and with the pommel of his sword he strikes him to the ground, and at first, because of his baseness, he was inclined to transfix him, but his heart relented. At that moment some of his own soldiers happened to come up, who were so incensed at this attack on their commanding officer, that they were ready to cut the Captain in pieces, if he had not been rescued out of their hands, and safely conveyed to prison, where he was put in irons, and continued in a most wretched condition somewhat more than a year."[96]

This passage highlights some of the technical aspects of the duel. It shows that the thrust was an important technique even when fighting for real, not just when practising in a fencing salle. The Captain uses a "back blow", showing that striking with the back edge of the sword was something that could be done powerfully and had tactical value in a fight. The Major uses a pommel strike to beat the Captain to the ground; he considers giving his

---

[96] Ibid. Pages 411-412.

opponent a lethal thrust to end the affair, but relents and shows mercy. This is an excellent example of a Highland soldier showing his moral strength and his skill at arms, as well as describing some interesting and unusual techniques with the broadsword.

In the army of the Duke of Marlborough in Flanders, just after the Battle of Wynendale in 1708, some Highland officers provoked the Master of Sinclair to fight duels. The Master of Sinclair was the more skilful fighter, so his challengers fared poorly. The Master of Sinclair killed his foe in each duel in an attempt to preserve his honour and integrity, even though this resulted in a court verdict of murder for his actions. The series of events began when the Ensign Hugh Schaw accused Sinclair of cowardice in battle:

> During the battle of Wynendale, in the midst of the fire, it appeared, in evidence afterwards taken, that Ensign Hugh Schaw, the first of the victims to the Master of Sinclair's wrath, was heard to call out to the Master "to stand upright;" it was afterwards publicly stated by Ensign Hugh Schaw, that he had done so upon seeing Sinclair bow himself down to the ground for a considerable time. This alleged act of cowardice on the part of Sinclair appears, however, not to have really taken place; but it was made the groundwork of a calumnious imputation. It must, however, be acknowledged, that there was nothing in the subsequent conduct of the Master of Sinclair, as far as the battle of Sherriff Muir was concerned, to raise his character as a man of personal bravery.[97]

Sinclair issued a challenge but Schaw refused to duel. This angered Sinclair greatly, and made him all the more intent upon fighting:

> On the following day, the Master met Ensign Schaw, and taking a stick from underneath his coat, struck the Ensign two blows over the head with it. They both drew, and fought with such fury that the Master's sword was broken, and that of the Ensign bent; upon which Sinclair retired behind a sentinel, desiring him "to keep off the Ensign, as his sword was broken." Schaw then said, "You know I am more of a gentleman than to pursue you when your sword is broken." But the young soldier Schaw had at this time

---

[97] A.T. Thomson, Vol. 1, 1845. "The Master of Sinclair."

received a mortal wound, of which he died; but not until after the verdict of the court-martial ultimately held on Sinclair.[98]

Within days, Schaw's brother, Captain Alexander Schaw, also became victim to the "vindictive and brutal notions at that period considered in the army to constitute a code of honour":

> Captain Schaw was naturally indignant at the death of his brother; he expressed his anger openly, and said, that the Master of Sinclair had "paper in his breast," against which his brother's sword was bent; and that he had received the fatal wound after his sword had thus become useless.
>
> The Master of Sinclair having heard of these assertions, resolved to avenge himself for these imputations cast upon him. On the thirteenth of September, as Captain Schaw was riding at the head of Major How's regiment, the sound of his own name, repeated twice, announced the approach of the hated Sinclair. Captain Schaw turned, and inquired of the Master what he wanted. Sinclair replied, by asking him to go to the front, as he wanted to speak to him; to which Captain Schaw rejoined, that he might speak to him there.
>
> "Yes," returned Sinclair, "but if I fire at you here, I may shoot some other body."
>
> Captain Schaw answered, that he might fire at him if he pleased, he bore him no ill-will. "If you will not go to the front," returned Sinclair, "beg my pardon."
>
> This was refused, some words of further aggravation ensued; then the Master of Sinclair drew his pistol and fired at Schaw. The Captain was also preparing to fire; his hand was in the act of drawing his pistol when it was for ever checked, whether employed for good or evil; the aim of Sinclair was certain, and Schaw fell dead from his horse. Sinclair, without waiting to inquire how far mortal might be the wound he had inflicted, rode away.[99]

Captain Schaw had merely expressed anger at the death of his brother, and had perhaps uttered some words to which Sinclair

[98] Ibid.
[99] Ibid.

took offence. That was enough provocation for Sinclair to duel. However, when Sinclair was court-martialled for his behaviour, he managed to escape the death penalty:

> On the seventeenth of October, 1708, a court-martial upon the Master of Sinclair was held at Ronsales by the command of the Duke of Marlborough. Upon the first charge, that of challenging Ensign Hugh Schaw (in breach of the twenty-eighth article of war), Sinclair was acquitted, the court being of opinion that the challenge was not proved.
>
> Of the second accusation, that of killing Captain Alexander Schaw, the Master of Sinclair was found guilty, and sentenced to suffer death. He was, however, recommended to the mercy of the Duke of Marlborough, in consideration of the provocation which he had received,—the prisoner having declared that, not only on that occasion, but upon several, and in different regiments, Captain Schaw had defamed him; that he was forced to do what he did, and that he had done it with reluctance.
>
> The case was, however, afterwards referred to the Attorney General and the Solicitor General, who gave it their opinion that Sinclair was guilty of murder; for had the trial taken place in England before a common jury, the judge must have directed the jury to find him guilty of murder, no provocation whatever being sufficient to excuse malice, or to make the offence of killing less than murder, when it is committed with premeditation. How far the provocation was to be considered as a ground of mercy, these legal functionaries declined to judge.[100]

This account shows a difference in the method of handling death by duelling between military and civil courts. The death penalty was the standard response for killing another person in a pre-meditated fashion; but the military court took provocation into account, while a civil court in England would not have considered any provocation to excuse murder.

In another instance, the Duke of Hamilton fought a duel with the Lord Mohun:

---

[100] Ibid.

Certain offensive words spoken by Lord Mohun in the chambers of a Master in Chancery, and addressed to the Duke of Hamilton, brought a long-standing enmity into open hostility.[101]

In this encounter not only did the principals fight each other, but the seconds (General Macartney and Colonel Hamilton, respectively) also became embroiled in the duel. This affair was conducted with smallswords rather than broadswords. The two principals died in the duel, but the two seconds survived the ferocious and bloody engagement:

"I must ask your Lordship," said Lord Mohun, "one favour, which is, that these gentlemen may have nothing to do with our quarrel."

"My Lord," answered the Duke, "I leave them to themselves."

The parties then threw off their cloaks, and all engaged; the seconds, it appears, fighting with as much fury as their principals. The park-keepers coming up, found Colonel Hamilton and General Macartney struggling together; the General holding the Colonel's sword in his left hand, the Colonel pulling at the blade of the General's sword. One of the keepers went up to the principals: he found Lord Mohun in a position between sitting and lying, bending towards the Duke, who was on his knees, leaning almost across Lord Mohun, both holding each other's sword fast, both striving and struggling with the fury of remorseless hatred. This awful scene was soon closed for ever, as far as Mohun was concerned. He expired shortly afterwards, having received four wounds, each of which was likely to be mortal. The Duke was raised and supported by Colonel Hamilton and one of the keepers; but after walking about thirty yards, exclaimed that "he could walk no farther," sank down upon the grass, and expired.[102]

Lord Mohun died first, after receiving four separate mortal wounds. The Duke of Hamilton expired shortly afterwards, most likely due to receiving a thrust from General McCartney:

General Macartney escaped. It appeared on oath that he had made a thrust at the Duke, as he was struggling with Mohun; and

---

[101] A.T. Thomson, Vol. 1, 1845. "John Erskine, Earl of Mar."
[102] Ibid.

it being generally believed that it was by that wound that the Duke died, an address was presented to her Majesty by the Scottish Peers, begging that she would write to all the kings and states in alliance with her, not to shelter Macartney from justice.[103]

From this story, and from the account of Sinclair's duel with Ensign Schaw, it is clear that sometimes a fighter could deal a mortal wound in a duel, yet the fight might continue. The victim would then die later, and this could cause legal problems for the man who killed him, even if the death was unintentional. In a similar situation, Donald McBane fled after he thought he killed his opponent in a duel (described later in this chapter), because he did not want the hangman's noose as a result of his actions.

Duels were sometimes conducted on horseback, and the weapon of choice was not limited to just the swords. This following excerpt describes an affair of honour between the Earl of Glencairn and Sir George Monro in the mid-1650s:

> Both the combatants were on horseback, and it was arranged that each was to discharge one pistol, and then fight with broadswords. The pistols were fired without injuring either of them, and then they drew their swords. After a few thrusts and passes Sir George got a sore stroke on the bridle-hand, which induced him to call out that he was not able to guide his horse – "And I hope," he added, "you will fight me on foot."
>
> "You carle," replied Glencairn, "I will let you know that I am a match for you either on foot or on horseback." At the first onset Sir George received a severe cut on the brow, which bled so profusely that he could not see. He was not completely at the mercy of the Earl, who was on the point of thrusting him through the body, when his trumpeter, who also acted as his valet, pushed his sword aside, saying – "You have enough of him, my Lord." His master gave him a slap on the shoulders, and rose back to his lodgings, leaving Sir George to reach his quarters in whatever way he pleased, which he did with great difficulty, and in a very weak state.[104]

---

[103] Ibid.
[104] John Parker Lawson, Vol. 2, 1839. Page 219.

The thrust is painted as a lethal blow in this passage, in a similar fashion to the accounts of the duels between the Lord Mohun and the Duke of Hamilton and between Major Sommerville and Captain Crawford. During their duel with smallswords, both the Lord Mohun and the Duke of Hamilton died of the thrusts they received. Major Sommerville and the Earl of Glencairn won their duels, and considered giving their opponents a lethal thrust to finish the matter, but decided to show mercy and restrain from delivering such a killing blow.

Duels did not have to be lethal, and in fact the Highlanders often preferred to show their mastery by disabling or wounding strikes rather than by killing their opponents. It normally needed more skill to spare a life in a duel than to take it.[105] The memoirs of Sergeant Donald Macleod provide several examples of duels that he fought, where he tried to minimise the injury to his opponent. For example, in Lisle, he fought with a brave German officer, and tried not to kill the man, as his opponent had done nothing wrong:

> On another occasion, and in another town, to the best of his remembrance Lisle, as he was walking with two ladies on the rampart, a German trooper, looking sternly at our hero, said in German, "The Devil take the whole of such dogs."
>
> "What is that you say?" – The German repeated it – Macleod immediately drew his sword – the trooper ran off: but a German officer, who had come up to take his part, faced Macleod, and a sharp conflict ensued. The officer had more courage and strength, than skill, at the broad-sword, and it would have been an easy thing for Macleod to have cut him off; but he had no quarrel with the gentleman who had generously come up to the assistance of his countryman when his life was threatened. He, therefore, finding that he was fully master of his man, determined to proceed by degrees. He first cut off a part of the calf of his large and thick leg. The Captain still persevered in the combat – the Serjeant wounded him smartly in the sword-arm.
>
> He gave up the contest on this, and said, "It is enough." The officer was assisted to his quarters; and, wounded as he was,

---

[105] Christopher Scott Thompson. *Broadsword Academy*. 1st edition, Lulu, 2012. Volume 1. Page 57.

insisted on Macleod's accompanying him home, and drinking with him; which they did very plentifully. They both cried, and kissed at parting.– Such is the nature of man, divided by selfish and social passions, according to various situations! Duelling, in those days, was more frequent in the army than now, but less common among all ranks in civil life.[106]

In this fight, Macleod's opponent was a brave and honourable man, and so Macleod did not want to kill him. The German captain was not the person who insulted Macleod, so it would be wrong for Macleod to kill him. Instead, the Highland sergeant did the only reasonable thing under the circumstances: with control and skill, he wounded his opponent enough to end the duel, refraining from delivering a killing blow.

In a similar fashion, Macleod fought a single combat with Captain Macdonald in 1715. Without killing his opponent, Macleod demonstrated his superior skills and won the fight:

> They met accordingly, without seconds, unaccompanied, and all alone, at a place appointed, nearly midway between the two armies. Macdonald pulled out a large canteen, willed with whiskey; and, before he should begin his attack on our hero, Donald, offered to drink with him. "No, the Devil a drop," said Donald, and calmly stood on his defence. Macdonald began; assailing Macleod with great fury, but with little skill. The Serjeant did not think that his life, or limb, was any object: he cut off his purse, and immediately demanded a parley.– "I have cut off your purse," said he, "is there any thing more I must cut off before you give up?" Macdonald acknowledged himself inferior in prowess to our Serjeant, and leaving his purse, in token of his inferiority, went back, with a very bad grace, to Marr's camp.[107]

Sometimes Macleod had no opportunity to win the fight without killing his opponent. In battle, there was less opportunity to win in such a non-lethal fashion. At Sheriffmuir, he was engaged first by a French officer and then by a cavalryman, and was forced to kill both of them in order to survive:

---

[106] William Thomson, 1791. Pages 35-37.
[107] Ibid. Pages 39-40.

The famous battle of the Sheriffmuir, near Dumblane, had lasted upwards of an hour, when a French officer, perceiving that our hero was making great havoc, with his broad sword, wherever he went, had the courage to oppose him; but, in a few minutes, his head was, by a touch of Macleod's hand, severed from his body. A horseman, seeing this, sprung forward on Donald like a tyger. A small water-course was between them, with the aid of which Donald was able to make a stand. But the horseman with his long sword wounded him in the shoulder, and was pressing him sorely, when he leaped forward, across the water-course, and plunged his sword into the horse's belly. The animal fell down, and his rider was immediately hewn in pieces by the enraged Serjeant, who, in the act of stabbing his horse, had been cut in the head by the horsemen's sabre, into the very brain. He bound his head fast with a handkerchief, otherwise, as he says, he verily believed it would have fallen into pieces.[108]

This excerpt was shown previously, as an example of athleticism as an important aspect of Highland martial training. It also serves to show that Macleod was not averse to taking life when the situation demanded, although he had the morals and ethics to spare lives when possible. Furthermore, it shows that Macleod received a painful wound to his head, yet still managed to survive: it is important to realise that not all touches are fatal, and even a strong cut to a vital location (such as the head) is not always a guarantee of death.

Battles were usually messy affairs, and could become even more complicated and dangerous when people felt that their honour was involved. For example, this following excerpt about the Battle of Falkirk Muir in 1746 describes a situation where an Irish dragoon bested a Highland opponent, but then because of honour, was unable to survive the engagement when his opponent was rescued:

The Highland weapons gave opportunity for many exertions of personal courage, and sometimes for single combats in the field; like those which occur so frequently in fabulous wars. At Falkirk, a gentleman now living, was, I suppose after the retreat of the King's troops, engaged at a distance from the rest with an Irish

---

[108] Ibid. Pages 40-41.

dragoon. They were both skilful swordsmen, and the contest was not easily decided: the dragoon at last had the advantage, and the Highlander called for quarter; but quarter was refused him, and the fight continued till he was reduced to defend himself upon his knee. At that instant one of the Macleods came to his rescue; who, as it is said, offered quarter to the dragoon, but he thought himself obliged to reject what he had before refused, and, as battle gives little time to deliberate, was immediately killed.[109]

It was often possible to force an opponent to capitulate in a duel, but sometimes it took several wounds before a man would take the hint and give up. In one occasion in 1757 in Ireland, Donald Macleod duelled with a tailor, and had to give the man several nasty wounds before his opponent was rendered unable to continue the fight. Macleod did his very best to end the fight without causing death, even though his opponent was determined to fight until he died, and luckily he succeeded in disabling his opponent:

> About the year 1757, after the 42nd regiment was ordered to America, Serjeant Macleod was sent over, on the business of recruiting, to Glasgow. At Belfast, where he halted with the party he commanded for a few days, he had an adventure, in the fighting way, with one Maclean a taylor, and a native of Inverness. This man, having heard of the prowess of Donald, and particularly how he had, a great many years ago, maimed a Maclean, came to a resolution, one day, when he was in his cups, of doing nothing less than challenging the Serjeant to single combat with broad-swords. Macleod, perceiving that the man was flustered, and unwilling to take any unfair advantage, advised him to re-consider the matter; telling him, that if he should persevere in his determination of fighting, he would meet him on the following day. But the more the Serjeant was pacifically inclined, the more obstreperous and insolent was the taylor; so that an encounter at last became inevitable.

> They went, with their seconds, to a field behind a garden, in the out-skirts of the town, and set to work immediately. The taylor, who was a well-made and a very nimble fellow, attacked his opponent with a great alacrity, and not without a considerable degree of art; but he soon exhausted his spirits and strength, and

---

[109] Samuel Johnson, 1775. Pages 264-266

was entirely at the mercy of the veteran, whom he had rashly dared to provoke to an engagement. Donald first cut off one of his ears, and then another; yet the taylor, with a foolish obstinacy, still maintained the conflict, and swore that he would rather die on the spot, than yield to any Macleod in the British Isles; so that the Serjeant, in self-defence, would have been obliged, as he expressed it, to *lay open the Taylor's belly*, if he had not fortunately brought him to the ground, but cutting a sinew of his hough.[110]

Macleod did his best to defuse the situation, and to avoid fighting, but his opponent was set on that course of action. The duel was unavoidable, yet still Macleod tried to spare the man's life, by cutting at extremities until eventually the tailor was rendered unable to continue. Deliberately cutting off the ears, one by one, without cutting into the head, would require some very careful targeting and control of the sword!

Returning to the concept of battle, where the concept of mercy or quarter could be withheld and where killing was more often the intention than sparing an opponent's life, men often wore metal skullcaps to protect their heads from the swords of the Highlanders. At the Battle of Falkirk Muir, the government cavalry wore such head protection. This caused some difficulties for MacPherson of Cluny, who was astonished at his inability to break the heads of his opponents:

> Polyaenus says that the Gauls always struck at the head with their swords. It was by slashing at the heads of the horses that the Highlanders were able so effectually to repulse and defeat the most numerous bodies of cavalry. They also struck at the heads of the infantry; and, to guard against the consequences of this mode of attack, it was represented as necessary for all to wear a skull cap, or horse shoe under their hat. The onset of the Highlanders, in the language of Johnstone, was "so terrible that the best troops in Europe would with difficulty sustain the first shock of it; and if the swords of the Highlanders once came in contact with them, their defeat was inevitable." Mac Pherson, of Cluny, not aware that the cavalry of the royal army at Falkirk wore head pieces of iron, declared, with astonishment, that he

---

[110] William Thomson, 1791. Pages 69-71.

never met with skulls as hard as those of the Dragoons, for he had struck at them until he was tired, and was scarce able to break one![111]

This passage illustrates the Highland predilection for striking to the head, and shows that horsemen tried to do this even when engaging other cavalrymen. Many different sources describe that the Highlanders frequently cut at the head with powerful downward blows, and that this was one of the most common targets and wounds on the battlefield. This is an important point worth bearing in mind when trying to reconstruct the Highland method of fighting.

However, sometimes the metal skullcap saved the Highlanders from the government troops. This following passage about Rob Roy MacGregor shows how a skullcap saved the famous robber when government dragoons attacked him:

> He was not always so fortunate as to avoid imminent danger; yet he had a faithful friend who watched over his safety, and who would have willingly sacrificed his life for that of Macgregor. This was the chieftain's lieutenant, Fletcher, or Mac-analeister, "the Little John of his band," and an excellent marksman. "It happened," writes Sir W. Scott, "that Mac Gregor and his party had been surprised and dispersed by a superior force of horse and foot, and the word was given to split and squander. Jack shifted for himself; but a bold dragoon attached himself to pursuit of Rob Roy, and overtaking him, struck at him with his broadsword. A plate of iron in his bonnet saved Mac Gregor from being cut down to the teeth; but the blow was heavy enough to bear him to the ground, crying as he fell, 'O Macanaleister, there is naething in her,' (i. e. in the gun:) the trooper at the same time exclaiming, 'D—n ye, your mother never brought your nightcap;' had his arm raised for a second blow, when Macanaleister fired, and the ball pierced the dragoon."[112]

Sometimes cleverness and outwitting the enemy was the best way to win a confrontation, rather than brute force. This next anecdote describes a situation in 1746 where a Highlander called Robert

---

[111] James Logan, 1831. Pages 211-212.
[112] A.T. Thomson, Vol. 2, 1845. "Rob Roy MacGregor Campbell."

Bane engaged a party of nine redcoat soldiers and used his wits to rob them of their weapons:

> In autumn 1746, a party, consisting of a corporal and eight soldiers, marching north to Inverness, after passing Tummel Bridge, halted on the road-side, and placed their arms against a large stone some yards behind them. Robert Bane observed the soldiers, and the manner in which they disposed of their arms. This, as he said, was a good opportunity to make a dash at his old friends the Seidaran dearag, or red coat soldiers, whom he had met at Gladsmuir, Falkirk, and Culloden. None of his neighbours were at home to assist him; but he sallied out by himself, armed with his gun, pistols, and broadsword, and, proceeding with great caution, got close to the party undiscovered, when he made a sudden spring, and placed himself between the soldiers and their arms. Brandishing his sword in one hand, and pointing his gun with the other, he called out to them in broken English, to surrender instantly, or he would call his party, who were in the wood behind, and would kill them all. The soldiers were so taken by surprise, that they permitted the kearnach to carry off their arms for the purpose of delivering them, as he said, to his companions in the wood. He quickly returned, however, and desiring the soldiers to follow him quietly, else those in the woods would be out, he conducted them to Tummel Bridge inn, where he left them, and repairing to the wood, took possession of the arms as fair spoil of war. The soldiers soon discovered the truth, and hurried back to recover their arms, and get hold of the man who, by his address and courage, had thus disgraced them; but the kearnach had taken care to place himself and his prize out of danger. When the soldiers reached Inverness, they were tried and punished for the loss of their arms.[113]

Not every fight was conducted with swords. Sometimes there was not a sword to hand, and an individual would need to fight with whatever he had available: for a Highlander, usually his dirk. For example, in 1776 during the American campaign, Major Murray was almost taken prisoner by a small detachment of American soldiers. He was unable to use his dirk because it slipped too far behind him on his belt, and he was so fat that he could no longer reach it. Thus bereft of his preferred weapon for close quarters, he

---

[113] David Stewart, 1825. Part 1, "Section II – System of Clanship."

had to defend himself with his musket until he was able to disarm the American officer and take the man's sword, which he then used to save himself from the situation.[114]

Disarming actions are not commonly described in the Scottish broadsword treatises, but they do appear from time to time. Some fencing masters across the centuries believed that disarms were too dangerous to attempt, and that fencers should stick to secure, safe fundamental actions when fighting for real. There might be some merit in this notion, but nonetheless, some skills at disarming an opposing swordsman managed to save Major Murray's life in America.

Another Highlander who fought several duels over the course of the late 17th and early 18th centuries was Donald McBane. Although he was a military man, a foot soldier in various Highland Regiments, he often used a smallsword or spadroon rather than the broadsword. In 1692, he fought his first duel, and was defeated due to his lack of knowledge and experience, so he took more lessons and improved his skills. In his second duel, shortly afterwards, he fought with the same person as before, and this time he won:

> We looked about to see if any person were in view, then we drew, and after two or three turns, he making a great stroke at my leg [with his broadsword], I slipped him, and thrust him through the body [with a smallsword] before he could recover himself. Finding he was wounded, he struck furiously, and giving way, he fell forward. (...) it was half a year before he fully recovered of his wounds.[115]

The thrust from the smallsword in this case was not lethal, merely serious. It is interesting that McBane "slipped" the leg cut by drawing back his leading leg; an action common in broadsword manuals, but not so common in smallsword texts where cuts to the leg are rare to non-existent. Apparently McBane's teacher had thought it worthwhile to teach him this movement in his first few lessons with the smallsword. Also, it is worth noting that McBane's

---

[114] David Stewart, 1825. Part 3, "Section VII – American War."
[115] Mark Rector, 2001. Page 27.

opponent received a thrust, then struck furiously for revenge, and only then fell to the floor. There are countless examples of such "afterblows" in accounts of fighting, so it is important to return to a safe, guarded position after striking or thrusting an opponent. This is an important point to bear in mind for modern practitioners of historical fencing.

One day in Perth, McBane fought a duel with a corporal, and thought he had killed the man. A few years later, in Holland, he met the same man and was very happy that his former opponent had managed to survive:

> One day [in Perth], being on guard, I happened to be absent from my duty. The Corporal being angry, upon my appearing he obliged me to stand four hours sentry, and beat me for my absence, at which my Highland blood warmed. ... I told the Corporal he had affronted me on the guard, for which I would have satisfaction, which he was very willing to give. ... We drew on each other. After some turns, he received a thrust on the breast bone. He, falling backward, cried, "You rogue! Run, for I am killed!" I said I wished it were otherways. He again desired that me to run away, for if I were catch'd, I would be hanged. (...) During my abode there [in Holland] our regiment went to the Bush at Brabin. There I met with the Sergeant I had killed in Perth. I asked him if he was ever a Corporal in Perth. He said he was. I said, "Was you not once kill'd at Perth, as you said yourself?" He said, "Almost, but not altogether, by a roguish fellow called Daniel Bane, and I believe you are the man!" I took him by the hand, so we went and took a bottle.[116]

Donald McBane was very much a rogue, and often not a very nice or honourable fellow. He was a gambler, a thief and a pimp, as well as a fencing master, and sometimes his duels were motivated for less than honourable reasons. In this excerpt, he had lost eight crowns at a game of gambling, and wanted his money back:

> At last I fell upon the fellow who got the money and took sixty crowns from him. Then he called for his companions; they were seven in number. All fell upon me with their swords. I drew my Spadroon in my own defence, with a stick in my left hand. I

---

[116] Ibid. Pages 28-30.

resolved to die rather than part with the crowns. O, how the bystanders laught to see the battle: swords broken, legs and arms cut, and five of them so wounded that they could do no more. The other two engaged me pretty hard. But I made a retreat until I got back to my camp and came to my good wife (...) I desired her to call for a surgeon. When he came, he dressed my wounds I got in the skirmish.[117]

It would be wrong to assume that duels were only ever fought for noble reasons of honour. Sometimes, fights broke out over base and unsavoury quarrels.

His final duel was against the Irishman O'Bryan in 1726, at the ripe old age of 62.[118] Here again, he avoided killing his opponent, although he had to land several blows before O'Bryan finally yielded:

In 1726 I fought a clean young man at Edinburgh. I gave him seven wounds and broke his arms with the Fauchion.[119]

McBane also describes a form of duelling between gentlemen that seems very unusual to the modern reader:

When Gentlemen are so desperate as to engage in this manner, they in honour ought to have regard to do one another justice, and each to take a fast hold of a cloak or plaid, holding it so high in the left hand that they cannot see their adversary, and cock on the other if he be ready. So by cocking their Pistols they may be so advertised, as by Slipping to the right or left they may very probably avoid each other's shot. Then may they apply to their Swords for the decision of their quarrel.[120]

Not only was duelling an activity that could break out for ignoble reasons, it was also an activity that could be conducted in various different ways. The subject of duelling is fascinating, often quite far removed from modern conceptions of the activity, and well worth further study.

---

[117] Ibid. Page 32.
[118] Ibid. Page 5.
[119] Ibid. Page 45.
[120] Ibid. Page 79.

It is clear from these excerpts that Highlanders were able to fight skilfully and bravely in many different circumstances, both on the battlefield and in affairs of honour (or in dishonourable altercations, as the case might be). Many Highlanders possessed great skill with their weapons and also immense bravery, physical strength and athleticism. Many Highlanders often had a strong moral code and would do what they could to avoid killing their opponent – sometimes because of the legality of such an action, but also sometimes because they simply did not want to kill their opponent and would rather spare a life.

By themselves, the Highlanders were fighters to be reckoned with. When they grouped together into regiments and performed the Highland charge on the battlefield, they often became unstoppable.

1.4   The Highland Charge

The "Highland Charge" was a tactic used by Highland clans and regiments on the battlefields of the 17th and 18th centuries. Generally speaking, the Highlanders would advance, shoot their muskets and discard them, then charge into close combat with broadsword and targe. There was no single method used by all the clans; accounts from battles illustrate differences in how the charge was conducted by different forces and at different times.

In his 19th century work *The Scottish Gael*, Logan describes the charge and compares it to the tactics of the ancient Celts. Given the time period in which Logan was writing, and taking into account how liberal with historical accuracy authors of that period could sometimes be, it is worth taking this comparison with a pinch of salt. However, his description of the Highland charge of the Jacobite era is similar to other descriptions, so we can trust that part of his description:

> The first assault of a Celtic army was tremendous. They ran on with such fury that they made whole legions recoil; but it has been also observed that they were always most vigorous in the first onset, their ardor gradually subsiding if unsuccessful, for

their best qualifications were strength and audacity. The strong resemblance of the Celts of modern times to their remote ancestors, in this respect, is remarkable. The Highlanders of 1745 retained all the bravery and heroism of the race, but "the chiefs knew no other manoeuvre than that of rushing upon the enemy, sword in hand, as soon as they saw them." At Flodden Field, "The Highland battalion so forward and valiant, They broke from their ranks and rushed on to slay; With hacking and slashing and broad swords a dashing, Through the front of the English they a' full way."

And at Prestonpans the rebels advanced with a swiftness not to be conceived. Dio described the Caledonian infantry as swift as running and firm in standing. An old writer, describing the Irish, says they were impetuous in their first onset, clashing their swords as they advanced; but, if repulsed, they speedily retreated to the bogs.[121]

However, the Highlanders did not just rush forwards with swords in hand. First of all, they advanced to musket range and discharged one or two volleys at their opponents:

The Highlanders advanced with rapidity, and reserved their fire until within musket length of the enemy, when they gave a general discharge, and threw them down. They then drew their swords, and, grasping their target, darted with fury on their adversaries, and fought in the manner before described. They frequently used the dirk, also, in their left hand, in which case the target was borne on the wrist.[122]

There is a critical piece of information in the final sentence of this passage: that when the dirk was held in the left hand, the targe (a small round shield) "was borne on the wrist." This would make it much easier than trying to grip both the targe and dirk together in the same hand, as has often been assumed to be the method. A large hand might be able to accommodate both handles for the targe and the dirk, but this can be problematic for people with smaller hands.

---

[121] James Logan, 1831. Pages 112-113.
[122] Ibid. Pages 239-240.

If the Highlanders had pistols as well as muskets, then these too would be fired, and then the empty pistols would be discarded like the muskets. However, unlike the muskets, the pistols could be discarded by throwing them at the enemy:

> The Highlanders were accustomed, after they had discharged their pistols, to throw them forcibly at the heads of their enemy, and it must be allowed that a blow from so hard a weapon would make no slight impression, but the policy of relinquishing either pistols or musket, during an engagement, may well be questioned. The Gaël alleged that they were relieved of encumbrances, and that if they won the battle, they could easily regain their arms, and, if defeated, their loss was not of so much consequence, that their possession could only incommode them, and retard the speed of retreat. This reasoning, I am afraid, is not altogether satisfactory, but the practice was observed at Preston Pans, and at Falkirk, in 1745.[123]

Major General David Stewart noted that the Highlanders were often very accurate and effective with their volleys, due to the short distance at which they fired and also due to their "constant practice as marksmen".[124] This shows that not only were the Scots well practised with the sword, they were also skilled with firearms, and could fight effectively at a distance as well as up close.

Donald McBane, author of *The Expert Sword-Man's Companion*, was on the receiving end of some Highland charges in his youth, and wrote about the experience in his memoirs. He fought at the Battle of Mulroy in 1688, where he received his first Highland charge and fled the battlefield:

> We drew up in a line of battle as best we could, our Company being on the right. We were no sooner in order but there appears double our number of the Mcdonalds, which made us then to fear the worst, at least for my part. I repeated my former wish [that he had still been spinning tobacco, rather than being a soldier] (I never having seen the like). The Mcdonalds came down the hill upon us without either shoe, stocking, or bonnet on their head. They gave a shout and then the fire began on both sides and

---

[123] Ibid. Pages 238-239.
[124] David Stewart, 1825. Part 3, "Section IV – Arms of the Clans."

continued a hot dispute for an hour. Then they broke in upon us with their sword and target and Lochaber axes, which obliged us to give way. Seeing my Captain sore wounded and a great many more with heads lying cloven on every side, I was sadly affrightened, never having seen the like before. A Highland-man attacked me with sword and targe and cut my wooden-handled bayonet out of the muzzle of my gun. I then clubbed my gun and give him a stroke with it, which made the butt-end to fly off. Seeing the Highlandmen to come fast upon me, I took to my heels and run thirty miles before I looked behind me.[125]

And in similar fashion, at the Battle of Killiecrankie just one year later, the Highland charge broke his unit and caused him to flee once more:

At length our enemy made their appearance at the top of a hill. We then gave a shout, daring them, as it were, to advance, which they quickly did to our great loss. When they advanced, we played our cannon for an hour upon them. The sun going down caused the Highlanders to advance on us like mad men, without shoe or stocking, covering themselves from our fire with their targes. At last they cast away their muskets, drew their Broad Swords and advanced furiously upon us, and were in the middle of us before we could fire three shots apiece, broke us and obliged us to retreat. ... I fled to the baggage and took a horse in order to ride the water. There follows me a Highland man with sword and targe in order to take the horse and kill my self. You'd laugh to see how he and I scampered about. I kept always the horse betwixt him and me. At length he drew his pistol and I fled. He fired after me. I went above the pass where I met with another water very deep. It was about eighteen foot over betwixt two rocks, I resolved to jump it, so I laid down my gun and hat and jumped and lost one of my shoes in the jump.[126]

At Killiecrankie, 2500 Highlanders fought against 4000 government troops. The government army was led by a Highland general, Hugh Mackay, who provided another account of the Highland charge that threw his army into disarray:

---

[125] Mark Rector, 2001. Page 25.
[126] Ibid. Page 26.

After firing once or twice, Highlanders "throw away their firelocks, and everyone drawing a long broad sword, with his targe ... they fall a running toward the enemy."[127]

Sir Ewen Campbell of Lochiel, who led the charge against the government troops, presents another account of the charge:

> His men "fell in pell-mell among the thickest of them with their broadswords". A strange quiet, Lochiel remembers, descended across the battlefield, "the fire ceasing on both sides", and "nothing was heard" save for "the sullen and hollow clashes of broadswords, with the dismall groans and crys of dyeing and wounded men."[128]

One of the problems faced by the royal troops in this battle was that the use of the bayonet was not as advanced a discipline as it was by the time of Culloden, nor was the bayonet itself as useful a tool at this earlier engagement. General Mackay learned from his defeat at Killiecrankie and helped to develop the strategy that helped the royal army ensure victory at Culloden:

> It was with the most intense anxiety that General Mackay beheld the sun rapidly sinking towards the horizon, and when this feeling was excited to the highest pitch, he perceived an extraordinary motion among the Highlanders, and all at once they moved slowly down the hills barefooted, and stripped of their coats. They soon rushed forward and with tremendous fury, uttering such a yell as the wild solitudes of Killiecrankie probably never before heard. They commenced the attack by a discharge of their fire-arms and pistols, which, on account of their being drawn up without regard to regularity, made little impression on Mackay's men, who were marshalled according to the strictest rules of discipline then followed, and who reserved their fire until within a few paces of the Highlanders, when they poured it into them. They discharged in platoons, they were enabled to take a steady aim, and their fire told with dreadful effect on the disorderly masses opposed to them.

---

[127] Fergus Cannan. *Scottish Arms and Armour*. Oxford: Shire Publications, 2009. Page 88.
[128] Ibid.

But this was almost all they were allowed to do. At that time the present plan of fixing bayonet was not known, and before the troops had time to screw their side-arms on their guns, and present a shining array of steel to their assailants, the Highlanders rushed in upon them sword-in-hand. It is said that General Mackay invented the present plan of firing with the bayonet screwed on from the complete defeat which he was now destined so briefly to experience, for the whole affair lasted only a few minutes, and may be described as a general discharge of fire-arms and then a carnage.[129]

At the Battle of Sheriffmuir in 1715, the plan of opposing the Highland charge with bayonet fixed around the barrel of the musket fared slightly better in the initial stage of the fight, allowing the royal army to fire volleys and cause casualties. The Highlanders almost gave up their charge because of these volleys, but the noble Glengarry roused them to complete their charge, whereupon they made short work of the royal army:

> As soon as the Earl of Mar perceived that Argyle's line was only partially formed, he resolved instantly to attack him before he should be able to complete his arrangements; and having sent orders to his right and left to fall simultaneously upon the enemy, Mar placed himself at the head of the clans; and being apprized by a firing on his left that the action had commenced, he pulled off his hat, which he waved, and with a huzza led forward his men upon the half-formed battalions which composed the left wing of the enemy.
>
> Arrived within pistol-shot, the Highlanders, according to custom, poured in a volley upon the English infantry. The fire was instantly returned; and, to the dismay of the Highlanders, Alan Muidartach, the captain of Clanranald, was mortally wounded. He was instantly carried off the field, and, as his men clustered around him, he encouraged them to stand firm to their posts, and expressed a hope that the result of the struggle in which they were engaged would be favourable to the cause of his sovereign. The loss of a chief, who, from the stately magnificence with which he upheld his feudal rank, and the urbanity of his disposition, had acquired an ascendancy over the minds of his people, could not fail to depress their spirits, and make them almost overlook the

---

[129] John Parker Lawson, Vol. 2, 1839. Page 454.

danger of their situation. While absorbed in grief, they were in a moment roused from their dejection by Glengarry, who, observing their conduct at this juncture, sprung forward, and, throwing his bonnet in the air, cried aloud, in the expressive language of his country, "Revenge! Revenge! Revenge to-day and mourning to-morrow!" No sooner had this brave chieftain pronounced these words, than the Highlanders rushed forward, sword in hand, with the utmost fury upon the royalist battalions.

The government troops attempted to stem the impetuosity of the attack, by opposing the Highlanders with fixed bayonets, but the latter pushed them aside with their targets, and rushing in with their broad swords among the enemy spread death and terror around them. The three battalions on Argyle's left, which had never been properly formed, unable to rally, instantly gave way, and falling back upon some squadrons of horse in their rear, created such confusion, that within seven or eight minutes after the assault, the form of a battalion or squadron was no longer discernible. A complete rout ensued; and there seems no doubt that the whole of Argyle's left would have been completely destroyed, had not General Whitham, at the head of the squadrons which were upon the left of the battalions, checked the advance of Mar's horse by a charge, in which he succeeded in capturing a standard.[130]

The charge was devastating when it worked, and sometimes it worked even better than usual. At the Battle of Prestonpans in 1745, the Highland charge routed not just the regiment that received the initial charge, but a further two regiments behind them. The Highlanders began their charge and kept going forwards, routing a unit of infantry and two units of cavalry in the process:

Observing the squadron of dragoons under Lieutenant-colonel Whitney advancing to charge them, the Camerons set up a loud shout, rushed past the cannon, and, after discharging a few shots at the dragoons, which killed several men, and wounded the lieutenant-colonel, flew upon them sword in hand. When assailed, the squadron was reeling to and fro from the fire; and the Highlanders, following an order they had received to strike at the noses of the horses without minding their riders, completed the

---

[130] John Parker Lawson, Vol. 4, 1839. Pages 287-288.

disorder. In a moment the dragoons wheeled about, rode over the artillery guard, and fled followed by the guard. The Highlanders continuing to push forward without stopping to take prisoners, Colonel Gardiner was ordered to advance with his squadron, and charge the enemy. He accordingly went forward, encouraging his men to stand firm; but this squadron, before it had advanced many paces, experienced a similar reception with its companion, and followed the example which the other had just set.

After the flight of the dragoons, the highlanders advanced upon the infantry, who opened a fire from right to left, which went down the line as far as Murray's regiment. They received this volley with a loud huzza, and throwing away their muskets, drew their swords and rushed upon the foot before they had time to reload their pieces. Confounded by the flight of the dragoons, and the furious onset of the Highlanders, the astonished infantry threw down their arms and took to their heels. Hamilton's dragoons, who were stationed on Cope's left, displayed even greater pusillanimity than their companions; for no sooner did they observe the squadrons on their right give way, than they turned their backs and fled without firing a single shot or drawing a sword. Murray's regiment being thus left alone on the field, fired upon the Macdonalds, who were advancing, and also fled. Thus, within a very few minutes after the action had commenced, the whole army of Cope was put to flight. With the exception of their fire, not the slightest resistance was made by horse or foot, and not a single bayonet was stained with blood. Such were the impetuosity and rapidity with which the first line of the Highlanders broke through Cope's ranks, that they left numbers of his men in their rear, who attempted to rally behind them; but on seeing the second line coming up, they endeavoured to make their escape. Though the second line was not more than 50 paces behind the first, and was always running as fast as it could to overtake the first line, and near enough never to lose sight of it, yet such was the rapidity with which the battle was gained, that, according to the Chevalier Johnstone, who stood by the side of the Prince in the second line, he could see no other enemy on the field of battle than those who were lying on the ground killed and wounded. [131]

---

[131] Ibid. Pages 117-119.

The Highlanders must have been covering ground swiftly, because the second line tried to overtake the first, but remained around 50 paces behind. This charge inflicted terrible casualties upon the government troops, mainly from the broadswords of the Camerons and the scythes that were carried by the Macgregors:

> The impetuosity of the attack, however, and the sudden flight of the royal army, allowed little leisure for the exercise of humanity; and before the carnage ceased several hundreds had fallen under the claymores of the Highlanders, and the ruthless scythes of the Macgregors. Armed with these deadly weapons, which were sharpened and fixed to poles from seven to eight feet long, to supply the place of other arms, this party mowed down the affrightened enemy, cut off the legs of the horses, and severed, it is said, the bodies of their riders in twain.[132]

As described, sometimes the charge worked superlatively, and achieved resounding success. At other times, it failed dismally. At the Battle of Culloden, the Highland charge failed to break the government lines as had been achieved so well in previous battles. An excerpt from the Duke of Cumberland's orderly-book describes the manner in which the Highlanders conducted this charge, and the response with which the government troops should meet the attack:

> Field-officer for the day: to-morrow Major Willson. The manner of the Highlander's way of fighting, which there is nothing so easy to resist, if officers and men are not prepossessed with the lyes and accounts which are told of them. They commonly form their front rank of what they call their best men, or true Highlanders, the number of which being allways but few, when they form in battallions they commonly form four deep, and these Highlanders form the front of the four, the rest being Lowlanders and arrant scum; when these battallions come within a large musket-shott, or three-score yards, this front rank gives their fire and immediately throw down their firelocks and come down in a cluster with their swords and targets, making a noise and endeavouring to pearce the body, or battallions before them. Becoming twelve or fourteen deep by the time they come up to the people, they attack. The sure way to demolish them is at three deep to fire by ranks diagonally to the centre where they

---

[132] Ibid Pages 117-119.

come, the rear rank first, and even that rank not to fire till they are within ten or twelve paces; but if the fire is given at a distance you probably will be broke, for you never get time to load a second cartridge; and if you give way, you may give your foot for dead, for they being without a firelock, or any load, no man with his arms, accoutrements, &c. can escape them, and they give no quarters; but if you will but observe the above directions, the are the most despicable enemy that are.[133]

Clearly the Duke and his orderlies believed that there was nothing too difficult in stopping the Highland charge, describing it as "nothing so easy to resist" as long as the government troops and officers did not believe the stories about the Highlanders. It seems that his army followed these tactics, because the Highland charges at Culloden were met with "a murderous fire" that critically reduced the effectiveness of the charge:

Unable any longer to restrain their impatience, Lord George [Murray] had just resolved upon an immediate advance; but before he had time to issue the order along the line, the Mackintoshes, with a heroism worthy of that brave clan, rushed forward enveloped in the smoke of the enemy's cannon. The fire of the centre field-pieces, and a discharge of musquetry from the Scotch Fusiliers, forced them to incline a little to the right; but all the regiments to their right, led on by Lord George Murray in person, and the united regiment of the Maclauchlans and Macleans on their left, coming down close after them, the whole moved forward at a pretty quick pace.

When within pistol-shot of the royalist line, they received a murderous fire, not only in front from some field-pieces, which for the first time were not loaded with grape-short, but in flank from a side-battery supported by the Campbells, and Lord Loudon's Highlanders. Whole ranks were literally swept away by the dreadful fire of the royalists. Yet, notwithstanding the dreadful carnage in their ranks, the Highlanders continued to advance, and, after giving their fire close to the royalist line, which, from the density of the smoke, was scarcely perceptible even within pistol-shot, the right wing, consisting of the Athole Highlanders and the Camerons, rushed in sword in hand, and broke through Barrel's and Monroe's regiments, which stood on the left of the

---

[133] A.T. Thomson, Vol. 1, 1845. "Cameron of Lochiel."

first line. These regiments bravely defended themselves with their spontoons and bayonets; but such was the impetuosity of the onset, that they would entirely have been cut to pieces had they not been immediately supported by two regiments from the second line, on the approach of which they retired behind the regiments on their right, after sustaining a loss in killed and wounded of upwards of two hundred men.

After breaking through these two regiments, the Highlanders, passing by the two field-pieces which had annoyed them in front, hurried forward to attack the left of the second line. They were met by a tremendous fire of grape-shot from the three field-pieces on the left of the second line, and by a discharge of musquetry from Bligh's and Semphill's regiments, which carried havoc through their ranks, and made them at first recoil; but, maddened by despair, and utterly regardless of their lives, they rushed upon an enemy whom they felt but could not see, amid the cloud of smoke in which the assailants were buried. The same kind of charge was made by the Stewarts of Appin, the Frasers, Mackintoshes, and the other centre regiments in their front, which they drove back upon the second line, which they also attempted to break; but finding themselves unable they gave up the contest, but not until numbers had been cut down at the mouths of the cannon.

While advancing towards the second line, Lord George Murray, in attempting to dismount from his horse, which had become unmanageable, was thrown; but, recovering himself, he ran to the rear and brought up two or three regiments from the second line to support the first; but although they gave their fire, nothing could be done,– all was lost. Unable to break the second line, and being greatly cut up by the fire of Wolfe's regiment, and by Cobham's and Kerr's dragoons, who had formed *en potence* on their right flank, the right wing also gave up the contest, and turning about, cut their way back, sword in hand, through those who advanced and formed on the ground they had passed over in charging to their front.[134]

An interesting note is that some of the Highlanders were "unable to fire their customary volley" because of difficult terrain and the heavy fire that they received. Instead, they discarded their primed and loaded guns, and charged into close quarters where they

---

[134] John Parker Lawson, Vol. 3, 1839. Pages 387-389.

could use their bladed weapons to greater effect than their firearms.[135]

The Highlanders managed to penetrate through the first line of government troops, where a second line of fresh soldiers met them. The charge stalled, and the Highlanders had to retreat; however, government troops had formed up in the space through which the Highlanders had charged, which meant that the Highlanders needed to charge back over that same ground in order to withdraw:

> Before commencing the attack, they frequently put off their jackets and shoes, that their movements might not be impeded. Their advance to battle was a kind of trot, such as is now, in our light infantry discipline, called double-quick marching. When they had advanced within a few yards of the enemy, they poured in a volley of musketry, which, from the short distance, and their constant practice as marksmen, was generally very effective; then dropping their muskets, they dashed forward sword in hand, reserving their pistols and dirks for close action. "To make an opening in regular troops, and to conquer, they reckoned the same thing, because, in close engagements, and in broken ranks, no regular troops would withstand them." [Dalrymple's Memoirs.]

> When they closed with the enemy, they received the points of the bayonets on their targets; and thrusting them aside, resorted to their pistols and dirks, to complete the impression made by the musket and broadsword. It was in this manner that the Athole Highlanders and the Camerons, who were on the right of Prince Charles Edward's followers at Culloden, charged the left wing of the royal army. After breaking through Barrell's and Munroe's (the 4th and 37th regiments), which formed the left of the royal army, they pushed forward to charge the second line, composed of Bligh's and Semple's (the 20th and 25th regiments). Here their impetuosity met an effectual check, by the fire of those corps, when they came within a few yards, and still more by Wolfe's (the 8th foot), and Cobham's and Lord Mark Kerr's (the 10th and 11th Light Dragoons), who had formed en potence on their right flank, and poured in a most destructive fire along their whole line. At the same moment they were taken in rear by the Argyle, and some companies of Lord Loudon's Highlanders, who had advanced

---

[135] Peter Harrington, 1991. Pages 61-62.

in that direction, and had broken down an old wall that covered the right of the rebels. By this combination of attacks in front, right flank, and rear, they were forced to give up the contest, and to charge back again, sword in hand, through those who had advanced and formed on the ground they had passed over in charging to their front. In this desperate conflict they left half their number dead on the field.

The same kind of charge was made by the Stewarts of Appin, Frasers, and Mackintoshes upon the regiments in their front. These were the Scotch Fusileers and Ligonier's (the 21st and 48th regiments,) which they drove back upon the second line, but, being unable to penetrate, numbers were cut down at the mouths of the cannon, before they gave up the contest.[136]

Major General David Stewart notes that even when the charge did not work, the Highlanders were able to "amaze and confound regular troops" with the "strength and dexterity" with which they used their weapons:

The Reverend Dr Shaw, in his manuscript History of the Rebellion, says, "The enemy's attack on the left wing of the royal army was made with a view to break that wing, to run it into disorder, and then to communicate the disorder to the whole army. This could not easily be effected, when a second and third line were ready to sustain the first. But it must be owned the attack was made with the greatest courage, order, and bravery, amidst the hottest fire of small arms, and continued fire of cannon with grape-shot, on their flanks, front, and rear. They ran in upon the points of the bayonets, hewed down the soldiers with their broad-swords, drove them back, put them into disorder, and possessed themselves of two pieces of cannon.

The rebels' left wing did not sustain them in the attack, and four fresh regiments coming up from the Duke's second line under General Huske, they could not stand under a continual fire both in front, in flank, and rear, and therefore they retired. It was in this attack that Lord Robert Kerr, having stood his ground, after Barrell's regiment was broke and drove back, was killed."

And farther we learn from the Lockhart papers, that "Lord George Murray attacked, at the head of the Atholemen, who had the right

---

[136] David Stewart, 1825. Part 3, "Section IV – Arms of the Clans."

of the army that day, with all the bravery imaginable, as the whole army did, and broke the Duke of Cumberland's line in several places, and made themselves masters of two pieces of cannon,—though they were both fronted and flanked by them, who kept a close firing from right to left,—and marched up to the points of their bayonets, which they could not see for smoke till they were upon them." Such were the strength and dexterity with which these people used their arms, if not always to conquer, at least to amaze and confound regular troops.[137]

Another surviving account of the Highland charge describes the stepwise process of the closing the distance towards the enemy regiment:

> When descending to battle, [the Highlander] was to place his bonnet on his head with an emphatic "scrugg"; his second, to cast off or throw back his plaid; his third to incline his body horizontally forward, cover it with his targe, rush to within 50 paces of the enemy's line, discharge and drop his fusee or musket; his fourth to dart within 12 paces, discharge and fling his claw-butted steel stocked pistols at the foeman's head; his fifth to draw his claymore and dirk at him![138]

Always willing to embrace useful equipment and techniques, the British Army adopted and modified the Highland charge tactic for their own use. The Highland Regiments performed such charges on the battlefields in Europe, India and North America. By the time of the Napoleonic Wars, the Duke of Wellington used the general tactic of firing volleys then advancing towards the enemy with cold steel to make them flee, with many of his regiments – not just the Scottish units.[139]

During the campaign in the West Indies, the Highlanders were part of the British force besieging Morne Tortueson in 1762, when they came under attack by "the enemy's whole force". They

---

[137] David Stewart, 1825. Part 3, "Section IV – Arms of the Clans."

[138] Peter Harrington, 1991. Page 40.

[139] Paul Wagner and Mark Rector. *Highland Broadsword: Five Manuals of Scottish Regimental Swordsmanship*. Highland Village: Chivalry Bookshelf, 2004. Pages 11-13.

repulsed this attack, then took the offensive themselves, charging with their broadswords, routing their enemy and seizing victory:

> The enemy's whole force descended from the hill, and attacked the British in their advanced posts. They were immediately repulsed; and the troops, carried forward by their ardour, converted defence into assault, and passed the ravines with the fugitives. "The Highlanders, drawing their swords, rushed forward like furies; and, being supported by the Grenadiers under Colonel Grant (Ballendalloch), and a party of Lord Rollo's brigade, the hills were mounted and the batteries seized, and numbers of the enemy, unable to escape from the rapidity of the attack, were taken.[140]

A year earlier in this campaign, the Highlanders had attacked some entrenchments during the siege of Roseau. The swiftness of their advanced helped to limit the number of casualties they suffered:

> Lord Rollo resolved to attack without delay, particularly as he had learned that a reinforcement from Martinique was shortly expected. This service was performed by his Lordship and Colonel Melville, at the head of the Grenadiers, Light infantry, and Highlanders, with such vigour and success, that the enemy were driven, in succession, from all their works. So rapid was the charge of the Grenadiers and Highlanders, that few of the British suffered.[141]

This information is similar to an account of the Battle of Fontenoy in 1745, during the War of the Austrian Succession. Again, the Highlanders made their charge, and the swiftness of their advance at Fontenoy meant that they sustained many fewer casualties than the Dutch, who advanced more cautiously and sustained fire for a longer period of time:

> Comparing the loss sustained by this [42nd] regiment in the field with that of other corps, it has generally been less than theirs, except in the unfortunate affair of Ticonderoga. I have conversed with several officers who served in the corps at that period, and

---

[140] David Stewart, 1825. Part 3, "Section V – Montgomery's Highlanders."
[141] Ibid.

they uniformly accounted for the moderate loss from the celerity of their attack, and the use of the broadsword, which the enemy could never withstand. This, likewise, was the opinion of an old gentleman, one of the original soldiers of the Black Watch, in the ranks of which, although a gentleman by birth and education, he served till the peace of 1748. He informed me that, although it was believed at home that the regiment had been nearly destroyed at Fontenoy, the thing was quite the reverse; and that it was the subject of general observation in the army, that their loss should have been so small, considering how actively they were engaged in different parts of the field.

"On one occasion," said the respectable veteran, who was animated with the subject, "a brigade of Dutch were ordered to attack a rising ground, on which were posted the troops called the King of France's own Guards. The Highlanders were to support them. The Dutch conducted their march and attack as if they did not know the road, halting and firing, and halting, every twenty paces. The Highlanders, losing all patience with this kind of fighting, which gave the enemy such time and opportunity to fire at their leisure, dashed forward, passed the Dutch, and the first ranks giving their firelocks to the rear rank, they drew their swords, and soon drove the French from their ground. When the attack was concluded, it was found that of the Highlanders not above a dozen men were killed and wounded, while the Dutch, who had not come up at all, lost more than five times that number."[142]

Before the Battle of Fontenoy, the Black Watch (the 42nd regiment) and the Scottish Foot-Guards had fought the French at Veson. Entrenchments protected the French, and the only way to secure victory was to resort to cold steel and close range use of explosive grenades. James Grant provides the following story in his *Legends of the Black Watch*:

The Guards and we—the old Black Watch—began the engagement at Veson—the well-known affair of outposts. There the Dauphin commanded, and his soldiers were the flower of the French line, a splendid brigade, all clad in white coats laced with gold, long ruffles, tied perriwigs, and little plumed hats. They were intrenched breast high, and defended by an abattls.

---

[142] Ibid. Part 3, "Section VI – Fraser's, Montgomery's, and Royal Highlanders."

We fell furiously on; the Scottish Foot-guards with their clubbed muskets and fixed bayonets; the Black Watch with swords, pistols, and dirks, and the struggle was terrible, as the action ensued at a place which was swept by the fire of a redoubt mounted with cannon and manned by six hundred of the noble Regiment de 'Picardie. Old Captain Maclean, at the head of his grenadiers and which his seven sons by his side, rushed up the glacis to storm the palisades.

"Open pouches—blow fuses—dirk and claymore, fall on" were his rapid orders, as the hand-grenades fell like a hissing shower over the breastwork, from which a sheet of lead tore through the ranks of our stormers. Maclean fell at the foot of the palisades with one hand upon them and the other on his sword. All his sons perished with him, falling over each other in a gory heap as they strove to protect his body. The last who fell was the youngest, Angus Dhu, who, after slaying a French field officer, had driven a bayonet into his head, thrusting it through the ears using it as a lever, he strove furiously to twist, tear, or wrench off the Frenchman's skull as a trophy, of vengeance; for the young Celt was beside himself with grief and rage, when a volley of bullets from the white-coated Regiment de Picardie laid him on the grass to rise no more, just as Sir James Campbell carried the intrenchment sword in hand, and totally routed and destroyed the soldiers of the Dauphin.[143]

It seems that "dirk and claymore" may have been a common battlecry, as it is also recorded in this account of the Montgomery Highlanders at the siege of Fort du Quesne:

The moment the soldiers of [Major] Grant were within range, the French cannon opened upon them, and under cover of this fire, the infantry made a furious sortie.

"Sling your muskets! Dirk and claymore," cried the major as the foe came on. A terrible conflict ensued, the Highlanders fighting with their swords and daggers, and the Provincials with their fixed bayonets; the French gave way, but, unable to reach the fort, they dispersed and sought shelter in the vast forest which spread in every direction round it.[144]

---

[143] James Grant, 1859. "The Seven Grenadiers."
[144] Ibid. "The Lost Regiment – A Love Story."

The Highlanders were always willing to do what needed to be done in order to secure victory, as long as they trusted and respected their leader, and felt that they were not being insulted. Likewise, some Irish regiments had similar strategies and similar characteristics to their Highland cousins, as shown by this excerpt from *The Legends of the Black Watch*:

> When the Comte d'Tastaing madly proposed to take the fortress [of Savannah] by a coup-de-main, M. le Comte Dillon, anxious to signalize his Irishmen, proposed a reward of a hundred guineas to the first grenadier who should plant a fascine in the fosse, which was swept by the whole fire of the garrison; but his purse was proffered in vain, for not an Irishman would advance. Confounded by this, Dillon was upbraiding them with cowardice, when the sergeant-major said—
>
> "Monsieur de Comte, had you not held out a sum of money as an incentive, your grenadiers would one and all have rushed to the assault."
>
> The count put his purse in his pocket.
>
> "Forward!" cried he—forward went the Irish grenadiers, and out of 194 who composed the company, 104 left their bodies in the breach.[145]

At the Battle of Camden in 1780, one of the British victories in the American War of Independence was achieved by the charges of the Highland Regiments. Lord Cornwallis led the British army, opposed by the American general Horatio Gates. The two armies marched towards each other, both intending to attack. They surprised each other; and while the British line was forming:

> Captain Charles Campbell, who commanded the Highland light companies on the right, placed himself on the stump of an old tree to reconnoitre, and observing the Americans moving as with the intention of turning his flank, leaped down, and giving vent to an oath, called to his men, "Remember you are light infantry; remember you are Highlanders: Charge!"

---

[145] Ibid.

The attack was rapid and irresistible, and being made before the Americans had completed their movement by which they were to surround the British right, they were broken and driven from the field, prior to the beginning of the battle in other parts of the line. When the battle did commence the American center gained ground. Lord Cornwallis opened his center to the right and left, till a considerable space intervened, and then directed the Highlanders to move forward and occupy the vacant space. When this was done, he cried out, "My brave Highlanders, now is your time."

They instantly rushed forward accompanied by the Irish volunteers and the 33d, and penetrated and completely overthrew the American column. However the American right continued to advance and gained the ground on which the Highlanders had been placed originally as a reserve. They gave three cheers for victory; but the smoke clearing up they saw their mistake. A party of Highlanders turning upon them, the greater part threw down their arms, while the remainder fled in all directions. The victory was complete.[146]

Of course, just as the Highland charge sometimes failed in the British Isles, it sometimes failed elsewhere in the world. In 1781, during the North American campaign, the Highlanders and their charge were defeated by two lines of infantry, in a similar fashion to Culloden: the front line gave way and retreated after giving fire and causing casualties, then the second line managed to stop the Highlanders and force them to retreat. This engagement is said to have been "the first instance of a Highland Regiment [in the British Army] running from an enemy", and is described by this passage:

Colonel Tarleton was detached to disperse the little army of General Morgan, having with him, the 7th or Fusileers, the 1st battalion of Fraser's Highlanders, or 71st, two hundred in number, a detachment of the British Legion, and three hundred cavalry. Intelligence was received, on the morning of January 17, 1781, that General Morgan was drawn up in front on rising ground. The

---

[146] J.P. MacLean. *An Historical Account of the Settlements of Scotch Highlanders in America Prior to the Peace of 1783 together with notices of Highland Regiments and Biographical Sketches.* Glasgow: John MacKay, 1900. "Chapter 13 – Highland Regiments in American Revolution."

British were hastily formed, with the Fusileers, the Legion, and the light infantry in front, and the Highlanders and cavalry forming the reserve. As soon as formed the line was ordered to advance rapidly. Exhausted by running, it received the American fire at the distance of thirty or forty paces. The effect was so great as to produce something of a recoil.

The fire was returned; and the light infantry made two attempts to charge, but were repulsed with loss. The Highlanders next were ordered up, and rapidly advancing in charge, the American front line gave way and retreated through an open space in the second line. This manoeuvre was made without interfering with the ranks of those who were now to oppose the Highlanders, who ran in to take advantage of what appeared to them to be a confusion of the Americans. The second line threw in a fire upon the 71st, when within forty yards which was so destructive that nearly one half their number fell; and those who remained were so scattered, having run a space of five hundred yards at full speed, that they could not be united to form a charge with the bayonet. They did not immediately fall back, but engaged in some irregular firing, when the American line pushed forward to the right flank of the Highlanders, who now realized that there was no prospect of support, and while their number was diminishing that of their foe was increasing. They first wavered, then began to retire, and finally to run, this is said to have been the first instance of a Highland Regiment running from an enemy.

This repulse struck a panic into those whom they left in the rear, and who fled in the greatest confusion. Order and command were lost, and the rout became general. Few of the infantry escaped, and the cavalry saved itself by putting their horses to full speed. The Highlanders reformed in the rear, and might have made a soldier—like retreat if they had been supported.[147]

A good general summary of the Highland charge was written by Mrs Thomson in her *Memoirs of the Jacobites of 1715 and 1745*:

It was the custom of the Highlanders to give a general discharge of their fire-arms, and then to rush, sword in hand, upon their foes: and the only chance of a victory for their party that day, was a general shock of their whole line at once; for the fury and

---

[147] Ibid. "Chapter 13 – Highland Regiments in American Revolution."

valour of these northern warriors produced results almost incredible.[148]

The precise method of the charge differed from clan to clan and across different time periods. It depended on the general in question, the equipment of the Highlanders and the terrain over which they fought. Generally speaking, it involved an advance, a volley of musketry or pistols, and then a rush to enter close combat with broadsword and targe. The shock of the charge was immense and it could rout even the well-trained and disciplined regiments of the British Army, who adopted similar tactics in their wars elsewhere in the world.

The combination of advancing with cold steel, their fearsome reputation, and their personal skill and strength with their weapons was a potent mixture, able to cause some of the most famous soldiers in the world to retreat and flee.

1.5   Highlanders in the British Army

It would be a mistake to think that before the Highland Regiments were raised as part of the British Army, the Highlanders had little military discipline or structure. James Logan notes that the clan armies had military structure appropriate to their methods of fighting:

> The order observed in the armies of the Highlanders, before the abolition of their heritable independence, was this: every regiment or clan was commanded by the chief, if of sufficient age, who was consequently the colonel. The eldest cadet was lieut.-colonel, and the next was major. Each company had two captains, two lieutenants, and two ensigns, and the front ranks were composed of gentlemen who were all provided with targets, and were otherwise better armed than the rear. In the day of battle, each company furnished two of their best men as a guard to the chief, and in their choice consanguinity was always considered. The chief was posted in the centre of the column, beside the colors, and he stood between two brothers, cousins-german, or

---

[148] A.T. Thomson, Vol. 3, 1845. "Lord George Murray."

other relations. The common men were also disposed with regard to their relatives, the father, the son, and the brother standing beside each other.[149]

In terms of guarding the chief as described in this passage, there was often a specific body of men called the *Luchdtacht* (or sometimes *Luchdtachk*) who were given this job and who trained for it extensively:

> The Luchdtachk of the highlanders was a body of young men, selected from the best families in the clan, who were skilfully trained to the use of the sword and targe, archery, wrestling, swimming, leaping, and all military and athletic exercises; and their duty was to attend the chief wherever he went.[150]

In his thesis comparing Scottish training methods for the battlefield and for the duel, Ben Kerr notes that battlefield training placed great importance upon being able to work as a group. While "personal conditioning" and "personal tactics" were important, they had to assist the "wider group tactics" so that the group could function effectively as a whole.[151] Scottish children were given tuition with singlestick or cudgel to develop their personal fighting skills, but they still had to learn how to function as part of a team. This passage from the *Dewar Manuscripts* describes a typical school for sword exercise for young men in the early 18th century:

> It was a custom in the Highlands of Scotland before the year 1745 that the gentry kept schools to give instruction to youths in sword exercise, and the laird of Ardsheil kept a school for the instruction of the youth of his own district. He stored the cudgels behind his house. There were cudgels for the lads, and there were cudgels for the laddies, and lads and laddies went every day to Ardsheil to receive instruction on the cudgel from the laird. After the laddies had received their day's instruction each got a bannock and lumps of cheese. They were then sent to try who would soonest ascend a mountain and eat the bannock and

---

[149] James Logan, 1831. Page 127.

[150] Ibid. Page 126.

[151] Ben Kerr. "A Comparison of the Training and Application of Techniques Between War and the Formal Duel in Scotland from 1690 to 1740." MLitt Thesis, University of Glasgow, September 2010. Pages 48-49.

cheese; and whoever was first got another bannock and lumps of cheese home with him.[152]

It can thus be well established that the Highlanders were skilled fighters who managed to structure their clan armies effectively. When the Highland Regiments were raised as part of the British Army, the regimental army training gave the Highlanders additional skills and equipment, combining their natural skill, courage and initiative with greater discipline and leadership.[153] Wagner and Rector note that the "most absurd courage, obstinacy, and innate sense of superiority of the aristocratic British officer class", including the Scottish nobles with British Army officer training, gave the Highlanders steady, unwavering and effective leadership.[154]

In the memoirs of Donald Macleod, he notes that in the early 18th century the British Army was filled with courageous and moral men, not just the scum that filled it later in the century:

> The army was not then, as it is now [c.1703], the common receptacle of all that carry the name and appearance of men. The art was not then known, or professed, of bending the greatest black-guards and poltroons into brave men, by the power of discipline: Regard was had to morals, to personal courage and strength, and to political and personal attachments.[155]

Paul Macdonald suggests that it should be considered a valid option, rather than being considered mercenary, for a young Scot in the time of Donald McBane to join one of the Government Companies in the British Army.[156] It should be noted that many Scots (if not most, asserts Cannan) were loyal to the Government and to the Hanoverian kings rather than to the deposed Stuart kings.[157] There were many Scottish soldiers and officers in the British Army, and also many English soldiers who joined the

---

[152] John MacKechnie. *The Dewar Manuscripts. Volume 1: Scottish West Highland Folk Tales*. London: William MacClellan, 1963. Page 161.
[153] Paul Wagner and Mark Rector, 2004. Page 8.
[154] Ibid.
[155] William Thomson, 1791. Page 30.
[156] Mark Rector, 2001. Page 20.
[157] Fergus Cannan, 2009. Page 95.

Jacobite uprisings.[158] The Jacobite conflicts were not "Scottish versus English" as is so commonly assumed, but rather were rebels (justified or unjustified, depending on different points of view) against the government, with Scots and English on both sides of the affair. In terms of the Scots in the British Army, there were both Highlanders and Lowlanders, and at Culloden the Clan Campbell "provided the Hanoverians with the same kind of wild muscle that had served Charles so well."[159]

Serving in the Highland Regiments of the British Army carried a certain prestige of carrying arms that appealed to the martial spirit of the disarmed Highlanders.[160] David Stewart relates that the soldiers in the Black Watch regiment carried a selection of weapons very similar to those of their non-regimental cousins:

> The arms [of the Black Watch regiment] were a musquet, a bayonet, and a large basket-hiked broadsword. These were furnished by Government: such of the men as chose to supply themselves with pistols and dirks were allowed to carry them, and some had targets after the fashion of their country. Grose, in his Military Antiquities, speaking of the Black Watch, says, "I doubt whether the dirk is part of their regimental arms; but I remember, in the year 1747, most of the private men had them, and many were also permitted to carry targets. The regiment was then on service in Flanders."[161]

The Highland Regiments used these weapons in a very similar fashion to the clan armies, even after receiving their Army training. Stewart provides this account from a Lowlander who served in many campaigns with the Highland Regiments, describing their manner of service and fighting:

> A learned and ingenious author, who, though himself a Lowlander, had ample opportunity, while serving in many campaigns with Highland regiments, of becoming intimately acquainted with their character, thus develops their conduct in the field: (...)

---

[158] Ibid.
[159] Ibid. Page 103.
[160] David Stewart, 1825. Part 3, "Section I – Black Watch."
[161] Ibid.

84

"If ardour be the characteristic of Highlanders, it is evident that they are not calculated for mechanical manoeuvres, nor for demonstrations and encounters with a view to diversion; for unless the purpose be previously explained and understood in its full extent, the Highlander darts on the enemy with impetuosity, rushing into close action, where it was only intended to amuse. He does not brook disappointment, sustain a galling distant fire with coolness, or retire from an enterprise with temper. He may be trusted to cover the most dangerous retreat assigned to him as a duty; a retreat in consequence of his own failure is likely to degenerate into a rout. In action, the Highlander requires to see his object fully: he then feels the impression of his duty, and acts animately and consistently, more from impression and sentiment than from external impulse of command; for, when an enemy is before the Highlander, the authority of the officer may be said to cease. Different nations have different excellencies or defects in war. Some excel in the use of missile weapons: the power of the Highlander lies in close combat. Close charge was his ancient mode of attack; and it is probably from impression, ingrafted in his nature in consequence of the national mode of war, that he still sustains the approaching point of a naked weapon with a steadier eye than any other man in Europe. Some nations turn with fear from the countenance of an enraged enemy: the Highlander rushes towards it with ardour; and if he can grasp his foe, as man with man, his courage is secure."[162]

The Highland charge was still a part of the tactical repertoire of the Highland Regiments, although they could discipline themselves to hold fast and trade volleys if required, and would stand and carry out their duties as ordered – as long as the enemy did not come too close in front of them! The Highlanders in the Army were very proud of their country and heritage, and did not view their participation in the British Army as contradictory to this. They could not be tempted by money to do what they did not want to do; they chose to serve with their friends and family in the theatre of war in which they felt most inclined to enter:

It is well known that the bounty-money had no influence in the Highlands, when men were raised for the 42d and other Highland corps in the Seven Years' War, as well as in that which ended in 1783. In 1776, upwards of 800 men were recruited for the 42d in

---

[162] Ibid. Part 3, "Preliminary Observations."

a few weeks, on a bounty of one guinea, while officers who offered ten and twelve guineas for recruits, which they were raising for their commissions, could not get a man till the national corps were completed. I have also had frequent experience of this in my own person while serving in the 42d and 78th regiments. On many occasions, as I shall have to notice afterwards, numbers of young Highlanders inlisted for foreign service, (and this sometimes in bands together), on receiving less than one-half of the bounty-money given at the same time by officers for their commissions in the regular and fencible regiments for home-service, as likewise by others for militia substitutes. When I was recruiting for the 78th, the regiment was in the East Indies, and the prospect held out to the men of embarking for that country in a few months; yet they engaged with me, and other officers, for ten guineas, to embark immediately on a dangerous but honourable duty, when they could have got twenty guineas as militia substitutes, and to remain in their native country. This is very different from what some late authors have pretended to discover, that the youth of the Highlands have a notorious aversion to a military life.[163]

The Highlanders were often virtuous and moral men, well behaved and well disciplined. Stewart writes that they received little by way of punishment across the second half of the 18th century because of their good conduct:

And why, when they mount the cockade, are they found to be so virtuous and regular, that one thousand men have been embodied four and five years together, at different and distant periods, from 1759 to 1763, from 1779 to 1783, and from 1793 to 1798, without an instance of military punishment? These men performed all the duties of soldiers to the perfect satisfaction of their commanders, and continued so unexceptionable in their conduct down to the latest period, when embodied into the 93d regiment, that, according to the words of a distinguished general officer, "Although the youngest regiment in the service, they might form an example to all:" And on general parades for punishment, the Sutherland Highlanders have been ordered to their quarters, as "examples of this kind were not necessary for such honourable soldiers, who had no crimes to punish".[164]

---

[163] Ibid. Part 2, "Section III – Beneficial Results of Judicious Arrangements."
[164] Ibid. Part 2, "Section II – Causes and Consequences of this Change."

Sir John Dalrymple observed of the Highland character:

> That to be modest as well as brave, to be contented with a few things which Nature requires, to act and to suffer without complaining, to be as much ashamed of doing any thing insolent or ungenerous to others, as of bearing it when done to ourselves, and to die with pleasure to revenge affronts offered to their clan or their country; these they accounted their highest accomplishments.[165]

While these assorted accounts paint a very positive picture of the Highlander as a model soldier in the army, it was not always the case. In the late 18th century, Donald Macleod wrote that the Army was "the common receptacle of all that carry the name and appearance of men",[166] not just the brave and moral. Donald McBane writes freely in *The Expert Sword-Man's Companion*, providing anecdotes showing that he was a pimp, gambler and thief as well as a soldier and fencing master.[167] There will have been many unsavoury characters among the Highland Regiments as well as the perfect soldiers.

Nor did the Highland Regiments remain "special" forever, with the prerogative to choose their own weapons and do their own thing with regard to arms and dress; in 1784, for example, private soldiers in the Black Watch were no longer issued with broadswords as standard items of equipment.[168] By 1809, six of the Highland Regiments no longer wore the kilt, and instead wore the same kind of uniform as the rest of the British Army.[169]

So the Highlanders in the British Army maintained much of their tradition and heritage, much of their national character, and served with dignity at home and abroad. The Highland Regiments campaigned across the world and won respect and acclaim for their actions and courage. But they were not supermen – they had their failings, and their leaders had to understand just how to lead

---

[165] Ibid. Part 1, "Section VII – General Means of Subsistence."
[166] William Thomson, 1791. Page 30.
[167] Mark Rector, 2001. Pages 21-45.
[168] Paul Wagner and Mark Rector, 2004. Page 8.
[169] W.A. Thorburn. *Uniform of the Scottish Infantry: 1740 to 1900*. Edinburgh: Scottish United Museum Service, 1970. Page 4.

them correctly, else the Highlanders would not fight properly. Over time, the Highland Regiments became more similar to other regiments in the British Army in terms of equipment and dress.

This is a fascinating area of Scottish and indeed British history, worthy of much deeper study, but this chapter must conclude now in order to stay within the scope of this study guide.

1.6   Conclusions about Scottish Swordsmanship

Paul Wagner writes that:

> While a considerable amount of literature exists on the tactics used by the Gaels, such as the famous "Highland Charge," Gaelic swordsmanship itself has received little attention and is often dismissed as being "simple" or "crude." However, it could be argued that the secret of the Highlander's military success lay not in the tactics of the clan armies, but at the level of the individual swordsman.[170]

This is a very reasonable conclusion to draw, and one with which this study guide agrees. From the historical accounts and memoirs presented throughout this chapter, it is plain to see that there was more to Scottish warfare than simply charging and hoping for the best. Individuals trained themselves to be fit, strong and capable; children were given tuition and copious opportunity to practise with the singlestick, broadsword and the targe. Wrestling and knife fighting were important skills, as were long-range skills with bows, pistols, muskets and rifles.

Games, sports and physical strength were important elements of a Highlander's life. Individual Scots could perform amazing feats of athleticism on the battlefield, allowing them to bring their swords to bear wherever they were needed, or allowing them to escape from harm as the case might be.

---

[170] Mark Rector, 2001. Page 7.

It would be wrong to assume that there was no sensible or rigorous training to produce the skill at arms possessed by many fighters. It would be similarly ridiculous to suggest that they spent their time concentrating on swordsmanship to the detriment of their physical fitness and athleticism. They could fight by themselves, in small skirmishing or raiding parties, or as part of a clan or government regiment, so they were able to conduct themselves appropriately in many different forms of engagement.

Obviously not every single Scotsman would be renowned as a warrior like Rob Roy MacGregor. Not every Scot could be as capable or noble a general as the Viscount Dundee in the 1715 uprising, or as Lord George Murray in the 1745 uprising. There would have been many Highlanders who were not noble, moral or particularly skilful individuals.

Yet on the whole, Scottish swordsmanship can be characterised as powerful and dynamic, well practised and skilful, supported by physical fitness and athleticism. Scottish swordsmen (at least those about whom the stories are told) could be described as physically fit and well developed, moral and judicious, yet proud and swift to take arms against those who offered insult to themselves, their country or their fellow countrymen.

Chapter 2: Contextual Information

When working with historical sources, it is important to understand their context and place in the study of the discipline. Sources can always give us information, but sometimes it can be important to consider what they do not tell us. The author with all of his or her biases, points of view and potentially incomplete knowledge of the subject, can cast shadows on the validity and helpfulness of a source.[171] Therefore, the purpose of this chapter is to examine the chosen primary source for Scottish broadsword for this study guide, Charles Roworth's *The Art of Defence on Foot*, to provide contextual information about the book itself, the author, and the system contained within the source. Furthermore, the chapter will analyse the "Scottishness" of the system and discuss the various close-quarters weapons used by the Scots over the centuries, paying attention to the types of swords in use at the time of Roworth's treatise.

By the end of this chapter, readers should be aware of the necessary contextual information to understand Roworth's treatise and be able to use information from it in the study of historical Scottish swordsmanship.

2.1   About *The Art of Defence on Foot*

The first edition of the book was published in late 1798. It was printed by Charles Roworth, who worked at Bell Yard, and was published and sold by T. Egerton near Whitehall. The full title was *The Art of Defence on Foot, with the Broad Sword and Sabre: uniting the Scotch and Austrian Methods into one Regular System.*

In this edition, Mr. Bawtree provided the illustrations. The fencers were portrayed in civilian dress, using the spadroon and the

---

[171] Keith Farrell. "Analysing Historical Sources." *Encased in Steel*, 2011, accessed 1st October 2014. http://historical-academy.co.uk/blog/2011/ 09/17/analysing-historical-sources/

smallsword to demonstrate the guard positions and parries.[172] It contains some additional illustrations not found in later editions, such as the Prime Parade with the back of the blade.

In 1804, T. Egerton published another edition, printed again by Roworth. This version had a new, even longer title: *The Art of Defence on Foot, with the Broad Sword and Sabre: adapted also for the Spadroon, or Cut and Thrust Sword. Improved, and Augmented with the Ten lessons of Mr. John Taylor, Late Broadsword Master to the Light Horse Volunteers of London and Westminster.*

Some new text and lessons had been added to the end of the book, and it contained new illustrations by Sir Robert Ker Porter. The fencers are portrayed in military dress, with sabres and spadroons, rather than the civilian fashion of the 1798 edition.

In 1824, H. Durell published an American edition of the book in New York. This edition seems to be virtually the same as the 1804 edition, without any noteworthy differences. The same military-style illustrations from the 1804 edition appear to have been reproduced in the 1824 edition.

2.2   About its Authors

Charles Roworth was a printer at Bell Yard, and seems to have been an enthusiastic amateur. He was a friend of the famous Angelo dynasty of fencing masters, and was a pupil at their school, but he was not a fencing master himself.[173] He was tasked to print Rowlandson's posters of Angelo's *The Guards and Lessons of the Highland Broadsword* and also *Hungarian and Highland Broadsword*, but printed his own treatise on the art of fencing before completing these other tasks (although we do not know when the tasks were assigned, or in what order). In addition to his professional printing work, he enrolled in the Westminster Light

---

[172] Paul Wagner and Mark Rector, 2004. Page 52.
[173] J.D. Aylward. *The English Master of Arms*. London: Routledge & Kegan Paul, 1956. Page 219.

Horse Volunteers when these regiments were formed to help defend Britain against a possible French invasion. [174] It was probably in this regiment that he learned Taylor's ten lessons. Presumably he had learned the basics of fencing from the Angelo school of arms, as the current general consensus is that his treatise explains the Angelo method illustrated by Rowlandson's posters.[175] A more detailed comparison of Angelo's and Taylor's lessons can be found in section 5.5 Using Taylor's 10 Lessons.

The 1804 edition of *The Art of Defence on Foot* was "improved and augmented" with the "ten lessons of Mr. John Taylor, late broadsword master to the Light Horse Volunteers of London and Westminster." [176] Roworth is listed as the printer, and the publisher was T. Egerton. As Taylor's is the only name given in terms of ownership or creation of textual material in the book, for many years, people have attributed the entire book to Taylor[177] and have thought Roworth an "unlikely candidate" as author of the book.[178]

John Taylor might have been named as the "late broadsword master to the Light Horse Volunteers of London and Westminster" on the cover of the 1804 treatise, but J.D. Aylward notes that this was probably not a true representation of his position. Henry Angelo was the fencing master for the City of London Light Horse Volunteers, and continued in that capacity when this regiment and the Westminster Light Horse Volunteers amalgamated in 1803; Aylward suggests that perhaps Taylor had been the broadsword

---

[174] J.D. Aylward, 1956. Page 219.

[175] Paul Wagner and Mark Rector, 2004. Page 52.

[176] Charles Roworth. *The Art of Defence on Foot, with the Broad Sword and Sabre: adapted also for the Spadroon, or Cut and Thrust Sword. Improved, and Augmented with the Ten lessons of Mr. John Taylor, Late Broadsword Master to the Light Horse Volunteers of London and Westminster.* London: T. Egerton, 1804.

[177] Christopher Scott Thompson, Vol. 1, 2012. Page 103.

[178] www.Double-B-Books.com, where we bought our copy of the 1798 edition of *The Art of Defence*, noted in their description of the book: "Taylor was Broadsword Master to the Light Horse Volunteers of London and so very possibly could have written the entire work, whereas Roworth appears in the Liberty Rolls as a printer working in the Bell Yard and was regularly used by the publisher T. Egerton at around this time. And so while we may never know for sure who the author really was, Roworth seems an unlikely candidate to have written one of the best manuals on the use of the broadsword and sabre at the end of the 18th century."

master to the Westminster Light Horse Volunteers before the amalgamation. [179] Aylward also notes that whatever Taylor's occupation or title, "he does not seem to have been responsible either for the book or for the use of his name."[180]

There is very little information in the printed copies of the books themselves to answer the question of authorship. However, there is another opportunity to obtain an answer: a court case in which Roworth sued for damages after the book he authored was pirated.

In 1807, Roworth brought a court case against John Wilkes for reproducing a large part of the 1798 edition of *The Art of Defence on Foot* without permission. Wilkes had published the *Encyclopaedia Londinensis*, in which he transcribed seventy-five pages of Roworth's text,[181] and also copied several illustrations.[182] Wilkes argued that under the 1735 Act for copyright law, he had done nothing wrong and Roworth was not entitled to any remedy: the Act required that the owner of the copyright should engrave his name upon his illustrations and that the author should state his authorship in his text; Roworth had done neither of these things, so Wilkes argued that since Roworth had not followed the law with regard to claiming and asserting authorship and ownership of the material, the material was available for copying.[183] It is worth noting that Bawtree's name does appear on illustrations in this treatise, but this does not seem to have had any bearing on the case.

Lord Ellenborough, the judge presiding over the case, believed that "although the plaintiff's name is not engraved upon them, if there has been a piracy, I think the plaintiff is entitled to a verdict." He also stated that "the interest being vested, the

---

[179] J.D. Aylward, 1956. Pages 220-221.
[180] Ibid.
[181] Walter Arthur Copinger. *The Law of Copyright, in Works of Literature and Art.* Clark, NJ: The Lawbook Exchange, 2012. Page ix.
[182] Ronan Deazley. *Rethinking Copyright: History, Theory, Language.* Cheltenham: Edward Elgar Publishing, 2006. Page 35.
[183] Ibid.

common law gives the remedy."[184] He therefore established that common law could protect an author who did not put his name to his work; an interesting side effect of the decision was that even an author who did not put his name to his work would still need to deposit a copy of his published work with the British Library, as such deposit was required of any person "whose property is protected."[185]

The test to determine whether a copied work was indeed pirated or rather an abridgement or compilation (and therefore an original new work in the eyes of the law)[186] was whether any skill or learning had been used to create the new work.[187] Since Wilkes had bestowed no skill or learning upon the work, Maugham notes that the case was that of:

> *wholesale compilation*, in which seventy-five pages were successively transcribed, without addition or alteration, and on which no *skill or learning* had been bestowed, the exercise of which may be considered as the true criterion by which to determine the bona fide character of the abridgement or compilation.[188]

On the 17th of December 1807, the court decided in favour of Roworth, finding Wilkes guilty of pirating the text. It was decided that Wilkes had transcribed a large part of a fencing treatise, without necessarily any intention to damage the sale of the original, but that since it was not a "bona fide abridgement" and could serve as a replacement for the original volume while being sold at a considerably lower price, "it was held actionable."[189] Roworth was awarded £100 damages,[190] and the concept of author's copyright took a significant step towards how it is understood in Britain and America today.

---

[184] Ibid.

[185] Ibid.

[186] Robert Maugham. *A Treatise on the Laws of Literary Property*. Clark, NJ: The Lawbook Exchange, 2008. Page 130.

[187] Walter Arthur Copinger, 2012. Page ix.

[188] Robert Maugham, 2008. Page 130.

[189] Ibid. Page 130.

[190] Charles Henry Timperley. *A Dictionary of Printers and Printing*. London: H. Johnson, 1839. Page 832.

Roworth could not have been awarded these damages unless he was the author of *The Art of Defence on Foot*, published in 1798. Furthermore, Henry Angelo was Roworth's primary witness to establish that Roworth's work had been pirated. [191] Although Angelo left no written material about the case, his presence at court to support Roworth's claims to authorship of the book is a strong indication of what he believed. It is certain that Roworth was the author of the treatise, not just the printer.

Given Roworth's objection to the wholesale copying of his treatise by Wilkes, culminating in this court case, it is unlikely that he would have allowed another individual to copy the entirety of his text and append additional instructions and lessons, as can be found in the 1804 edition of the treatise, so Roworth is most probably the author of that treatise as well, not Taylor or any other individual.

As the 1824 edition of the treatise contains exactly the same text and illustrations as the 1804 edition, it seems we can establish that Roworth was the author behind all three editions (although the 1824 edition in the New York Public Library bears "Art of Defence, Taylor" on its spine;[192] when the treatise was reprinted in a different country, that was probably the same mistaken attribution that modern historians have made), as well as the printer behind the first two. He probably could not have brought legal action against H. Durell for pirating the book in 1824, because by that time America was a separate country with its own legal system.

It is likely that he simply included Taylor's ten lessons in his second edition of his own work, after he was introduced to them through his service in the Light Horse Volunteers where Taylor was the broadsword master from 1796 until 1803.

---

[191] J.D. Aylward, 1956. Pages 220-221.
[192] Paul Wagner and Mark Rector, 2004. Page 64, end note 188.

2.3   About the Weapons

Before discussing how to reconstruct the historical fencing system of Roworth, it is important to understand the weapons that they had to use and to teach, and also to understand where these weapons came from and how they developed. It is also useful to cover the issue of terminology, so that readers are equipped with the right knowledge of technical words and phrases to be able to indulge in further reading on the subject.

The Claymore

The first question to be addressed is that of the "claymore": what exactly is it?

The claymore is the basket-hilted broadsword.[193] The word is the Anglicised form of the Gaelic *claidheamh mor*, or "big sword", and the earliest known use of the phrase refers to the broadsword, not the two-handed sword.[194] The Victorians sometimes used the term claymore or *claidhheamh mor* to mean the two-handed sword,[195] and while this usage is also common today, it is incorrect to do so, as the Scots themselves used the term to mean the broadsword.

Other Highland Swords and Weapons

The two-handed sword of the Highlands is a unique design of sword that is very easily identifiable as Scottish. The crossguard slopes forward, and the terminals at the ends of the crossguard form a quatrefoil pattern. The blade tends to be reasonably broad and around three and a half feet in length, but the grip not overly long; James Logan notes that "the two-handed sword was a

---

[193] Fergus Cannan, 2009. Page 95.
[194] Christopher Scott Thompson. *Highland Broadsword: Lessons, Drills, and Practices*. Boulder: Paladin Press, 2010. Page 4.
[195] Charles Niven McIntyre North. *The Book of the Club of True Highlanders*. Vol. II, London: C.N. McIntyre North, 1881.

favourite weapon of the Highlands".[196] Unfortunately, there are not very many surviving examples of this kind of sword in museums around the world. The two-handed sword of the lowlands was often larger, but more plainly decorated, more resembling the two-handed swords from the rest of Europe.

There are no manuals or treatises that describe how the Scottish "twa-handit" sword was used. Probably incorrectly, a couple of 19th century sources suggest that the weapon was used in a fashion similar to that of the extended Liechtenauer tradition from the Holy Roman Empire in the 16th century. Logan refers to a treatise in the British Museum:

> In the British Museum is a black letter work entitled, "La noble Science des jouers de Spee," printed at Danviers, in 1538, which contains instructions for the exercise of the sword. It is embellished with twenty-two woodcuts, representing the different guards and positions. From this, it appears the weapon was often rested with the point on the ground, the hands not being always confined to the hilt or handle, but occasionally grasped the blade itself.[197]

Of course, this is none other than the book entitled *La noble science des ioueurs despee* (*The noble science of the players of the sword*), published in 1538 in Antwerp by Willem Vorsterman. It is a Middle Walloon translation of Andre Paurñfeyndt's fencing book *Ergrundung Ritterlicher Kunst der Fechterey* (*Foundation of the Chivalric Art of Swordplay*) that was printed in Vienna in 1516.

The original book presented Paurñfeyndt's teachings of the arts of fencing with the longsword, the dussack, and polearms. Furthermore, it included brief treatises on dagger and on sword and buckler, both by Andre Lignitzer.[198] In terms of the longsword material, there is some similarity with and connection to the Liechtenauer tradition of Bloßfechten (unarmoured combat), with some unique material (although this has its similarities to other

---

[196] James Logan, 1831. Pages 213-214.
[197] Ibid. Page 214.
[198] "Ergrundung Ritterlicher Kunst der Fechterey (Andre Paurñfeyndt)." *Wiktenauer*, accessed 21st July 2014. http://wiktenauer.com/wiki/ Ergrundung_Ritterlicher_Kunst_der_Fechterey_(Andre_Paurñfeyndt)

methods of longsword fencing in the 16th century, such as the Augsburg tradition).[199]

Another source from the 19th century makes the same sort of assumption: the second volume of *The Book of the Club of True Highlanders*, published in 1881, contains a plate with illustrations of medium Highland fencers holding two-handed swords in the same basic positions as Paurñfeyndt's illustrations of Liechtenauer's "vier leger", or "four positions" (also known as the four guards). The caption to the illustration reads: "Play with the Claidheamh-mor, the positions copied from Book dated 1538 'La noble science des joueurs d'espee'".[200]

There is no good reason to connect *La noble science des ioueurs despee* and Paurñfeyndt's system of longsword fencing with the methods of the Highlanders. Logan was probably aware that this book existed, and made the assumption that if some people used the longsword in that fashion, then perhaps other people might have used it similarly. It is not an unreasonable assumption to make for someone without access to proper scholarly material on the subject; indeed, various people today, even with access to good quality scholarly material, still subscribe to the "Pan-European Theory", a notion that everyone in Europe during the 14th-16th centuries used weapons like the longsword in the same way, without recognising different schools, traditions or styles. However, it is a wrong assumption to make,[201] and hopefully readers of this book will not fall into the trap of making this kind of assumption with regard to the Scottish two-handed sword.

There was another form of longsword in the 17th century, more or less peculiar to Scotland, with a certain style of complex hilt. Longswords with complex hilts were to be found in various places throughout history, but the "clam-shellit" sword was almost unique to Scotland. It had "clam shell" shaped guards that came

---

[199] This statement is based on the author's own studies of 15th and 16th century longsword traditions.

[200] Charles Niven McIntyre North, 1881. Plate LII.

[201] This statement is also based on the author's own studies of 15th and 16th century longsword traditions and various other disciplines from the same time period.

down from the crossguard to protect the hands, almost like the basket-guard on the broadsword. It has been theorised that as soldiers stopped wearing steel gauntlets, this seemed like a reasonable evolution of the swords to continue to provide some measure of protection.[202]

A shorter sword was the spadroon or shearing sword; a light straight bladed weapon that could be used for thrusting and for cutting. The hilt was usually just a simple crossguard, without a basket for protection. It was a civilian weapon in 17th and 18th century Scotland, but over the course of the 18th and 19th centuries it developed into a military sword for officers in the British Army.[203]

Similar to the shearing sword was the smallsword. It was small, light, fast and nimble. The blade tended to have a hexagonal or triangular cross-section, and although the edges were not sharp, the blade terminated in a lethal point.[204] It was a weapon designed for thrusting, and the method of its use reflected this fact. Many fencing masters taught the use of the smallsword across Europe, and even in Scotland it was a popular weapon of the upper class. Sir William Hope wrote several books about the smallsword from 1687 to 1724,[205] and John Xavier Tremamondo (brother of Domenico Angelo) taught smallsword at the Royal Academy of Exercises in Edinburgh from 1763 to 1805.[206] Even amongst the lower classes, it was a popular weapon: Donald McBane taught the smallsword at his fencing schools, and his stories show that even private soldiers and non-commissioned officers in the British Army used this weapon.[207]

A common sidearm for the Highlanders was the dirk: a long knife or dagger that was used for mundane everyday tasks as well as for armed conflict. James Logan remarks on the mundane

[202] Fergus Cannan, 2009. Page 79.
[203] Ben Kerr, 2010. Pages 20-21.
[204] Ewart Oakeshott. *European Weapons and Armour From the Renaissance to the Industrial Revolution*. Woodbridge: Boydell Press, 2012. Page 251.
[205] Mark Rector, 2001. Pages 87-88.
[206] J.D. Aylward, 1956. Page 227.
[207] Mark Rector, 2001. Pages 21-85.

purposes of the dirk:

> I have remarked that more broad swords than dirks are to be now seen, and the reason, I apprehend, is, that the latter were appropriated for domestic purposes, when it was no longer necessary or lawful to carry them as arms. Pennant observed the dirk frequently converted into a very useful knife, by the butchers of Inverness, being, like Hudibras's dagger, "a serviceable dudgeon, Either for fighting or for drudging."[208]

Logan also provides a short description of the dirk as a weapon:

> The dirk of the Highlanders is called bidag, or biodag, the bidawg of the Welsh, in the latter syllable of which we perceive the root of the English dagger.

> The bidag is adapted for fighting at close quarters, where the sword cannot be used, or where the party may, either in the heat of action, or otherwise, have been deprived of it. When dexterously wielded by a strong and resolute Highlander, this was a most terrific weapon. It was not held in the same way as the sword, but in a reverse position, pointing towards the elbow, and the manner in which it was carried allowed it to be drawn back with perfect facility. The belt which fastened the plaid, became the baldrick by which this trusty blade was secured. It was placed on the right side, and instead of hanging loosely as it is now generally worn, the belt was either slipped through a hook affixed to the sheath, sometimes steady, and frequently movable on a swivel, or a long hook, or slide, answered the same purpose. It was thus firmly attached to the thigh, and was consequently so judiciously suspended, that it could be drawn in an instant, and this was of some importance in the event of a sudden assault, or so close a contention as would prevent a free use of the sword. If it hung loosely, it would have incommoded the wearer, and could not be so promptly at command, but, carried as it was, the hand could instinctively be laid on the hilt.[209]

Even after Acts of Parliament disarmed the Highlanders, the dirk was the item with which they founded hardest to part.[210]

---

[208] James Logan, 1831. Page 217.
[209] Ibid. Pages 216-217.
[210] Ibid. Page 218.

The Highlanders often used the dirk alongside the targe: a small round shield, constructed of several layers, with bulletproof properties.[211] After a skirmish with dragoons near Clifton, in 1745, Lord George Murray found that the targe he had borrowed had absorbed the impact of several bullets, and had probably saved his life.[212] Various other accounts also talk of targes absorbing or deflecting musket balls.

This was the item that the Highlanders preferred to use to defend their bodies, rather than armour.[213] Sometimes the targe had a long spike protruding from the centre,[214] and there have been discussions over whether or not this spike could have been used offensively. Some spikes seem very weakly secured to the shield, so that they would likely break off if they were used offensively; other spikes seem better secured; others were screwed into place and could be removed or fitted at the user's leisure.[215] With the variations in methods for attaching the spikes, it is only reasonable to assume that some were built to be used offensively and others were not.

Regardless of the functionality of the spike, the targe was still an important part of the Highland charge, used to knock aside bayonets,[216] allowing the Highlanders to close into sword range. Sometimes the Highlanders held their dirk in their left hand, in which case the targe was "borne on the wrist" rather than grasped in the left hand.[217]

Staff weapons such as the scythe and the Lochaber axe (a large, two handed axe, with just a single cutting edge unlike other polearms)[218] were also used, although these had fallen into decline by the 18th century. Still, at the Battle of Prestonpans, the

---

[211] Ben Kerr, 2010. Page 26.

[212] Fergus Cannan, 2009. Page 95.

[213] Ibid. Page 84.

[214] John Parker Lawson, Vol. 1, 1839. Page 186.

[215] This statement is based on the author's discussions with Ben Kerr, who has collected a lot of information and data on the subject.

[216] Peter Harrington, 1991. Page 40.

[217] James Logan, 1831. Pages 239-240.

[218] Fergus Cannan, 2009. Pages 31-33.

fallen had been slain almost entirely by broadsword and scythe.[219] At the Battle of Killiecrankie, the Lochaber axe had broken and "snapt asunder" pikes, swords and muskets to clear obstructions from the path of the Highland charge.[220]

Sometimes, when there was little other option, the Highlanders armed themselves with simple clubs and sticks.[221] These could be very effective despite their primitive nature. In one skirmish between the Campbells and the McMartins, the Campbells used their dirks to cut themselves some branches from nearby trees, and used these makeshift cudgels to defend their position at a ford against the McMartins, who were armed with axes and other live steel weapons; the Campbells won the fight, killing nearly all of their attackers.[222]

The Scots used longer-range weapons as well as close quarters weapons. The bow was a traditional weapon of the Highlands; described sometimes as a "long bow" or "large bow", but nonetheless shorter than the "longbow" of the English and Welsh.[223] The Scots used archers in battle, but archers were never as prevalent in Scottish forces as they were in armies mustered south of the border.

Firearms such as the musket and rifle were used in Scotland, for hunting and for military purposes. The Scots developed a reputation for accuracy and precision with their fire,[224] and could wreak havoc both with their firearms and with their swords.

When the Highlanders carried muskets into battle, they did not always possess enough ammunition to indulge in a standing engagement. The European armies of the late 18th and early 19th century were trained to form line and engage each other at close range, trading volleys, which expended a significant amount of ammunition. However, the Highlanders did not carry a huge

---

[219] John Parker Lawson, Vol. 4, 1839. Page 122.
[220] John Parker Lawson, Vol. 2, 1839. Pages 461-462.
[221] James Logan, 1831. Page 201.
[222] Christopher Scott Thompson, Vol. 1, 2012. Pages 33-33.
[223] Fergus Cannan, 2009. Pages 33-34.
[224] John Parker Lawson, Vol. 4, 1839. Pages 289-290.

number of cartridges at any given time, and so could not afford to stand still and trade volleys. For example, at the Battle of Sheriffmuir in 1745, the Duke of Argyle issued further cartridges to his troops, but they still did not have enough for a long engagement:

> The Duke himself retired to a sheep-cote at the foot of a hill on the right of the army, where he passed the night sitting on a bundle of straw. Intelligence having been brought him at midnight of the near position of the enemy, he ordered six rounds of ammunition to be distributed to each man in addition to twenty-four which they had already received. This order was carried into effect before two o'clock in the morning.[225]

As a result, a common method for using muskets was to march up close enough to the enemy to pour accurate and deadly fire into them with just one or two volleys, then to drop the muskets and charge with the broadsword and targe. This tactic was discussed in greater detail in chapter 1.3: The Highland Charge earlier in this book.

Pistols were very popular in Scotland, and the country developed a unique style of building and decorating these firearms. The weapons were constructed entirely from metal and featured distinctive designs at the base of the butt. They were often richly decorated and ornamented. Of course, not every pistol manufactured in Scotland followed this pattern, but the all-metal construction was stylistically Scottish.[226]

A well-made pistol was a source of pride for its owner. There is an entertaining snippet in *The Scottish Gael* where a man shows off his pistols to an old man, who remains unimpressed and prefers his dirk:

> I recollect one John McBean, who fought at Culloden, and was among the McIntoshes, who made so furious an irruption on the king's army. This old man, who died at the age of 101, and was able to walk abroad some days before his death, never thought

---

[225] Ibid. Page 283.
[226] Fergus Cannan, 2009. Pages 61-63.

himself dressed without his belt and a small knife. A gentleman of my acquaintance had shown his pistols to an old man at Skellater, in Strathdon, who, in reply, drew his dirk, and, regarding it with a look of satisfaction, observed, "my pistol will no miss fire."[227]

The pistol was a comforting traveling companion. The Scots enjoyed carrying bladed weapons just as part of daily life, and regarded this as entirely normal. When they travelled, however, they took firearms with them just to be on the safe side:

> The habits of the Highlanders were also, at this time, essentially warlike. "The use of arms," to borrow a description from an anonymous writer, "formed their common occupation, and the affairs of war their ordinary pursuit. They appeared on all public occasions, at market, and even at church, with their broadswords and their dirks; and, more recently, when the use of fire-arms became general, they seldom travelled without a musket and pistol."[228]

Weapons were not all equally popular or common. The dirk was ubiquitous, but of the longer and more serious weapons, the broadsword was most common. In 1638, the Earl of Atholl conducted a survey of the "vapins and armour" possessed by a group of 523 men across the Perthshire parishes. Between them, they amassed: 448 swords, 3 two-handed swords, 112 guns, 11 pistols, 149 bows, 125 targes, 9 lochaber axes, 2 halberds, 11 breastplates, 8 "headpieces," 2 "steel bonnets," a pair of plate sleeves, and a coat of mail.[229]

An interesting piece of information is that after the Battle of Culloden, when the Duke of Cumberland's men were collected the discarded weapons from the field, they found 2320 firearms, but only 190 swords.[230] Either the sword was less prevalent on the battlefield than the musket, or the Jacobites who fled the field chose to hold onto their sword, and showed less regard for their

---

[227] James Logan, 1831. Page 218.
[228] A.T. Thomson, Vol. 2, 1845. "Rob Roy MacGregor Campbell."
[229] John Wallace. *Scottish Swords and Dirks: An illustrated Reference Guide to Scottish Edged Weapons*. Harrisburg, PA: Stackpole Books, 1970.
[230] Fergus Cannan, 2009. Page 95.

long and cumbersome muskets.

Sometimes the Highlanders were poorly armed when they went to war, if they were armed at all. For example, when the Highlanders joined Prince Charles before the Battle of Prestonpans (sometimes called the Battle of Gladsmuir) in 1745:

> In point of numbers the army of Cope was rather inferior to that of Charles; but many of the Highlanders were badly armed, and some of them were without arms.[231]

Some of them had managed to arm themselves with cudgels, and intended to use these as deadly weapons until they could find better armament:

> When the Highlanders joined Prince Charles, when they fought at Gladsmuir and even afterwards, many had no better weapon, but "With heavy cudgels of good oak, They vowed to kill at every stroke."[232]

In contrast, sometimes the Highlanders were exceptionally well armed. An account of a party of Highlanders under the command of Sir Humphrey Colquhoun, summoned to help deal with Rob Roy Macgregor and a band of raiders, describes them as appearing exceptionally well equipped to deal with the threat:

> On the evening of that day the crews in the pinnaces came on shore at Luss, where they were joined by Sir Humphrey Colquhoun, and his son-in-law Grant of Pluscardine, "followed by forty or fifty stately fellows in their short hose and belted plaids, armed each of them with a well-fixed gun on his shoulder, a strong handsome target, with a sharp-pointed steel, of above half an ell in length, screwed into the navel of it, on his left arm, a sturdy claymore by his side, and a pistol or two, with a dirk and knife by his side."[233]

Another description of well-armed Highlanders appears in an account of their march into Preston, shortly before Culloden:

---

[231] John Parker Lawson, Vol. 4, 1839. Pages 111-112.
[232] James Logan, 1831. Page 201.
[233] John Parker Lawson, Vol. 1, 1839. Page 186.

The very arms borne by the Highlanders were objects of curiosity and surprise, no less than of alarm, to the populace, who stood by the way-side expressing their good-will to the expedition, but who, when asked to join the insurgents, declined, saying, "they did not understand fighting."

The formidable weapons with which the Highlanders contrived to make themselves terrible to their enemies, consisted of a broadsword, girded on the left side, and a dirk or short thick dagger on the right, used only when the combat was so close as to render the broadsword useless. In ancient times, these fierce warriors brandished a small short-handled hatchet or axe, for the purpose of a close fight. A gun, a pair of pistols, and a target, completed their armour, except when ammunition failed, when they substituted for the gun, the lochaber axe; this was a species of long lance, or juke, with a formidable weapon at the end of it, adapted either for cutting or stabbing.

The lochaber axe had fallen into disuse since the introduction of the musket; but a rude, yet ready substitute had been found for it, by fixing scythes at the end of a, pole, with which the Highlanders resisted the attacks of cavalry. Such had been their arms m the early part of the Insurrection of 1745, and such they continued until, at the battles of Falkirk and Preston Pans, they had collected muskets from the slain on the battle-held.

In addition to these weapons, the gentlemen sometimes wore suits of armour and coats of mail; in which, indeed, some of the principal Jacobites have been depicted; but, with these, the common men never incumbered themselves, both on account of the expense, and of the weight, which was ill-adapted to their long marches and steep hills.[234]

It would be a mistake to assume that the Highlanders could never appear for battle well armed with a plethora of weapons at their disposal. At the same time, it would be a mistake to assume that the Highlanders were always in possession of several weapons. They enjoyed carrying weapons,[235] but this was not always possible.

---

[234] A.T. Thomson, Vol. 3, 1845. "Lord George Murray."
[235] David Stewart, 1825. Part 3, "Section I – Black Watch."

Development of the Broadsword

There are three schools of thought with regard to the origin of the basket-hilted broadsword: that it came to the British Isles from the continent,[236] that it came to Scotland from England,[237] and that in fact it was developed by the Scottish Highlanders around the middle of the 16th century.[238]

The first school of thought may well have the greatest merit. Anthony Darling believes it unlikely that the style of sword came to Scotland from England in the late 16th century, because the earliest examples of basket-guards from both countries from that period show significant differences.[239] Rather, he believes that the concept of the basket-hilted sword probably developed in Germany. From here the concept of a basket-hilted sword spread to the British Isles, first to England, and then later to Scotland. Both England and Scotland then developed national styles in their independent implementation of the concept.[240]

The earliest Scottish basket-hilts are sometimes known as "ribbon hilts", because "ribbons" or strips of flat steel were bent and welded into place to construct the basket.[241] Mazansky writes that the modern term for this style of basket is the "West Highland" hilt.[242] The tops of the ribbons were welded to the base of the crossguard, and at the bottom they slotted into grooves in the pommel.[243] These baskets are sometimes also known as "beak-nose" or "hog-snout" hilts. Darling notes that there are two styles of this type of hilt: an earlier pattern and a later pattern.

The earlier pattern may have originated as early as the late 16th

---

[236] Anthony Darling. "The Earliest Scottish Basket-Hilted Swords." *Man at Arms* (July/August 1979): 18-23. Page 19.

[237] Ibid.

[238] Paul Wagner. "Gaelic Swordsmanship." Mark Rector, 2001. Pages 8-9.

[239] Anthony Darling, 1979. Page 19.

[240] Ibid.

[241] Ibid.

[242] Cyril Mazansky. *British Basket-Hilted Swords*. Woodbridge: Boydell Press, 2005. Page 12.

[243] Anthony Darling, 1979. Page 19.

century. The medieval crossguard is still quite pronounced, and the terminals are "elongated and countercurved". From the crossguard, two languets protrude along the two flat sides of the blade (in a very similar fashion to the Highland single-handed and two-handed swords). The pommel tends to be roughly mushroom shaped.[244]

The later pattern retains the same form of pommel, but the languets disappear, and the length of the crossguard shortens – although the crossguard does not entirely disappear, inspiring the "snout" and "beak" names for the hilt. The basket extends slightly further to the rear with the addition of an extra vertical bar on each side of the hilt. This pattern probably developed in the mid 17th century, so perhaps half a century after the earlier pattern.[245]

Later in the 17th century, the "ribbon hilt" began to fall out of fashion, and the style of basket constructed from vertical bars connected with small junction plates seems to have been adopted almost universally.[246] This design was quite popular in England while the Scots had developed the "ribbon hilt", so the fashion of vertical bars seems to have moved northwards. The *pas d'anes*, the two loops protruding from the top of the front of the basket, were originally an English design, which was copied on the Scottish baskets.[247] Although they seemed to fall out of fashion in England in later centuries, they remained in fashion in Scotland and became part of the Glasgow and Stirling hilt designs.

Oakeshott notes that the main differences between Scottish and English basket-hilts in the 17th century were the shape of the pommel, the number of vertical bars (the Scottish basket had more bars and covered more of the hand), and additional horizontal links between the vertical bars on the Scottish basket.[248] Furthermore, Scottish broadswords with steel basket-hilts were often either "japanned or oxidised, as gunbarrels are

---

[244] Ibid. Page 20.
[245] Ibid. Page 21.
[246] Ibid.
[247] Ibid.
[248] Ewart Oakeshott, 2012. Page 177.

browned", to protect against rust.[249]

At different times in history, different linings were used inside the Scottish basket. From the mid 16th century until roughly 1730, the lining only covered the very base of the basket, and was made from very thick deerskin. From the 1730s until the 1770s, the lining expanded its coverage to roughly a "half-filling", still made from deerskin. From the 1790s onward, the lining tended to fill the whole basket, and could be made from soft leather covered with felt or velvet. Such soft chamois liners were often added to earlier hilts to improve the comfort.[250]

By the early 18th century, the Scottish basket-hilt adopted a general design that changed relatively little thereafter.[251] Darling suggests that this Scottish style of basket-hilt (mainly with a Glasgow hilt) was the most common type used on swords for many British regiments, but Mazansky is hesitant to accept that point of view, due to lack of evidence.[252]

The basket-hilted sword was sometimes referred to as the "highland hilt". The earliest written record of this term is found in the Inverness Burgh record of 1576.[253] However, Mazansky warns that the term did not always refer to a full basket-hilted sword; so early records such as this may be misleading.[254] The term became synonymous with the basket-hilted sword in the late 16th century and mid 17th centuries.[255]

In the early 17th century, the term "Irish hilt" was often used to describe the Scottish basket-hilted sword.[256] The English tended to refer to the Highlanders as "Irish" and that was what they called the Gaelic language; [257] they saw relatively little difference

---

[249] Ibid. Page 181.
[250] Ibid. Page 181.
[251] Anthony Darling, 1979. Page 23.
[252] Cyril Mazansky, 2005. Page 12.
[253] Anthony Darling, 1979. Page 19.
[254] Cyril Mazansky, 2005. Page 11.
[255] Ibid. Page 12.
[256] Ibid.
[257] Ibid. Page 13.

between the two peoples.[258] This term referred to both the plain "munitions-grade" hilts and the intricately decorated hilts of the nobility.[259]

In the early 18th century, two very special designs of hilt came into being. John Simpson the Elder, who practised his craft in Glasgow between 1638 and 1717, developed the famous "Glasgow hilt".[260] This style became that of the "traditional" Scottish basket-hilt,[261] but formally the term refers specifically to swords made in Glasgow in the 18th century; the main identifying feature is the manufacturer's signature on the hilt.[262] The Glasgow hilt was very common on broadswords used by cavalry units throughout the 18th century, and the style was also found on many infantry broadswords.[263]

John Allan the Elder undertook his journeyman apprenticeship in Glasgow with John Simpson the Elder from 1702 until 1707, then worked in Glasgow from 1707-1710.[264] Then, from 1710-1714, he worked in Doune.[265] In 1714, he moved to Stirling, where he eventually retired from his craft in 1741; during this time he developed the "Stirling hilt" style of basket.[266]

Mazansky notes that the Stirling hilts are characterised by their "lack of standardisation", and that "if the Glasgow hilt is viewed as the traditional Scottish hilt, then the Stirling ones might be seen as the artistic ones."[267] Generally speaking, the "Stirling hilt" was simply a hilt made in Stirling, not necessarily to a particular design.[268] However, all the known hilt manufacturers in Stirling probably produced somewhat similar designs, since they were all

---

[258] Anthony Darling, 1979. Page 19.
[259] Cyril Mazansky, 2005. Page 13.
[260] Richard Bezdek. *Swords and Sword Makers of England and Scotland.* Boulder: Paladin Press, 2003. Page 260.
[261] Cyril Mazansky, 2005. Page 12.
[262] Ibid.
[263] Ibid. Page 13.
[264] Richard Bezdek, 2003. Page 256.
[265] Ibid. Page 238.
[266] Ibid. Page 266.
[267] Cyril Mazansky, 2005. Page 31.
[268] Ibid. Page 13.

related either by family or by training and apprenticeships.[269]

Walter Allan (who practised from 1732-1765 in Stirling) was one of the sons of John Allan the Elder, and he "became the most famous maker of basket-hilted broadswords in Scotland."[270]

Sometimes the term "British hilt" is used by modern authors to indicate a type of hilt that was used in both England and Scotland, but not in Europe.[271]

Most broadsword blades were imported from Solingen in Germany, or from other well-known manufacturers on the continent; many bore the name "Andrea Ferrara", and it was not uncommon for them to bear an inspiring slogan.[272] Since most blades came from abroad, the majority of the sword makers in Scotland were actually "sword slippers", or cutlers, who made the baskets and assembled swords from imported blades rather than making every single component themselves.[273]

The Scottish swordsmiths did not just limit themselves to basket-hilted broadswords; they made other weapons as well. In 1694, James Masch the Elder made 12 bayonets and 12 sabres, and delivered them to Edinburgh Castle.[274] In 1699, John Davidson the Younger and John Simpson the Elder worked together in Glasgow to supply "250 horseman's sabres with basket hilts to the company of Scotland trading in Africa."[275]

The broadswords that were made were not always hilted with steel and many decorative baskets were made from silver. James Oliphant practised from 1760-1780 in Edinburgh, and he specialised in mounting silver basket-hilted broadswords and sabres.[276] John Rolla also practised in Edinburgh, from 1710-1737,

---

[269] Ibid.
[270] Richard Bezdek, 2003. Page 266.
[271] Cyril Mazansky, 2005. Page 13.
[272] Ewart Oakeshott, 2012. Page 178.
[273] Richard Bezdek, 2003. Page 233.
[274] Ibid. Page 248.
[275] Ibid. Pages 256 & 260.
[276] Ibid. Page 250.

and he mounted silver and brass basket-hilted broadswords, but also silver hilted hangers and cutlasses.[277]

The various Acts of Parliament to disarm the Highlanders had a negative effect on business for sword slippers. At least three cutlers in Glasgow were affected badly by these Acts: Robert Low (practised 1696-1731) was forced to surrender "70 swords, 40 scabbards, 1 two-handed sword, and 3 guns". Likewise, Charles McCulloch (practised 1715-1746) had to surrender "7 swords, 15 guns and 2 dirks", while William McDonald (practised 1712-1750) had to surrender "31 swords, 1 poinard, and 63 sword blades."[278] From the dates of their practice, it is clear that these three cutlers were able to continue business somehow, but such legal setbacks would not have made their lives any easier.

Swords and dirks were still carried in the Highland Regiments, even though they were banned for civilians. In true military fashion, these regimental weapons were manufactured to regulation patterns. After the bans on Highland weapons and dress were repealed in 1782, the style of swords produced for and worn by civilians had a rather military and regimental style.[279] The Highland Regiments had special permission to choose their own sword patterns, and so Highland soldiers exercised their right to carry broadswords even after muskets and bayonets had supposedly replaced swords as regulation weapons.[280] In 1784, broadswords were no longer issued as standard to the private soldiers in the Black Watch, but many such soldiers retained their swords or acquired them anyway.[281]

Sword slippers were still producing broadswords into the 18th and 19th centuries. In Perth, Alexander Fergusson practised from 1796-1806, and William Marshall practised from 1806-1822. During the Jacobite uprising, and then for almost a quarter of a century afterwards, John Scott V practised in Glasgow from 1745-1779. William Love also practised in Glasgow, from 1777-1815,

---

[277] Ibid. Pages 250-251.
[278] Ibid. Page 262.
[279] Fergus Cannan, 2009. Page 105.
[280] Paul Wagner and Mark Rector, 2004. Page 8.
[281] Ibid. Page 9.

and Robert MacDougall practised from 1840-1855 in Inverness. Clearly, the trade of the sword slipper was not restricted just to the 17th and early 18th centuries, but such craftsmen continued to supply basket-hilted broadswords long after the Jacobite uprisings.[282]

The Swords of Roworth and Angelo

In 1788, a regulation pattern broadsword was introduced that weighed only around 1 kilogram.[283] Earlier in the century, soldiers in other British regiments had noted that the broadswords carried in the Highland Regiments (around 1.4 to 1.6 kg) were much heavier than their own swords; the weight of the 1788 pattern broadsword became more similar to other military issue swords of the time.[284]

The 1796 pattern infantry broadsword weighed only 750 grams, a huge departure from the weight and handling characteristics of the Culloden-era broadswords.[285] Such light broadswords could be used very differently (and with much less effort, requiring considerably less strength in the wrist and forearm) than the broadswords of the Jacobite uprisings. Paul Wagner and Mark Rector note that with such dramatic decrease in the weight of swords, "it is not surprising that the style of swordplay also changed."[286]

From 1796 onwards, the sabres of the period tended to have just a simple knuckle-bow or maybe an asymmetric guard with three bars to help protect the fingers. Sometimes also a very simple shell, although this became more popular towards the second half of the 1800s.[287]

There was a 1798 regulation pattern broadsword, with brass

---

[282] Richard Bezdek, 2003. Pages 259-264.
[283] Paul Wagner and Mark Rector, 2004. Page 41.
[284] Ibid.
[285] Ibid. Pages 41-42.
[286] Ibid. Page 42.
[287] Richard Bezdek, 2003. Pages 286-292.

basket-hilt that provided very reasonable coverage for the hand. The blade was around 30-33 inches long and sharp on both edges.[288] However, the basket did not possess the two *pas d'anes* (the looping rings at the front of the hilt) that tend to be regarded as part of the traditional Scottish design. This pattern was discontinued in 1820.[289]

Generally speaking, the Scottish broadswords from around the period of Culloden, into the 19th century, tended to be fairly ornate pieces, and the general blade length did not really change.[290]

As well as the sabre and broadsword, there was the spadroon: a sword with a single-edged slender blade that could be used both for cutting and thrusting, with relatively little by way of hand protection. It was lighter than the sabre and broadsword, and could be used easily by officers familiar with the smallsword. However, officers in the Peninsular War against Napoleon found that it was a generally useless sword,[291] intended to be a jack-of-all-trades, but in fact a master of nothing. It had become so light that it could no longer function with the effectiveness of the spadroon described by Sir William Hope and Donald McBane, who praised the shearing sword as an excellent weapon.

In the period of 1798 to 1804, when Roworth released his first and second editions of *The Art of Defence on Foot*, and when Henry Angelo and Thomas Rowlandson produced *The Guards and Lessons of the Highland Broadsword* and *Hungarian & Highland Broadsword*, the broadsword tended to be a relatively light weapon compared to its Jacobite forebears, although still with a basket providing relatively good coverage of the hand. The sabre was coming into fashion, although it generally had very little hand protection, and the spadroon also had little hand protection. All the military swords tended to be quite light, not any more than around 1 kilogram, quite well balanced and could be used both for thrusting and for cutting.

---

[288] Ibid. Pages 341-343.
[289] Paul Wagner and Mark Rector, 2004. Page 23.
[290] Richard Bezdek, 2003. Pages 376-381.
[291] Paul Wagner and Mark Rector, 2004. Page 42.

Cavalry swords were sometimes heavier than infantry swords, with a point of balance further out from the hilt. These weapons suited a slightly different method of use, more appropriate for heavy cavalry charges than for protracted infantry fighting.

In summary, during the period of Roworth and Angelo, there was not a particularly large difference in the weight or handling characteristics of broadswords or sabres for infantrymen. The broadswords of the period were becoming lighter and more in line with the regimental pattern sabres. Cavalry swords handled differently to infantry swords, but they had different methods of use. The techniques and fencing concepts for fighting on foot that were proposed by Roworth and Angelo would be useful to officers armed with common issue patterns of broadsword, sabre or spadroon.

2.4 How "Scottish" is the Method?

It seems that Roworth's treatise provides a textual of description the Angelo system of broadsword,[292] illustrated by Rowlandson's posters. The name of his 1798 treatise claims to unite "the Scotch and Austrian methods into one Regular System", while Angelo's system claims to be that of the "Highland and Hungarian" methods of swordsmanship. It has been suggested that Roworth's treatise may include some of the ideas and lessons that Le Marchant learned in 1794 from the Austrians.[293]

It is possible that Roworth's "Scotch" method came from Angelo, although there are some clear links between Roworth's work and some of the earlier treatises on Scottish broadsword fighting. The system of traversing in Roworth's book is not just based on Thomas Page's 1746 treatise; the text is reproduced word for word, and the diagram is a perfect copy.

Page was an English civilian who ran a general hardware shop in Norwich. He had volunteered in the city's artillery militia when it

---

[292] Ibid. Page 52.
[293] Ibid.

was created for defence of the city during the Jacobite uprising.[294] He published a treatise in 1746 entitled *The Use of the Broad Sword*, in which he endeavoured to explain "the true method of fighting with that weapon as it is now in use among the Highlanders."[295] He had studied fencing under the gladiator Timothy Buck, so had most likely learned a system of broadsword fencing resembling that of the English gladiators,[296] rather than that of the Highlanders, but he may well have picked up some information about the Highland methods of fighting along the way.

Chris Thompson suggests that there was probably a very similar system of fighting used by gladiators (prize-fighters and stage-fighters) across the British Isles, and that it would be a mistake to view English gladiator fighting as completely different from Scottish gladiator fighting.[297] There are certainly many similarities between the broadsword treatises of the English gladiators and the Scottish fencing masters. Just as with singlestick, there may well have been very similar methods in use around the British Isles, with local variations. It is probably reasonable to say that Page's system is a fair representation of how some Scots used the broadsword.

Roworth was a student of the Angelo school of fencing, but was not a master himself, rather a very enthusiastic amateur.[298] Since his treatise is thought to be a textual description of the Angelo method of broadsword, the question is how much did he learn directly from Henry Angelo, and how much did he learn by reading earlier texts himself? We do not have any way to know the answer to this for certain; perhaps he took the basic Angelo method and supplemented it with additional information (which might explain why Henry Angelo (Angelo III) then drew inspiration from Roworth's 1798 textbook for his own *Sword Exercise for Infantry*

---

[294] Bethan Jenkins. "Contextualising Western Martial Arts." *Linacre School of Defence*, January 2007, accessed 2nd August 2014. http://www.sirwilliamhope.org/Library/Articles/Jenkins/Contextualising.php

[295] Thomas Page. *The Use of the Broad Sword*. Norwich: M. Chase, 1746.

[296] Christopher Scott Thompson, Vol. 1, 2012. Pages 106-107.

[297] Ibid. Page 107.

[298] J.D. Aylward, 1956. Page 219.

treatise in 1842,[299] rather than from his own father's work), or perhaps Angelo had performed the necessary research to include Scottish elements in his system and simply passed along the information.

My suggestion is that Roworth performed the research himself, and must have read some earlier textbooks to inform his work. He reproduced an exact copy Page's diagram and text about the traverse, and also reproduced Page's instructions for attacking the leg; this would not have been possible if he did not have access to that material for reference. Therefore, if he had access to the treatise in order to reproduce its content, and had read it enough to understand its merits and to describe Page as "an able writer on this science", [300] then he had probably read enough to supplement the knowledge he gained from studying with Angelo.

Furthermore, Chris Thompson asserts that the Roworth treatise draws material from Captain Sinclair's *Anti-Pugilism* treatise published in 1790.[301] Sinclair's system probably derived from a combination of his military training as an officer in the Black Watch and of his experience of traditional Highland methods.[302] According to Wagner and Rector, after the disarming Acts following the Jacobite uprisings, the only sword-like weapon available to the Highlanders was the singlestick or cudgel, and so 18th century Highland singlestick methods probably found their way into Sinclair's system. [303] They note that *Anti-Pugilism* contains some stylistic elements not found in other British treatises from the 17th and 18th centuries, hence their assertion of the "retention of old clan techniques through a Highland singlestick tradition".[304]

---

[299] Ibid. Pages 220-221.
[300] Charles Roworth, 1804. Page 90.
[301] Christopher Scott Thompson, Vol. 1, 2012. Page 103.
[302] Paul Wagner and Mark Rector, 2004. Page 43.
[303] Ibid.
[304] Ibid. Page 44.

Henry Angelo (Angelo II) had some experience of the Aberdeen methods of singlestick play,[305] which Chris Thompson believes must have occurred in 1798[306] before Angelo and Rowlandson published *The Guards and Lessons of the Highland Broadsword* posters.[307] However, Angelo could not have drawn upon this experience to help formulate his broadsword method; he devised the method in 1795, ready for formal adoption as the regulation sword exercise for the British Army in 1796.[308]

Aylward wonders where Angelo developed his understanding of the broadsword. Until 1795, Angelo's studies had been limited to the civilian smallsword.[309] Aylward suggests that perhaps Angelo "had no experience at all with the cavalry weapons for which he drew up a system" and that perhaps he "confined himself to a study of the single-stick play then still popular with the lower classes, removing some conventionalities, and returning to the original notion that the basket-hilted cudgel was a rough-and-ready substitute for a sword, and not a weapon in itself."[310]

After further study, Aylward suggests that perhaps calling the system "Highland broadsword" was a falsehood that covered "a trail which leads to Figg, Miller and Godfrey" and early 18th century English backsword play.[311] Figg, Miller and Godfrey (amongst others) were masters of English backsword fighting; Chris Thompson believes that this discipline was probably similar to Scottish broadsword or singlestick fighting.[312] Nonetheless, these men were English masters of an English art, hence Aylward's hesitation to recognise Angelo's system as of Scottish origin.

---

[305] Henry Angelo. *Reminiscences of Henry Angelo, With Memoirs of his late Father and Friends*. Vol. II, London: Henry Colburn and Richard Bentley, 1830. Pages 312-313.

[306] As this was the year when James Perry was imprisoned in Newgate Prison, where Angelo met him, and where the practised singlestick.

[307] Christopher Scott Thompson, Vol. 1, 2012. Pages 102-103.

[308] J.D. Aylward, 1956. Page 214.

[309] J.D. Aylward. *The House of Angelo*. London: The Batchworth Press, 1953. Pages 168-170.

[310] Ibid. Pages 168-170.

[311] J.D. Aylward, 1956. Page 220.

[312] Christopher Scott Thompson, Vol. 1, 2012. Page 107.

It is worth noting that Egerton Castle concluded his "sketch of the character of English swordsmanship" by referring to Angelo and Roworth.[313] However, he may not have meant that there was no link to a Scottish method of fencing, just that these sources were good examples of the development of the English tradition.

If the dates provided by Aylward and Thompson are correct, and Angelo developed his system before learning singlestick from Perry, then it is likely that Roworth's knowledge of Scottish treatises such as those by Page and Sinclair cannot have come from Angelo. Therefore, it is likely that Roworth undertook the research necessary to include these Scottish influences in *The Art of Defence on Foot*, rather than simply reproducing the Angelo method. Chris Thompson asserts that "the works associated with the Angelo family" show that they had studied Page and Sinclair;[314] however, I believe that Roworth studied these treatises, and did not simply reproduce the methods of the Angelo school of arms.

Nonetheless, Aylward feels that the Angelo method is best understood when studied alongside Roworth's treatise,[315] and there are indeed great similarities between the illustrations of guard positions by Rowlandson and in Roworth's 1804 edition. Furthermore, Thompson notes that the ten lessons of John Taylor are virtually identical to the ten divisions of Highland broadsword set down by Angelo.[316] However, Taylor probably learned the Angelo method when it became regulation for the Army, so this may explain the similarity.

To answer the question of just "how Scottish" is the system, we must examine the role of the Scottish broadsword over a longer time period.

As described in Chapter 1: Scottish Swordsmanship, the broadsword was often used for personal defence, for skirmishes

---

[313] Egerton Castle. *Schools and Masters of Fencing.* Mineola, NY: Dover Publications, 2003. Page 219.
[314] Christopher Scott Thompson, Vol. 1, 2012. Page 124.
[315] J.D. Aylward, 1956. Page 219.
[316] Christopher Scott Thompson, Vol. 1, 2012. Page 103.

and for battles. Soldiers in the Highland Regiments were issued with broadswords as one of their standard weapons.

Earlier in the 18th century, before Page's *The Use of the Broad Sword* in 1746 and Sinclair's *Anti-Pugilism* in 1790, no Scottish treatises survive that describe in significant detail the use of the broadsword. [317] The sources by Page and Sinclair provide a snapshot of what Scottish broadsword fencing potentially looked like in the mid to late 18th century; since Roworth's system involves elements from these two sources, there is a clear link to 18th century Scottish broadsword fighting, even if the swords of his time had become lighter and more akin to the other regimental weapons of standard issue.[318]

Some elements of Roworth's system do not resemble elements of earlier Scottish systems. For example, Roworth's method of making a swift pushing cut on the lunge is different to the Highland method of striking on the passing step with the full weight of the body, as described by Mathewson.[319] It is evident that Roworth's system has similarities to the earlier Highland traditions, but also some differences. That being said, it is highly unlikely that Scotland had any single ubiquitous tradition; most likely there were regional differences and developments over time. So Mathewson's method of striking may have been a snapshot of just one of the Highland methods, there may have been other Highland methods involving cuts from the wrist that were more similar to Roworth's preferred striking mechanics.

In 1796, when Angelo's broadsword and sabre system became the formal regulation method for the British Army, all cavalry regiments had to send sergeants to London to receive tuition in the system, in order to bring the information back to the

---

[317] Both Hope and McBane talk about the use of the broadsword in their books, written in the first few decades of the 18th century. Hope explains that his New Method can be used for the broadsword as well as the smallsword, and McBane talks a little about the use of the broadsword and the broadsword and targe. However, neither author described a system designed specifically for a basket-hilted cutting weapon, in the same fashion as Roworth does in his treatise; the primary weapon described by both Hope and McBane was the smallsword.
[318] Paul Wagner and Mark Rector, 2004. Page 41.
[319] Ibid. Page 57-58.

regiments for training. [320] Presumably the system must have spread to the infantry regiments in some fashion as well, and so the Highland Regiments would have adopted this new system as their regulation practice. Therefore, the Highland Regiments in the 19th century would have fought using such training; Roworth's treatise (assuming it describes the Angelo method, as has been asserted by Aylward, Thompson and others, or is at least very similar) is therefore indicative of Scottish broadsword fighting of the 19th century.

Great quantities of ink could be spent discussing whether or not the system is at all similar to the earlier Highland methods of fighting, from the early 18th or 17th centuries. At least in the 19th century, this was the system that was trained and used by Highland Regiments and Scottish officers. It is therefore entirely reasonable to describe Roworth's system as a Scottish broadsword system, even if it is not a perfect description of the Highland methods of the early 18th century.

---

[320] J.D. Aylward, 1956. Page 214.

Chapter 3: History of Singlestick in Britain

Singlestick is a historical game and training method practised in many different countries across different time periods, usually with different rules and styles of play, and sometimes with different objectives. It is often misunderstood by modern practitioners, due to the lack of specificity of the word "singlestick", and due to the amount of well-meaning but often incorrect information available on the subject. It is the intention that this chapter will examine singlestick through the ages in the British Isles, showing the differences between implementations and rules of the game, and also showing the modern survival of the discipline in post-war Scotland through to the current day.

3.1   Singlestick in Scotland

It is important to note that the terms "singlestick" and "cudgel" sometimes apply to a type of weapon, sometimes to an activity. At different times in history, and in different places in Britain, the terms were used interchangeably or to mean different things.

The Oxford English Dictionary cites the word "singlestick" as first appearing in the late 18th century. In many of the sources that mention stick fighting in Scotland in the 17th, 18th and 19th centuries, the phrase "cudgel" is more common than "singlestick", but often seems to refer to the same activity. There does not appear to have been a major difference in concept between "singlestick" and "cudgel" in Scotland, unlike in England where the words referred to quite different styles of fighting.

At least in this section, we can probably understand "singlestick" and "cudgel" to be more or less synonymous. However, we should be aware that the terms are being used more loosely than in the section about stick-play in England, found later in this chapter, and so these excerpts may not all describe exactly the same weapon or activity.

In the Highlands of Scotland, during the 17th and early 18th centuries, singlestick was used as a method to teach children and adults the rudiments of sword fighting. This skill was not limited to the nobles and their warriors; even common people learned some skills for fighting with the sword, mainly through singlestick play.[321] After the Disarming Act of 1716 and the Proscription Act of 1746, possession of weapons was banned in the Highlands. However, sticks were not banned, and so playing with singlestick and cudgel remained popular in Scotland throughout the 18th and 19th centuries.[322]

The singlestick or cudgel was not only a training sword; sometimes it could be a real weapon, and could be wielded by otherwise unarmed men to defeat armed attackers.[323] In one skirmish between the Campbells and the McMartins, the Campbells used their dirks to cut some branches from nearby trees. They then utilised these makeshift cudgels to defend their position at a ford against the McMartins, who were armed with axes and other sharp steel weapons. The Campbells won the fight, killing nearly all of their attackers.[324]

In *The Scottish* Gael, Logan describes another occasion when cudgels were used in place of steel swords:

> A club is another simple implement of destruction. In cases of necessity, combatants will avail themselves of any thing that can be converted into arms, and, at all times, those who can find nothing better will provide themselves with a good stick. Three or four hundred of the king's army went to the battle of Edgehill with nothing but a cudgel. When the Highlanders joined Prince Charles, when they fought at Gladsmuir and even afterwards, many had no better weapon, but "With heavy cudgels of good oak, They vowed to kill at every stroke."[325]

---

[321] Christopher Scott Thompson. *Highland Martial Culture.* Boulder: Paladin Press, 2009. Page 7.
[322] Paul Wagner and Mark Rector, 2004. Page 43.
[323] Christopher Scott Thompson, 2009. Page 8.
[324] Christopher Scott Thompson, Vol. 1, 2012. Pages 33-33.
[325] James Logan, 1831. Page 201.

Admittedly, in this two accounts, there is the possibility that the "cudgels of good oak" were larger than one-handed singlesticks. Perhaps in this case the cudgels were more like two-handed short staffs. From these brief accounts, we cannot say for certain exactly what these "cudgels" may have looked like.

However, most of the time, the cudgel or singlestick was not a weapon of war, but a weapon of training. As a boy, Donald Macleod spent much of his time engaged in the practice of the one-handed cudgel:

> He was an apt and diligent apprentice, learned his trade with great facility, and pleased his masters well. Both here, and when he was at the school of Bracadill, his spare hours, like those of other boys, were wholly employed in training up himself, by cudgel-playing, to the use and management of the broad-sword and target.[326]

Logan recounts that Highland boys spent a lot of their time practising with the stick, and that sometimes there was a gymnasium of sorts where such training could take place:

> The boys of the Highlanders were trained, from an early age, to cudgel playing, that they might become expert at the broadsword exercise. Their whole time is said to have been so occupied; and, besides training at home, there was a sort of gymnasium in Badenoch, to which the youth resorted.[327]

What was this "sort of gymnasium", and how was training conducted? According to John Dewar, in his *Dewar Manuscripts* of 1875, the gentry schooled the local youths in how to fight:

> It was a custom in the Highlands of Scotland before the year 1745 that the gentry kept schools to give instruction to youths in sword exercise, and the laird of Ardsheil kept a school for the instruction of the youth of his own district. He stored the cudgels behind his house. There were cudgels for the lads, and there were cudgels for the laddies, and lads and laddies went every day to Ardsheil to receive instruction on the cudgel from the laird. After

---

[326] William Thomson, 1791. Page 13.
[327] James Logan, 1831. Page 211.

the laddies had received their day's instruction each got a bannock and lumps of cheese. They were then sent to try who would soonest ascend a mountain and eat the bannock and cheese; and whoever was first got another bannock and lumps of cheese home with him.[328]

This school was known as the Taigh Suntais, and was the Highland equivalent of a *salle d'armes* to provide martial training for young gentlemen.[329]

Logan writes about the nature and management of the singlestick practice in preparation for the use of the broadsword. He describes the system as simple and elegant, as he believes that such skill with a stick was useful both historically and in his own century:

> The management of the broadsword, or single stick, which it closely resembles, as now taught, may be comprehended in thirty-one lessons. The old Highland exercise was not less remarkable for its simplicity and elegance, than utility. By seven cuts, oblique, horizontal, and diagonal, and one guard, in which the sword is held vibrating, as a pendulum, ready to turn aside the thrusts of an enemy, the adversary was assailed and the person effectually protected. The salute of the Celtic swordsman was peculiarly graceful. The importance of this exercise was evinced by enabling undisciplined troops to make head against numerous armies, and even defeat skilled veterans. Its utility in the present day, to officers of both army and navy, is apparent, and many occasions may arise to show the advantage of knowing properly how to use a stick. With this simple weapon, a skilful player can defend himself with ease from the simultaneous attacks of three or four, and put to defiance the efforts of the most renowned pugilists. It is to be regretted that this desirable accomplishment and healthy exercise is now so little attended to.[330]

However, Logan's description of the system might be slightly suspect. His description is probably based on the broadsword method described in the *Anti-Pugilism* treatise, published in 1790

---

[328] John MacKechnie, 1963. Page 161.
[329] Christopher Scott Thompson, Vol. 1, 2012. Page 116.
[330] James Logan, 1831. Page 212.

by "A Highland Officer" of the Black Watch.[331] This officer was most likely Captain Sinclair,[332] who published a very similar treatise in 1800 entitled *Cudgel-playing Modernized and Improved*, which was almost an exact copy of *Anti-Pugilism* other than for the correction of a printing error.[333] *Anti-Pugilism* contained 32 lessons: 31 lessons about fencing, and one lesson about the salute. Logan probably found a copy of *Anti-Pugilism* or *Cudgel-playing Modernized and Improved*, and chose to base his description of the Highlanders' singlestick system upon this treatise, just as he suggested that the book *La noble science des ioueurs despee* exemplified the Highland method of fighting with the two-handed sword.

Sinclair's system of singlestick and broadsword could have been developed as a synthesis of his military sword experience in the Black Watch regiment and knowledge of civilian Highland swordplay traditions.[334] In some ways, *Anti-Pugilism* is similar to later regimental broadsword treatises, but it does differ in some instances. It has been suggested that these differences are the result of Highland singlestick systems retaining old clan techniques.[335]

In Aberdeen, singlestick remained popular into the 19th century, and even as late as the 1830s, youths in that city excelled in its practice.[336] Furthermore, from Angelo's reminiscences, we find that it was a man from Aberdeen who taught Henry Angelo the method of singlestick play:

> I have passed many pleasant days in Newgate [Prison]. My old friend, James Perry, of the Morning Chronicle, who was confined there some months for a libel, was always glad to see me, so that I often partook his *fortune de pot*, enjoying ourselves, whilst many a distressed object, under the same roof, was loaded with fetters, and perhaps the very next hour might bring his death warrant. We often went to the top of the prison, as he found

---

[331] Christopher Scott Thompson, Vol. 1, 2012. Page 123.
[332] Ibid. Pages 121-122.
[333] Paul Wagner and Mark Rector, 2004. Page 45.
[334] Ibid. Page 43.
[335] Ibid. Page 44.
[336] Christopher Scott Thompson, Vol. 1, 2012. Page 111.

exercise very necessary for preserving his health, his apartment being confined, far different to the incarceration of my clerical friend in the Bench, for every body knows, that in that prison there is plenty of space to play at racket, which serves for an amusement, as well as to improve the health. Often we mounted the top of the prison there; nobody could see us where we were on the leads, and we amused ourselves, secure from being seen, with playing the Highland broadsword, at which he was very expert, being his favourite national diversion; and often I have seen him at the masquerade, dressed in the true costume of a Highlander, with a party of Scotch lassies, dancing Scotch reels.[337]

Chris Thompson notes that James Perry hailed from Aberdeen, and that Angelo learned singlestick from Perry in the same year that he published his posters about Highland broadsword.[338]

The practice of singlestick and cudgel (terms which appear to have been roughly synonymous in Scotland) seems to have been found throughout the country, particularly in the Highlands, both for play and in preparation for serious fighting with real weapons. The latter seems to have been more likely during the 17th and early 18th centuries, but after Culloden, it seems to have persisted as a martial game that then became useful for training the Highland Regiments and later the other regiments in the British Army and Navy.

3.2   Singlestick and Cudgelling in England

Singlestick and cudgel-play seem to have been quite different activities in England, although sometimes the terms may have been used interchangeably, or may have had different meanings. Generally speaking, however, singlestick seems to have been played with just one stick, and cudgel seems to have been played with two sticks. The aim of both games was usually to defend yourself successfully and to draw blood from the opponent's head:

---

[337] Henry Angelo, Vol. 2, 1830. Pages 312-313.
[338] Christopher Scott Thompson, Vol. 1, 2012. Page 111.

> Single-stick playing is so called to distinguish it from cudgelling, in which two sticks are used: the single-stick player having the left hand tied down, and using only one stick to defend himself and strike his antagonist. The object of each gamester in this play, as in cudgelling, is to guard himself, and to fetch blood from the other's head; whether by taking a little skin from his pericranium, drawing a stream from his nose, or knocking out a few of those early inventions for grinding – the teeth.[339]

It was not always the case that the left hand was tied down, so this is an unusual description of singlestick. Comparatively, cudgel-play was conducted with two sticks, one for offence and one for defence:

> In cudgelling, as the name implies, the weapon is a stout cudgel; and the player defends himself with another having a large hemisphere of wicker-work upon it. This is called the pot, either from its likewise in shape to that kitchen article, or else in commemoration of some ancient warfare, when the "rude forefathers of the hamlet," being suddenly surrounded with their foes, sallied forth against them, armed with the pot and ladle.[340]

The etymology of "pot" in this case is probably rather fanciful, but the description of cudgelling is quite representative of the sport. Sometimes just one stick would have a basket-guard; sometimes both sticks would possess a basket-guard.[341]

Another difference between singlestick and cudgel was that in some places, the rules held that singlestick should be conducted in a static fashion,[342] without moving the feet,[343] while presumably cudgelling allowed footwork and movement. Of course, other rulesets for singlestick permitted the movement of the feet, and

---

[339] William Hone. *The Year Book of Daily Recreation and Information*. London: Thomas Tegg, 1832. Page 1525.
[340] Ibid.
[341] Mark Hathaway. "Cudgelling and Singlestick." Tony Collins, John Martin and Wray Vamplew. *Encyclopedia of Traditional British Rural Sports*. Abingdon: Routledge, 2005. Page 89.
[342] Ibid.
[343] "Singlestick." *Encyclopaedia Britannica*, accessed 20th July 2014. http://www.britannica.com/EBchecked/topic/546008/singlestick

even encouraged good form such as lunging and slipping the lead leg.

The games of singlestick and cudgel differed from each other, but there were also various different ways to play singlestick, depending on region, time period and context. For example, in Wiltshire, players could use their left arm to defend their heads, their left hands holding a handkerchief tied around the left thigh. However, in Gloucestershire, the left hand was tied securely to the thigh, so the left arm could not be used in defence of the head.[344] Generally speaking, the game was won when an inch of blood was drawn from the head.[345]

In 1711, some correspondence was written to Eustace Budgell, one of the writers for *The Spectator*, describing a "country wake" with a game of cudgelling:

> A Country Wake, which you know in most Parts of England is the Eve-Feast of the Dedication of our Churches. I was last Week at one of these Assemblies which was held in a neighbouring Parish; where I found their Green covered with a promiscuous Multitude of all Ages and both Sexes, who esteem one another more or less the following Part of the Year according as they distinguish themselves at this Time. The whole Company were in their Holiday Cloaths, and divided into several Parties, all of them endeavouring to shew themselves in those Exercises wherein they excelled, and to gain the Approbation of the Lookers on.
>
> I found a Ring of Cudgel-Players, who were breaking one another's Heads in order to make some Impression on their Mistresses Hearts. I observed a lusty young Fellow, who had the Misfortune of a broken Pate; but what considerably added to the Anguish of the Wound, was his over-hearing an old Man, who shook his Head and said, That he questioned now if black Kate would marry him these three Years. (...)
>
> In short, I found the men endeavoured to shew the Women they were no Cowards, and that the whole Company strived to recommend themselves to each other, by making it appear that

[344] Mark Hathaway, 2005. Page 89.
[345] J.R. Daeschner. *True Brits: A Tour of 21st Century Britain in All its Bog-Snorkelling, Gurning and Cheese-Rolling Glory*. London: Arrow, 2004. Page 77.

they were all in a perfect State of Health, and fit to undergo any Fatigues of bodily Labour.[346]

Such country wakes and fairs were common across England in the 18th and 19th centuries. From the early 17th century, the annual Olimpick Games were held in Cotswold. A man named Robert Dover started this tradition,[347] and the games of backsword and cudgelling were popular parts of this event. The frontispiece for the *Annalia Dubrensia*, published in 1636 in celebration of Dover's Games, shows a pair of cudgellers fighting in the top right corner, each armed with a long stick and a short stick, both sticks protecting the hands with basket-guards.[348]

The practice of physical exercise, Dover believed, was something that was important for the defence of the country. The reigning monarch, King James, agreed with this sentiment, and had expressed to his own son that it would be sensible to appoint days in the year for people to play games and for the "exercise of arms". However, the outbreak of the English Civil War in 1642 heralded the end of the Cotswold Olimpick Games.[349]

Dover died in 1652, but at some point after 1660, the Games were revived. Without Dover's leadership, the Games seem to have devolved into a drunken country festival, and in 1740 William Somerville wrote the mock-heroic poem *Hobbinol* that shows the coarseness of the Games. Eventually, the local fields where the Games were held were enclosed, and so in 1852 the Games could no longer continue due to lack of common land upon which to take place.[350] The Games were revived yet again in 1951 as a one-off event, and have been a regular annual event since 1966.[351]

---

[346] Eustace Budgell. *The Spectator* 161 (September 1711).
[347] "A Brief History of Robert Dover's Games." *Robert Dover's Cotswold Olimpicks*, accessed 20th July 2014. http://www.olimpickgames.com/history/
[348] Alexander Grosart. *Annalia Dubrensia, or Celebration of Captain Robert Dover's Cotswold Games*. Manchester: Charles E. Simms, 1877.
[349] "A Brief History." http://www.olimpickgames.com/history/
[350] Mark Hathaway, 2005. Page 89.
[351] "A Brief History." http://www.olimpickgames.com/history/

Backswording was one of the events held at these Games. The game of singlestick was commonly known as "backswording", and the singlestick itself was often called a "backsword". Some of the posters for the Games from the early 19th century advertise prizes for the activity:

> The sports will commence with a grand match of Backswords for a purse of guineas, To be played by 9 or 7 men on a side. Each side must appear in the ring by 3 o'clock in the afternoon. Or 15s. each pair will be given for as many as will play.[352]

And on another poster:

> There will be a purse of twenty guineas, To be played for at Backswords, By Men, as shall be agreed upon, to begin play at three o'clock in the afternoon.[353]

Various meetings, festivals and competitions for singlestick and cudgel took place in the 17th and 18th centuries, with increasing frequency – although at the same time, in London, the frequency of such sports decreased in popularity.[354] In counties such as Somerset, Gloucester, Wiltshire and Berkshire, such contests had become major attractions. Sometimes the gentry hosted events where singlestick or cudgel would be the only activity, and these could bring together large numbers of competitors. For example, in 1753, a cudgelling contest in Bristol brought together 70 players to compete against each other.[355]

Up until the late 18th century, cudgelling was apparently the more popular sport. However, as the 19th century dawned, singlestick seems to have overtaken cudgelling in popularity.[356]

In the early 19th century, there was some measure of discussion in Parliament about abolishing traditional games such as boxing, singlestick and wrestling. As a result, various publications showed their support for these traditional games, publishing stories and

---

[352] An advertising flyer for the Games in 1812.
[353] An advertising flyer for the Games in 1819.
[354] Mark Hathaway, 2005. Page 88.
[355] Ibid.
[356] Ibid.

correspondence showing why these games were valuable for the nation.

This rather long excerpt from *The Mirror of Taste, and Dramatic Censor* shows an example of this sort of pro-game publication:

> In the discussions which have arisen in and out of parliament in England about the abolition of the Briton's old favourite sports, it was conceded by all but a few, that from the custom of boxing, singlestick and backsword playing, wrestling, &c. arose the good temper which distinguishes that people – Englishmen being less subject to violent fits of anger than the people of any other nation in the world. In the compass of eighteen pages of a work now before us we have details of no less than two grand matches of singlestick, one Wiltshire against Somerset, and the other Somerset against all England, for large purses. In both cases the champions of Somerset country beat; and what must astonish those who hear it, the victors (though men in the lowest classes of life in one case) shared the prize with the vanquished. In the former, Somerset gave nine broken heads and received seven – in the latter, gave eight and received six. The Wiltshire men went to Trowbridge in Somersetshire, the appointed place of meeting, attended by some of the leading gentry of Wiltshire, and the gentleman who was appointed by them to preside, bore public testimony to the liberal and kind treatment his countrymen experienced.
>
> Any person who has seen the farce of Hob in the Well, performed, will remember to have seen a specimen of this kind of prize fighting, for which as well as wrestling, the people of Somersetshire have for ages been renowned. In Scotland they excel at the backsword – the Irish too are admirable hands – but neither have the temper of the English; "Oppression makes a wise man mad;" what should it do then with a poor peasantry? The tempers of the English have not had that to irritate them. We will close this subject with a letter from an intelligent Londoner, who was travelling through Hampshire.
>
> PASSING, sometime since, through Ralpey Dean, Hants, my attention being attracted by a crowd of rustics on a little green near the road I turned my horse thither, and arrived in time when a lame elderly man, who I afterwards found was the knight marshal of the field, from the middle of a ring made by ropes, proclaimed, that "a hat worth one guinea was to be played for at

the backsword; the breaker of most heads to bear away the hat and honour," and inviting the youth there to contend for it. A little after, a young fellow threw his hat into the ring and followed, when the lame umpire called out "a challenge," and proceeded to equip the challenger for the game. His coat and waistcoat were taken off, his left hand tied by a handkerchief to his left thigh, and a stick, with basket hilt, put into his hand; he then walked round the ring till a second hat was thrown in, and the umpire called out, "the challenge is answered."

As soon as prepared, the knights met, measured weapons, shook hands, walked once round, turned and began the contest. In about a minute, the umpire called out "About," when they dropped the points of their weapons and walked round, and this called I observed, was repeated as often as the umpire judged either distressed. After some twenty minutes play, some blood trickled down the challenger's head; the umpire called "Blood;" and declared the other to have won a head.

When both left the ring another hat was thrown in, and the challenge again accepted, and played off in the like manner, till the umpire announced there were four winners of heads, and proceeded to call the ties, that is, he called on the winners of the first two heads play together, and afterwards on the winners of the third and fourth heads; after which the winners of two heads each played for the hat, and the proud victor (Morgan) thus to earn it, broke three heads. I was much struck with the amazing temper with which the game was played: not a particle of ill will was shown, two young fellows, who played together forty-five minutes, and in the course of it gave each other many severe blows, one alone of which would have satisfied the most unconscionable taylor or man-milliner breathing, drank frequently together between the bouts, shaking hands as often as the weight of the blows given seemed to require it of their good-nature. Indeed it appeared to be a rule with each pair that played, to drink together after the contest, and a general spirit of harmony seemed to prevail. This game is certainly of great antiquity, and the only relick (with the exception of wrestling) of the ancient tournament. The knight defied with throwing down his hat or gauntlet – the rustic gamester does the same, and is equally courteous with the knight towards his opponent: nor were there in this instance village dames or damsels wanting, to animate the prowess of the youth.

It has been asserted, that these exhibitions engender a ferocious spirit; but were I to judge from what I saw, and from the inquiries I made into the characters of the players at Ropley Dean, from the farmers on my right and left, I should pronounce quite the contrary; and think that as long as the sword is used by our cavalry and navy, and as long as we wish to entertain in the nation a fearless, generous, martial spirit, we should encourage the like pastimes at our fairs and revels.[357]

The same volume contained some other passages describing local British events where backsword was played:

BACKSWORD PLAYING – MIDDLESEX PASTIME.

At Wilsden Green, a hat, and a purse of twenty shillings, were played for at backsword, and, as an encouragement for young players, five shillings were given to the winner of every head, and two shillings to the loser. On the umpire's proclaiming the game, a hat was thrown into the ring (being the ancient mode of defiance) another soon followed, and the owners entered and played several bouts with much good humour, till the blood trickled down the head of the least fortunate. Other gamesters followed, to the number of seventeen, affording most excellent sport to a numerous and well-dressed field. The prize was won by a Dorsetshire lad, who, by breaking four heads provided himself to be the best man.[358]

This is an interesting passage, because it shows that simply participating was enough to secure a small payment, even if you lost and had your head broken. Winners received a greater monetary reward, and the overall winner (of four separate rounds) received the purse and the new hat.

Another excerpt describes the game at a different event, which was "the most lively picture of war", with many broken heads and yet little or no animosity between the competitors:

Twenty-four gamesters contended manfully at Harrow-on-the-Hill for a prize of a hat and purse, at the right valiant game of

---

[357] *The Mirror of Taste and Dramatic Censor.* Vol. I, Philadelphia: Bradford and Inskeep, 1810. Pages 93-95.
[358] Ibid. Page 266.

backsword. Many a crown was cracked, and many a heavy blow was given with right good will, and received with true humour. Much skill also in assault and defence in this game (the most lively picture of war) was evinced. Jack Martin of Harrow played the best stick among the Harrow lads – but the prize, alas was actually borne away by – a LONDON TAILOR. Fourteen broken heads graced the ring.[359]

This passage shows that the combatants gave and received heavy hits without bad feeling or anger. It certainly paints the picture that such games were good for one's temper and civility.

Sometimes, only amateurs attended these competitions. At other times, the events involved professional fighters, or at least well-known and skilful individuals would participate:

WILTSHIRE PASTIME.

The play at singlestick at Salisbury races on Wednesday was very dull, there being no players of note to meet the Somerset men, who carried off the prize easily. On Thursday, however, James Lyne arrived, on his return from Magdaline bull fair, and Maslen came in from Devizes. Some fine play was now displayed – Maslin and John Wall had no less than thirty-five bouts, and at length Wall gave in, not being able longer to keep his guard.

But the crack play was between James Lyne (of Wilts.) and Wm. Wall (Somerset) and it afforded a high treat to the amateurs of the art. At length Lyne won Wall's head, and the play concluded for the morning. In the afternoon when the tyes were called on, the Wiltshire men had four heads, and only one Somerset man (Bunn) had gained a head. The odds were too great for Bunn to have any hope of success, he therefore gave in, and the Wiltshire men divided the prize.

Two master gamesters, a Berkshire and a Hampshire man then entered the ring on a particular challenge, and showed much skill, intrepidity and good bottom [courage]. Berkshire triumphed. The sport lasted five hours. The bouts played were one hundred and sixty-one. The heads broken seventeen.[360]

---

[359] Ibid. Page 267.
[360] Ibid. Page 411.

The concept of "tyes" in the above account refers to the winners of the previous rounds. This following excerpt describes how the different rounds were arranged, and also describes how teams could enter the contests:

Back-sword, or Single-stick, is a game of high antiquity and the most warlike extant. When the fate of nations was principally decided in battle by the sword, it was the policy of our ancestors to render its use familiar to the bulk of the population; hence arose the courtly tournament, and the plebeian exhibitions at wakes and festivals of courage and skill, in sword and dagger, sword and pot-lid, cudgels, back-sword, &c. &c. The prizes for which still remain annually given in many parts: thus were formed those heroes, who carried triumphant the British standard, "o'er the vine covered hills and gay vallies of France;" and though the fire of artillery now generally rules the battle, yet the use made of the sword in modern warfare, warrants every encouragement being given to a game, so productive of intrepidity and confidence beyond its use, which the practice of back-sword must, in combats of hand to hand, inspire. With a view to its more general encouragement, I send you the following rules of the game, premising that the stage should not be less than sixteen feet square, the ring of ropes from forty to fifty feet diameter.

The basket sticks to be three feet two inches in length.

The winner of most heads to carry the prize.

Should a stick break, or fall out of the hand, and the adversary, not observing, strike, and the blow so given draw blood, the head nevertheless, is not to be allowed.

No head to be allowed, except the blood runs an inch above the chin.

The umpire to decide all disputes.

The tyers to play with one another in the order they become tyers; that is, the winner of the first head to play with the winner of the second, the winner of the third with the fourth, and so on.

The first tyer being on the stage, the second is called, and if he appears not to play the first, after being repeatedly called, he loses his right to further play, and the third tyer is called; if he appears not, the fourth is called, &c. &c. and if none appears to dispute the prize, it is adjudged to the first tyer.

If the tyers are played regularly off, supposing the tyers to be four, being each winners of one head, then the two winners of these four being then tyers of two heads each, play for the prize.

If the number of tyers is uneven (suppose three), then the winner of the first head plays with the winner of the second, and the winner of these plays the remaining tyer, the prize belonging to the victor.

When two parties play together, if on gets six heads out of seven, and supposing the players to be seven aside, yet the seventh may insist on playing till he loses his own or wins the other heads, in which case he carries the prize.

Wilts and Somerset are the most famous counties for this pastime; it is partially practised in Hants, Berks, Dorset, Bucks and the neighbouring counties, where, perhaps it is only necessary to bring it into more general use, to furnish at the several fairs the prizes usually given; viz. a hat with gold or silver lace of from fifteen to thirty shillings value, or a purse of from twenty to fifty shillings.

The lord of the manor of Buckelsbury, Berks, gives the first Monday in August, a hat value 25s. and 2s. to the winner and 1s. to the loser of each head; also a hat of the value of 10s. 6d. to the best wrestler.[361]

Sometimes the cudgel was used to settle arguments, and was not such a sterling example of good British nature:

With such provocations of mutual irritations, they quickly appealed to the law of arms; and after putting the eyes of each other into half mourning, they agreed to adjourn the battle till Saturday morning, and to decide it like jontlemen – by the *cudgel*. The meeting took place accordingly, and each was attended to the field by a numerous train of partizans, male and female, from the warlike purlieus of Dyott-street and Saffron-hill. They were armed with blackthorn cudgels of no ordinary

---

[361] Ibid. Page 190.

dimensions; and having set to, without ceremony or parade, each belaboured his antagonist for above an hour, in a style that would have struck terror into the stoutest of the Burkes and Belchers, and enameled each other from head to foot, with lasting testimonies of vigour and dexterity. The air was rent by the triumphant shouts of their respective partizans, as either alternately bit the ground. At length, Mr. O'Chaugnessy yielded the victory; and Mr. O'Flannagan was borne off the field, with his browns enwreathed by the Sunday shawl of a milkwoman, his sweetheart, who witnessed the combat, and crowned the conqueror with own fair hands.[362]

People sometimes looked upon singlestick or cudgel as a barbarous and uncivilised form of entertainment. When played by novices, certainly that might be the case, but skilled players could make an art of the game, as this correspondence by "a real lover of old English Pastimes" wrote in 1826:

At the southern extremity of the hill is a thick wood, called Weston Park; under the shade of the trees on the borders of this wood the booths are built, and the principal sports are carried on, (on the Thursday and Friday in Whitsun-week) they consist of single-stick, (in Gloucestershire called backsword) wrestling, running, jingling, morris-dancing, and other sports of a minor importance. (...)

Backsword is looked upon by the cockneys, and those living in counties where it is rarely practised, as a most barbarous and bloodthirsty piece of business; but I think there is no game that shows the courage, hardihood, and manliness of the British character like it; on Dover's Hill, it is practised in its greatest perfection, I have seen two scientific men play nearly an hour and a half before one could break the other's head, and when it was over, it could not be seen that more than one blow had been struck on either side. Certainly when two novices contend it is thrashing work, and the blows fall heavily, then they are not obliged to enter the ring, but there it is they show their courage.

There are generally about twelve couple play at backsword, the prize is a guinea each couple, eighteen shillings goes to the victor and three shillings to the vanquished. (...)

---

[362] Ibid. Page 412.

138

I am certain that if any of our rigid mirth-destroying moralists, possessing the least sensibility or liberality of feeling towards the youth of both sexes, were to witness the innocent mirth and happy countenances at Dover's meeting, and at our country wakes and revels they would not strive as they do to the utmost of their power to cramp the amusements of the humbler classes, but would regret with every generous mind that the old English pastimes are so much upon the decline.[363]

Doubtless these "rigid mirth-destroying moralists" disapproved of games that led to death and serious disfigurement, and the Dover Games were shut down in 1852. Shortly before this date, there took place a backsword match between a local champion called "Nezzy" Plested and another man called Spiers. After a long fight, potentially as long as an hour and a half, Plested was announced the winner. However, in the process of winning the fight, he lost an eye. His opponent Spiers was completely incapacitated and died from his injuries two weeks later.[364]

The publications that stood up in favour of these games tried to show that while the activities might be bloody, they helped develop good character among the participants. There were lots of inter-county events that took place, giving people a chance to test themselves against the best players in the neighbouring counties.

I think it may be generally allowed that Wiltshire, and the western counties, keep up their primitive customs more than any counties. This is greatly to the credit of the inhabitants; for these usages tend to promote cheerful intercourse and friendly feeling among the residents of the different villages, who on such occasions assemble together. In Wiltshire I have remarked various customs particularly at Christmas, which I have never seen or heard of in any other place. If these customs were witnessed by a stranger, I am sure he must fancy the good old days of yore, where every season brought its particular custom, which was always strictly adhered to.

Wiltshire consists of beautiful and extensive downs, and rich meadow and pasture lands, which support some of the finest

[363] *The Mirror of Literature, Amusement, and Instruction: containing Original Essays*. Vol. VII, London: J. Limbird, 1826. Pages 354-355.
[364] J.R. Daeschner, 2004. Page 79.

dairies and farms that can be met with in the kingdom. The natives are a very strong and hardy set of men, and are particularly fond of robust sports; their chief and favourite amusement is back-swording, or singlestick, for which they are as greatly celebrated as the inhabitants of the adjoining counties, Somerset and Gloucestershire.

At this game there are several rules observed. They play with a large round stick, which must be three feet long, with a basket prefixed to one end as a guard for the hand. The combatants throw off their hats and upper garments, with the exception of the shirt, and have the left hand tied to the side, so that they cannot defend themselves with that hand. They brandish the stick over the head, guarding off the adversary's blows, and striking him whenever an opportunity occurs. Great skill is often used in the defence. I have seen two men play for upwards of half an hour without once hitting each other. The blood must flow an inch from some part of the head, before either party is declared victor.

Blackford, the backsword player, was a butcher residing at Swindon; he died a few years ago. His "successor" is a blacksmith at Lyddington, named Morris Pope, who is considered the best player of the day, and generally carries off the prizes at the Hungerford revel, which he always attends. This revel is attended by all the best players in Wiltshire and Somersetshire, between whom the contest lies. To commence the fray, twenty very excellent players are selected from each county; the contest lasts a considerable time, and it is always severe, but the Wiltshire men are generally conquerors. Their principal characteristics are skill, strength, and courage – this is generally allowed by all who are acquainted with them.[365]

The fairs and contests could also be smaller in scale, giving villages a regular opportunity to pit their best players against each other to make local traditions:

The spot whereon Purton fair is annually celebrated is a very pleasant little green called the "close" or play-ground, belonging to all the unmarried men in the village. They generally assemble there every evening after the toils of the day to recreate themselves with a few pleasant sports. Their favourite game is

[365] William Hone. *The Every-Day Book; or, Everlasting Calendar of Popular Amusements*. Vol. II, Part II, London: Hunt and Clarke, 1827. Pages 399-400.

what they call backswording, in some places called singlestick. Some few of the village have the good fortune to be adepts in that noble art, and are held up as beings of transcendent genius among the rustic admirers of that noted science. They have one whom they call their umpire, to whom all disputes are referred, and he always, with the greatest possible impartiality, decides them. (...)

The next day, several champions enter the field to contest the right to several prizes, which are laid out in the following order:-

1st. A new smock.
2nd. A new hat with a blue cockade.
3rd. An inferior hat with a white cockade.
4th. A still inferior hat without a cockade.

A stage is erected on the green, and at five o'clock the sport commences; and a very celebrated personage, whom they call their umpshire, (umpire,) stands high above the rest to award the prizes. The candidates are generally selected from the best players at singlestick, and on this occasion they use their utmost skill and ingenuity, and are highly applauded by the surrounding spectators. I must not forget to remark that on this grand, and to them, interesting day, the inhabitants of Purton do not compete against each other. No – believe me, sir, they are better acquainted with the laws of chivalry. Purton produces four candidates, and a small village adjoining, called Stretton, sends forth four more. These candidates are representatives of the villages to which they respectively belong, and they who lose have to pay all the expenses of the day; but it is to the credit of Purton I record, that for seven successive years their candidates have been returned the victors. The contest generally lasts two hours, and, after that, the ceremony of chairing the representatives takes place, which is thus performed:- Four chairs made with the boughs of trees are in waiting, and the conquerors are placed therein and carried through the village with every possible demonstration of joy, the inhabitants shouting "Purton for ever! Huzza! My boys, huzza!" and waving boughs over their triumphant candidates. After the chairing they adjourn to the village public-house, and spend the rest of the evening as before.[366]

---

[366] William Hone, 1827. Pages 1207-1210.

In the latter half of the 19th century, singlestick was often taught in private schools, giving children a form of physical exercise with traditional roots and martial applications.[367] However, towards the end of the century, the singlestick had mostly fallen out of favour, other than as a light training weapon for the sabre.[368]

3.3 1740: *Hobbinol*

In 1740, William Somerville wrote a mock-heroic poem entitled *Hobbinol, or the Rural Games*, named after the main character and his adventures at a county fair. I have provided a transcription of the two sections that deal with singlestick, because the poem contains some excellent descriptions of the style of fighting and the techniques and tactics that could be used. The poem is both educational and entertaining.

In this first excerpt, Milonides the marshal arrives to announce the game of singlestick:

FORTHWITH in hoary Majesty appears
One of gigantic Size, but Visage wan,
MILONIDES the Strong, renown'd of old
For Feats of Arms, but, bending now with Years,
His Trunk unwieldy from the verdant Turf
He rears deliberate, and with his Plant
Of toughest Virgin Oak in rising aids
His trembling Limbs; his bald and wrinkled Front,
Entrench'd with many a glorious Scar, bespeaks
Submissive Rev'rence. He with Count'nance grim
Boasts his past Deeds, and with redoubled Strokes
Marshalls the Croud, and forms the Circle wide.
Stern Arbiter! like some huge Rock he stands,
That breaks th'incumbent Waves; they thronging press
In Troops confus'd, and rear their foaming Heads
Each above each, but from superior Force
Shrinking repell'd, compose of stateliest View
A liquid Theatre. With Hands uplift,
And Voice *Stentorian*, he proclaims aloud

---

[367] Mark Hathaway, 2005. Page 88.
[368] "Singlestick." http://www.britannica.com/EBchecked/topic/546008/singlestick

Each rural Prize. "To him whose active Foot
" Foils his bold Foe, and rivets him to Earth,
" This Pair of Gloves, by curious Virgin Hands
" Embroider'd, seam'd with Silk, and fring'd with Gold.
" To him, who best the stubborn Hilts can wield,
" And bloody Marks of his Displeasure leave
" On his Opponent's Head, this Beaver white
" With Silver Edging grac'd, and Scarlet Plume.
" Ye taper Maidens! whose impetuous Speed
" Outflies the Roe, nor bends the tender Grass,
" See here this Prize, this rich lac'd Smock behold,
" White as your Bosoms, as your Kisses soft.
" Blest Nymph! whom bounteous Heav'n's peculiar Grace
" Allots this pompous Vest, and worthy deems
" To win a Virgin, and to wear a Bride."[369]

In this second excerpt, the champions meet to fight. Hobbinol is a "stripling" compared to his massive opponent Gorgonius, yet he manages to conduct himself with great skill:

NOW Front to Front the fearless Champions meet;
GORGONIUS like a Tow'r, whose cloudy Top
Invades the Skies, stood low'ring; far beneath
The stripling HOBBINOL, with careful Eye
Each Op'ning scans, and each unguarded Space
Measures intent. While negligently bold,
The bulky Combatant, whose Heart elate
Disdain'd his puny Foe, now fondly deem'd
At one decisive Stroke to win unhurt
An easy Victory; down came at once
The pond'rous Plant, with fell malicious Rage,
Aim'd at his Head direct; but the tough Hilts,
Swift interpos'd elude his Effort vain.
The cautious HOBBINOL, with ready Feet
Now shifts his Ground, retreating; then again
Advances bold, and his unguarded Shins
Batters secure; each well-directed Blow
Bites to the Quick; thick as the falling Hail,
The Strokes redoubled peal his hollow Sides.
The Multitude amaz'd with Horror view
The rattling Storm, shrink back at ev'ry Blow,

[369] William Somerville. *Hobbinol, or the Rural Games. A Burlesque Poem, in Blank Verse*. London: J. Stagg, 1740. Pages 12-14.

And seem to feel his Wounds; inly he groan'd,
And gnash'd his Teeth, and from his Blood-shot Eye
Red Light'ning flash'd, the fierce tumultuous Rage
Shook all his mighty Fabric; once again
Erect he stands, collected, and resolv'd
To conquer, or to die: Swift as the Bolt
Of angry *Jove*, the weighty Plant descends.
But wary HOBBINOL, whose watchful Eye
Perceiv'd his kind Intent, slip'd on one Side
Declining; the vain Stroke from such an Height,
With such a Force impell'd, headlong drew down
Th' unwieldy Champion: On the solid Ground
He fell rebounding; breathless, and astunn'd,
His Trunk extended lay; sore maim'd, from out
His heaving Breast, he belch'd a crimson Flood.
Full leisurely he rose, but conscious Shame
Of Honour lost his failing Strength renew'd.
Rage, and Revenge, and ever-during Hate,
Blacken'd his stormy Front; rash, furious, blind,
And lavish of his Blood, of random Strokes
He laid on Load; without Design or Art
Onward he press'd outrageous, while his Foe
Encircling wheels, or Inch by Inch retires,
Wise Niggard of his Strength. Yet all thy Care,
O HOBBINOL! avail'd not to prevent
One hapless Blow; o'er his strong Guard the Plant
Lapp'd pliant, and its knotty Point impress'd
His nervous Chine; he wreath'd him to and fro
Convolv'd, yet thus distress'd, intrepid bore
His Hilts aloft, and guarded well his Head.
So when th' unwary Clown, with hasty step,
Crushes the folded Snake, her wounded Parts
Grov'ling she trails along, but her high Crest
Erect she bears; in all its speckled Pride,
She swells inflam'd, and with her forky Tongue
Threatens Destruction. With like eager Haste,
Th' impatient HOBB'NOL, whose excessive Pain
Stung to his Heart, a speedy Vengeance vow'd,
Nor wanted long the Means; a Feint he made
With well dissembled Guile, his batter'd Shins
Mark'd with his Eyes, and menac'd with his Plant.
GORGONIUS, whose long-suff'ring Legs scarce bore
His cumb'rous Bulk, to his Supporters frail
Indulgent, soon the friendly Hilts oppos'd;

Betray'd, deceiv'd, on his unguarded Crest
The Stroke delusive fell; a dismal Groan
Burst from his hollow Chest, his trembling Hands
Forsook the Hilts, across the spacious Ring
Backward he reel'd, the Crowd affrighted fly
T'escape the falling Ruin. But, alas!
'Twas thy hard Fate, TWANGDILLO! to receive
His pond'rous Trunk; on thee, on helpless thee,
Headlong, and heavy, the foul Monster fell.
Beneath a Mountain's Weight, th'unhappy Bard
Lay prostrate, nor was more renown'd thy Song,
O Seer of *Thrace*! nor more severe thy Fate.
His vocal Shell, the Solace, and Support
Of wretched Age, gave one melodious Scream,
And in a thousand Fragments strow'd the Plain.
The Nymphs, sure Friends to his harmonious Mirth,
Fly to his Aid, his hairy Breast expose
To each refreshing Gale, and with soft Hands
His Temples chafe; at their persuasive Touch
His fleeting Soul returns, upon his Rump
He sate disconsolate; but when, alas!
He view'd the shatter'd Fragments, down again
He sunk expiring; by their friendly Care
Once more reviv'd, he thrice assay'd to speak,
And thrice the rising Sobs his Voice subdu'd:
'Till thus at last his wretched Plight he mourn'd.[370]

Hobbinol triumphs against his foe Gorgonius by playing skilfully, not taking chances, ensuring his own defence at every point. Interestingly, Hobbinol uses the action of striking to the shins of his opponent as a feature of his strategy. This could only have been a safe tactic by working with lightning-fast strikes in between returning to a high guard position to keep his head protected (similar to the actions found in some of Taylor's lessons, described in chapter 5.5: Using Taylor's 10 Lessons later in this book).

As Gorgonius makes a particularly strong blow, Hobbinol slips out of distance, and Gorgonius loses his balance. In a few places, Hobbinol is described as possessing and performing with skilled

---

[370] William Somerville, 1740. Pages 36-40.

and clever footwork. This definitely works in his favour by allowing him to avoid powerful blows.

After Gorgonius returns to his feet, he makes a wild flurry of strikes, fuelled by rage and revenge. This flurry is described as "rash, furious, blind," and "without design or art". Eventually this onslaught proves too much for Hobbinol's careful defence, and "one hapless blow" strikes him over his strong guard, into his chin. Yet nonetheless, Hobbinol kept up his guard, kept defending himself, and endeavoured to end the fight swiftly.

A feint to the shins drew a parry from Gorgonius after receiving so many painful hits to that location earlier in the match. Hobbinol used this opportunity to land a mighty blow upon Gorgonius's chest, illustrating the interesting tactic of feinting low to strike high: the reverse of the usual tactic of feinting high in order to strike low. Gorgonius reeled from this blow and fell, landing on a bard named Twangdillo, and could no longer continue the fight. Hobbinol had won.

We can consider this poem to give a reasonably accurate representation of a game of singlestick at one of the English county fairs or at the Dover Games. The tactics and techniques described resemble those found in fencing treatises and also those that are seen when modern singlestick fencers engage in a sparring match. For this reason, the poem is worth using as a source for fighting with the singlestick.

3.4   1840: *Defensive Exercises*

In 1840, Donald Walker published a treatise with a very long name, entitled *Defensive Exercises; comprising Wrestling, as in Cumberland, Westmoreland, Cornwall, and Devonshire; Boxing, both in the usual mode and in a simpler one; Defence Against Brute Force, by various means; Fencing and Broad Sword, with simpler methods; the Gun and its Exercise; the Rifle, and its exercise; &c. &c. &c.*

As part of these vital skills for ensuring personal safety and the protection of one's country, Walker found it important to include information about games such as singlestick, boxing, and the Irish Shilelah, as well as more serious disciplines such as broadsword, the musket and the rifle.

He begins his book by introducing his rationale for the need for defensive exercises and skill:

> I AM not a less ardent lover of peace than those who inculcate non-resistance. I only differ from them as to the means of ensuring peace. (...) Universal skill in the arts of defence, and the protection of a country entrusted to all its males from the age of eighteen to nineteen, are, therefore, in aid of knowledge, the surest means of freedom, and PERPETUAL PEACE.[371]

He describes a method for the use of the broadsword, but also recommends that fencers gain experience in loose play or sparring, so that they can learn to use their skills against an uncooperative opponent. To this end, he advises that fencers use singlesticks instead of broadswords, just as foils were used instead of smallswords:

> Of the Practice Drill with Sticks.
>
> As no exercise with the Sword can be brought to perfection without some species of loose or independent practice, Sticks

---

[371] Donald Walker. *Defensive Exercises*. London: Thomas Hurst, 1840. Pages v-vi.

should be substituted for Swords in the present instance, as, in Fencing, Foils are used for the acquirement of the art.

The Point also is to be occasionally substituted for the Cut, and defended by the same Guard as for the latter; and as a thrust should always be given, if a good opportunity and opening is offered, such an advantage should be taken of the practice with sticks, and the thrust delivered by an immediate extension of the arm, when the point is in the proper line of direction.

In the following directions, the word Sword is retained, although the practice is with sticks, which should be about thirty-eight inches long, and not so weak as to bend; and the leather practising-hilts merely large enough to cover the hand, without confining it: strike wire masks ought always to be used, as it enables those who practise to cut of thrust with more confidence.[372]

Furthermore, he emphasised the need to use the stick like a sword, with attention to edge alignment, correctness, and common sense:

As it is supposed that the Stick is a substitute for the Sword, the cut is considered fair, and effective, only when given with that part which would, of course, correspond with the edge; nor should anything be attempted with the Stick, which could not be performed with the Sword.[373]

When sparring with sticks, there is of course the need to protect the legs. He mentions that the "military school" at the time (still using the Angelo system) had seven guards, and that trying to parry low cuts would make the fencer vulnerable to feints (as shown by the final blow in the poem *Hobbinol*, in the previous section). Therefore, he prefers the method of slipping and counter-cutting, rather than trying to parry low strikes:

The legs are protected by drawing the right back behind the left, and thrusting straight at the adversary's head or breast the moment he attacks them.

---

[372] Ibid. Pages 115-116.
[373] Ibid. Page 116.

The great advantage which this method has over the preceding, is, that it is so much more easily acquired. The difficulty of following, with the seven guards of the military school, all the feints which the adversary may make, is very great.

It has been objected, that the mode of defending the legs according to this plan, is dangerous in practising with the sticks. This objection is easily avoided by the players agreeing before they begin not to attack the legs.[374]

He is not very clear whether "the plan" that is "dangerous in practising with the sticks" is that of slipping the leading leg or that of trying to parry using the military guards. His solution to the problem, though, is not very practical – agreeing not to target the legs before beginning play is not a helpful way for fencers to develop the defensive skills they need to ensure personal safety while protecting their country.

In additional to discussing the use of singlestick to represent the broadsword in loose play, he includes a chapter about the use of singlestick as a civilian form of recreation:

Basket-sticks, similar to those used in the broad-sword exercise, but rather heavier, are used for this exercise. Both parties strip to the shirt. In some parts of the country, paddings are used to save the arms, especially the elbows; but this is never done in London.

Most players prefer to stand with the right foot forward; but some prefer the left.

The body is held upright; the head, backward; the leg, straight; the right arm, advanced and nearly straight; the hand, opposite the forehead, but rather higher; the stick, slanting towards the left shoulder. The left hand grasps a handkerchief, which is tied loosely round the left thigh; and the left elbow is elevated and thrown forward, so as to protect the head.

The principal point of attack is the head; first blood from it, or from the face or neck, above the level of the lower jaw, being decisive.

---

[374] Ibid. Page 121.

In the position already described, the head is thoroughly protected. It is, therefore, necessary to get the adversary out of that position before attacking his head. This may be attempted by attacking him under the arm, at the point of the elbow, or on the ribs; or you may wait till he attacks you, and then try to strike at his head before he can get back to guard.

All the blows are to be made from the wrist; the great art being to strike them as quickly as possible, and return to the primary position, in which the head of thoroughly protected, before the adversary can get at it.

The usual blow at the head is struck by suddenly twisting the wrist round from a state of pronation to supination; the point of the stick describing a semicircle round the hand. To stop this, raise the hand a little. The return is the same as the attack.

Striking over is done when the adversary, through inattention or fatigue, lets his hand sink below the level of his head. In this blow, the stick passes over the adversary's hand; the wrist is not twisted round to supination; and the blow is altogether more horizontal and passes somewhat diagonally from left to right. The arm moves more. To guard this, raise the hand.

The usual return after this attack, is a blow at the left side of the face, which is likely to succeed on account of difficulty of the other party returning to guard after striking over.

Striking at the ribs is done chiefly to fatigue the adversary, and make him bring down his hand so as to expose the head. It is the right ribs that we attack. Some players guard this by throwing the stick down, while others do not guard at all, but strike at the head.

The right fore-arm and elbow are also frequent points of attack. A blow on the inside of the elbow just between the two bones which project there, deadens the ulnar nerve passing down to the third and fourth fingers, and prevents the stick being felt with them.

The wrist is sometimes attacked, and must be guarded by moving the hand a little to the right.[375]

---

[375] Donald Walker, 1840. Pages 66-71.

In terms of strategy, it was important to draw the opponent away from his guarded position and to create an opening to strike at his head. This could be achieved be low feints, making him drop his sword, or by letting him make the attack, creating the opportunity for a lightning-fast riposte.

Curiously, Walker mentions that the right forearm and elbow are common targets, but does not say anything about he left arm. Perhaps sometimes the left arm was off-target, or perhaps players simply learned to absorb blows on their left arm and keep fighting!

The "usual blow at the head" is one also described by Roworth:

> Among cudgel players the blows from this position are effected by a turn of the wrist differing from that used with the broad sword, the large knuckles of the hand (instead of the middle ones) being directed towards the object at which the blow is discharged, and turned downwards at the instant of making it. If the opponent springs off from a blow made in this manner, the general consequence to the assailant, is a strain of the wrist, or the loss of his stick Another material disadvantage in this mode of striking is, that unless they engage very close they cannot reach to his their antagonist.[376]

Roworth describes the strike by referring to the direction of the large knuckles, while Walker describes it in terms of changing from pronation to supination, but both authors are describing the same sort of action. It is worth noting that Roworth merely describes a method of striking with the stick performed by some cudgel-players; this is not his preferred mechanic for striking with the broadsword.

A final interesting note is that the left leg could be forward; it did not need to be strictly a right-foot-forward sport, such as when fencing with the foil or broadsword.

---

[376] Charles Roworth, 1804. Pages 113-114.

3.5   1857: *Tom Brown's School Days*

In 1857, Thomas Hughes published a novel entitled *Tom Brown's School Days*, which included some scenes depicting the county fair of the 1820s. The description of a singlestick competition is one of the best descriptions of this activity in English literature.[377]

This first excerpt sets the scene for the competition that will follow:

> Benjy himself was come of a family distinguished in the Vale for their prowess in all athletic games. Some half-dozen of his brothers and kinsmen had gone to the wars, of whom only one had survived to come home, with a small pension, and three bullets in different parts of his body; he had shared Benjy's cottage till his death, and had left him his old dragoon's sword and pistol, which hung over the mantel-piece, flanked by a pair of heavy single-sticks, with which Benjy himself had won renown long ago as an old gamester, against the picked men of Wiltshire and Somerset in many a good bout at the revels and pastimes of the country-side. For he had been a famous back-sword man in his young days, and a good wrestler at elbow and collar.
>
> Back-swording and wrestling were the most serious holiday pursuits of the Vale, those by which men attained fame, and each village had its champion. I suppose that on the whole, people were less worked than they are now; at any rate they seemed to have more time and energy for the old "pastimes." The great times for back-sword came round once a-year in each village, at the feast. The Vale "Veasts" were not the common statute feasts, but much more ancient business. They are literally, so far as one can ascertain, feasts of the dedication, *i.e.* they were first established in the Church-yard, on the day which the village Church was opened for public worship, which was on the wake or festival of the patron Saint, and have been held on the same day in every year since that time.[378]

---

[377] J. Christoph Amberger. *The Secret History of the Sword*. Orange: Multimedia Books, 1999. Page 251.

[378] Thomas Hughes. *Tom Brown's School Days*. Cambridge: Macmillan and Co., 1857. Pages 29-30.

This second excerpt describes the singlestick competition as it occurred at the fair. Parts of this excerpt have been quoted in other books in an effort to describe the game of singlestick,[379] but the quoted part is usually very brief and does not give the whole feeling, flavour and description of the event. Thus, a more complete excerpt is provided here.

Excerpt from Chapter 2: The Veast[380]

And now, while they are climbing the pole in another part of the field, and muzzling in a flour-tub in another, the old farmer whose house, as has been said, overlooks the field, and who is master of the revels, gets up the steps on to the stage and announces to all whom it may concern, that a half-sovereign in money will be forthcoming for the old gamester who breaks most heads; to which the Square and he have added a new hat.

The amount of the prize is sufficient to stimulate the men of the immediate neighbourhood, but not enough to bring any very high talent from a distance; so, after a glance or two round, a tall fellow, who is a down shepherd, chucks his hat on to the stage and climbs up the steps, looking rather sheepish; the crowd of course first cheer, and then chaff as usual, as he picks up his hat and begins handling the sticks to see which will suit him.

"Wooy, Willum Smith, thee canst plaay wi' he arra daay," says his companion to the blacksmith's apprentice, a stout young fellow of nineteen or twenty. Willum's sweetheart is in the "veast" somewhere, and has strictly enjoined him not to get his head broke at backswording, on pain of her highest displeasure; but as she is not to be seen, (the women pretend not to like to see the backsword play, and keep away from the stage,) and his hat is decidedly getting old, he chucks it on to the stage, and follows himself, hopding that he will only have to break other people's heads, or that after all Rachel won't really mind.

---

[379] J. Christoph Amberger, 1999. Page 252.
[380] Thomas Hughes, 1857. Pages 36-44.

Then follows the greasy cap lined with fur of a half-gipsey, poaching, loafing fellow, who travels the Vale not for much good I fancy:

> "Full twenty times was Peter feared
> For once that Peter was respected"

in fact. And then three or four other hats, including the glossy castor of Joe Willis, the self-elected and would-be champion of the neighbourhood, a well-to-do young butcher of twenty-eight or thereabouts, and a great strapping fellow with his full allowance of bluster. This is a capital show of gamesters, considering the amount of the prize; so while they are picking their sticks and drawing their lots, I think I must tell you as shortly as I can how the noble old game of back-sword is played; for it is sadly gone out of late, even in the Vale, and may-be you have never seen it.

The weapon is a good stout ash-stick with a large basket handle, heavier and somewhat shorter than a common single-stick. The players are called "old gamesters," – why I can't tell you, – and their object is simply to break one another's heads: for the moment that blood runs an inch anywhere above the eyebrow, the old gamester to whom it belongs is beaten, and has to stop. A very slight blow with the sticks will fetch blood, so that it is by no means a punishing pastime, if the men don't play on purpose, and savagely, at the body and arms of their adversaries. The old gamester going into action only takes off his hat and coat, and arms himself with a stick; he then loops the fingers of his left-hand in a handkerchief or strap which he fastens round his left leg, measuring the length, so that when he draws it tight with his left elbow in the air, that elbow shall just reach as high as his crown. Thus you see, as long as he chooses to keep his left elbow up regardless of cuts, he has a perfect guard for the left side of his head. Then he advances his right hand above and in front of his head, holding his stick across so that its point projects an inch or two over his left elbow, and thus his head is completely guarded, and he faces his man armed in like manner, and they stand some three feet apart, often nearer, and feint, and strike, and return at one another's heads, until one cries "hold," or blood flows; in the first case they are allowed a minute's time, and go on again; in the latter, another pair of gamesters are called on. If good men are playing, the quickness of returns is marvellous; you hear the rattle like that a boy makes drawing his stick along palings, only heavier, and the closeness of the men in action to one another gives it a strange interest, and makes a spell at backswording a very noble sight.

They are all suited now with sticks, and Joe Willis and the gipsey man have drawn first lot. So the rest lean against the rails of the stage, and Joe and the dark man meet in the middle, the boards having been strewed with sawdust, Joe's white shirt and spotless drab breeches and boots contrasting with the gipsey's coarse blue shirt and dirty green velveteen breeches and leather gaiters. Joe is evidently turning up his nose at the other, and half insulted at having to break his head.

The gipsey is a tough active fellow, but not very skilful with his weapon, so that Joe's weight and strength tell in a minute; he is too heavy metal for him: whack, whack, whack, come his blows breaking down the gipsey's guard, and threatening to reach his head every moment. There it is at last – "Blood, blood!" shout the spectators as a thin stream oozes out slowly from the roots of his hair, and the umpire calls to them to stop. The gipsey scowls at Joe under his brows in no pleasant manner, while Master Joe swaggers about, and makes attitudes, and thinks himself, and shews that he thinks himself, the greatest man in the field.

Then follow several stout sets-to between the other candidates for the new hat, and at last come the shepherd and Willum Smith. This is the crack set-to of the day. They are both in famous wind, and there is no crying "hold;" the shepherd is an old hand and up to all the dodges; he tries them one after another, and very nearly gets at Willum's head by coming in near, and playing over his guard at the half-stick, but somehow Willum blunders through, catching the stick on his shoulders, neck, sides every now and then, anywhere but on his head, and his returns are heavy and straight, and he is the youngest gamester, and a favourite in the parish, and his gallant stand brings down shouts and cheers, and the knowing ones think he'll win if he keeps steady, and Tom on the groom's shoulders holds his hands together, and can hardly breathe for excitement.

Alas for Willum! His sweetheart getting tired of female companionship has been hunting the booths to see where he can have got to, and now catches sight of him on the stage in full combat. She flushes and turns pale; her old aunt catches hold of her, saying, "Bless'ee, child, doan't 'ee go a'nigst it;" but she breaks away, and runs towards the stage calling his name. Willum keeps up his guard stoutly, but glances for a moment towards the voice. No guard will do it, Willum, without the eye. The shepherd steps round and strikes, and the opint of his stick just grazes Willum's forehead, fetching off the skin, and the blood flows, and the umpire cries "Hold," and poor Willum's chance is up for the day. But he takes it very well, and puts on his old hat and coat, and goes down to be scolded by his sweetheart, and led away out of mischief. Tom hears him say coaxingly as he walks off –

"Now doan't'ee, Rachel! I would'nt ha' done it, I only wanted summut to buy'ee a fairing wi', and I be as vlush o' money as a twod o' veathers."

"Thee minds what I tells'ee," rejoins Rachel saucily, "and doan't'ee kep blethering about fairings." Tom resolves in his heart to give Willum the remainder of his two shillings after the back-swording.

Joe Willis has all the luck to-day. His next bout ends in an easy victory, while the shepherd has a tough job to break his second head; and when Joe and the shepherd meet, and the whole circle expect and hope to see him get a broken crown, the shepherd slips in the first round and falls against the rails, hurting himself so that the old farmer will not let him go on, much as he wishes to try; and that imposter Joe (for he is certainly not the best man) struts and swaggers about the stage the conquering gamester, though he hasn't had five minutes' really trying play.

Joe takes the new hat in his hand, and puts the money into it, and then as if a thought strikes him, and he doesn't think his victory quite acknowledged down below, walks to each face of the stage, and looks down shaking the money, and chaffing as how he'll stake hat and money and another half-sovereign "agin any gamester as hasn't played already." Cunning Joe! He thus gets rid of Willum and the shepherd, who is quite fresh again.

No one seems to like the offer, and the umpire is just coming down, when a queer old hat, something like a Doctor of Divinity's shovel, is chucked on to the stage, and an elderly quiet man steps out, who has been watching the play, saying he should like to cross a stick wi' the progidalish young chap.

The crowd cheer and begin to chaff Joe, who turns up his nose and swaggers across to the sticks. "Imp'dent old wosbird!" says he, "I'll break the bald head on un to the truth."

The old boy is very bald certainly, and the blood will show fast enough if you can touch him, Joe.

He takes off his long-flapped coat, and stands up in a long-flapped waistcoat, which Sir Roger de Coverley might have worn when it was new, picks out a stick, and is ready for Master Joe, who loses no time, but begins his old game, whack, whack, whack, trying to break down the old man's guard by sheer strength. But it won't do,– he catches every blow close by the basket, and though he is rather stiff in his returns, after a minute walks Joe about the stage, and is clearly a staunch old gamester. Joe now comes in, and making the most of his height, tries to get over the old man's guard at half-stick, by which he takes a smart blow in the ribs and another on the elbow and nothing more. And now he loses wind and begins to puff, and the crowd laugh: "Cry 'hold,' Joe – thee'st met thy match!" Instead of taking good advice and getting his wind, Joe loses his temper and strikes at the old man's body.

"Blood, blood!" shout the crowd, "Joe's head's broke!"

Who'd have thought it? How did it come? That body-blow left Joe's head unguarded for a moment, and with one turn of the wrist the old gentleman has picked a near little bit of skin off the middle of his forehead, and though he won't believe it, and hammers on for three more blows despite of the shouts, is then convinced by the blood trickling into his eye. Poor Joe is sadly crestfallen, and fumbles in his pocket for the other half-sovereign, but the old gamester won't have it. "Keep thy money, man, and gi's thy hand," says he, and they shake hands; but the old gamester gives the new hat to the shepherd, and soon after the half-sovereign to Willum, who thereout decorates his sweetheart with ribbons to his heart's content.

"Who can a be?" "Wur do a cum from?" ask the crowd. And it soon flies about that the old west-country champion, who played a tie with Shaw the Life-guardsman at "Vizes" twenty years before, has broken Joe Willis's crown for him.

Analysis of Excerpt

This lengthy excerpt shows some very interesting things. The prize is not just money, but also a new hat. Furthermore, to signal that one chooses to compete, a fighter must first throw his own hat into the ring. Sometimes the fights could be brief; sometimes they could take significantly longer. People fought with different styles and approaches.

When Willum fights against the shepherd, he receives several hits to his shoulders, neck and sides; but as long as he does not take a hit to the head, he is able to continue playing.

In Joe's final fight with the bald old man, he tries to win using strength and youthful energy, while the older competitor fights slowly and "stiffly", yet the old man's well-structured parries and defences manage to keep him safe against all of Joe's attacks. Finally, Joe ignores good advice, and strikes a blow to the old man's body, leaving his own head open. The old man takes the opportunity to strike to Joe's forehead, and wins the match.

It is clear that skill, patience and precision was a good method to win against aggression and strength. This still holds true in modern practice of historical fencing.

3.6   The Angelo School of Arms

The smallsword had been the primary weapon taught by many fencing masters in both England and Scotland.[381]

The broadsword had never really gone out of fashion in Scotland – the Disarming Act 1716 and the Act of Proscription in 1746 had attempted to remove the weapons from the country after the Jacobite uprisings, but members of the Black Watch regiment were allowed (required, even) to be armed in order to do their duty. Major-General David Stewart noted that "in the Highlands, men were accustomed to go continually armed,— a custom which they were most anxious to retain. (...) Young men, therefore, gladly availed themselves of the privilege of engaging in a profession which relieved them from the sense of degradation and dishonour attached to the idea of being disarmed."[382] After the Acts of disarmament, the singlestick was the best way for many civilians to continue their practice of swordsmanship.

Comparatively, in the 18th century, the cutting weapons came back into fashion in England.[383] In the late 18th century, and into the 19th century, the broadsword, sabre and cutlass received significantly more attention from English fencing masters than they had during the previous two hundred years.

The Angelo school of arms was one establishment that helped to popularise singlestick in England. In 1787, Thomas Rowlandson made a coloured etching of Harry Angelo's salle at the Royal Opera House in London. On the wall was a pair of singlesticks, which would not have been hanging there unless the school taught the discipline.[384] In 1820, an illustration by Cruikshank in the book *Life in London* showed the salle in Bond Street. Along the walls were racks for foils and for singlesticks.[385] Only 33 years after

---

[381] In Scotland, masters such as Donald McBane, Sir William Hope and John Xavier Tremamondo mainly taught use of the smallsword.
[382] David Stewart, 1825. Part 3, "Section I – Black Watch."
[383] J.D. Aylward, 1956. Page 250.
[384] Ibid. Page 148-149.
[385] Ibid. Page 157-158.

Rowlandson's etching, the singlestick had gone from being just a pair on the wall to being a regular training weapon stored in racks alongside the foils.

When Harry and his son Henry taught cutlass drills to the Royal Navy in the 1820s and 1830s, they used singlesticks for the task. Aylward notes dryly that "unless Mr. Clapperton and his colleagues differed remarkably from the traditional inhabitant of the gun-room, they must have enjoyed the humour of the situation as, with faces as wooden as the single-sticks so much beloved of Harry, they went through the elegant motions adapted from the 'Highland' broadsword exercise as taught by Messrs. Angelo & Son."[386]

However, Aylward does criticise Harry Angelo's relationship with the singlestick. He claims that Angelo was obsessed with the stick, and that since it is difficult to observe edge alignment with a stick, this obsession led him to overlook the importance of training this skill with their sabres.[387] Furthermore, Aylward asserts that Angelo's obsession with the stick as a cutting weapon meant that he completely ignored the thrust and any use of the point, both in offence and defence; this led to problems for the troops who received this training, when they went to fight on the continent and met French cavalry who used thrusts against them.[388] This is a very strange state of affairs, considering that Angelo's early training had all been with the foil and smallsword, until the final few years of the 18th century; as the 19th century dawned, Angelo was becoming more enamoured with the singlestick, and it took a place of greater importance in his salle.

Comparatively, Hutton noted that in the first half of the 19th century, the activities of backswording and cudgelling had become less common with the demise of the Cotswold Games, but that singlestick in London nonetheless persisted. It was "recognised as the medium for studying and practising the use of the officer's

---

[386] Ibid. Page 182.
[387] Ibid. Page 170.
[388] Ibid.

sword."[389] Furthermore, Hutton believed that Angelo's salle was the meeting place for many of the top fencers and gentlemen in the country: "at Angelo's famous rooms in St. James's Street the best gentlemen in England were wont to assemble to receive their lessons".[390] Henry Angelo required that his students wore a proper fencing mask, but allowed them to show their toughness by wearing no other protective or padded garments.[391]

Even in the Angelo school of arms, fencing with singlestick was not always a friendly contest between gentlemen. There was a student called Mr. Rolland, described as a man with "consummate skill" and with "imperturbable command of his temper". There was another student, named only as T---y, who was a Sergeant in the Royal Artillery, and who was a bit of a bully. The two men had played at singlestick at a previous encounter, agreeing to regard blows to the leg as foul play, but T---y had broken the rule and had won the bout unfairly by cutting Rolland "inside the leg".[392]

One day T---y walked into Angelo's salle, and Henry Angelo suggested that Rolland and T---y should spar again. The two men duly engaged at singlestick once more. Rolland defended himself admirably, letting T---y tire himself and spend all his energy. Then, at the most opportune moment, Rolland "all of a sudden crouched like a tiger, like a tiger sprang forward, and with all the force of his spring and the weight of his mighty arm landed a fearful blow exactly on the point of the inside of his adversary's right knee."[393] T---y shrieked and fell; he was taken to hospital, where he stayed for more than a month, and it was more than three months after that before he was able to mount a horse again.[394]

At a later date, Sergeant T---y returned to the salle. This time, his opponent was a man called Jackson, one of the assistant

---

[389] Alfred Hutton. *The Sword and the Centuries*. London: Greenhill Books, 2003. Page 356.
[390] Ibid.
[391] Ibid.
[392] J. Christoph Amberger, 1999. Page 252.
[393] Alfred Hutton, 2003. Page 359.
[394] Ibid.

instructors at the school, and recently retired from the Household Brigade. Jackson was not a great fencer with the foil as his fist was too big and clumsy for the necessary fine manipulation, but he was excellent with the singlestick.

The two men fought with the singlestick, both hitting hard, when Jackson's stick broke just above the leather basket. T---y took the opportunity to bully his opponent, and rather than giving Jackson a chance to take a fresh stick or resign from the bout, he hit Jackson five or six times. Jackson was furious, and used his buffalo-hide hilt to punch T---y as hard in the face as he possibly could. T---y's mask saved his face, but he fell from the force of the blow. Henry Angelo had been in a different room, but returned just in time to see this whole exchange. He went up to where T---y lay on the ground, kicked him, ordered him to take his clothes and leave, and never to return to the school.[395]

Even in an eminent *salle d'armes*, singlestick was not always a gentlemanly affair. However, Angelo's school was one of the bastions of singlestick play, which kept the discipline alive even while it was becoming less popular as a method of civilian recreation.

3.7 1882: Hutton's Rules

Later in the 19th century, Alfred Hutton continued to use singlestick as a method of teaching his students, keeping the discipline alive until the beginning of the 20th century. In his book *Bayonet-Fencing and Sword-Practice*, published in 1882, Alfred Hutton set down some "rules for independent practice with sabre or stick":

> 1. No one to play, on any pretence whatever, without wearing a helmet.
>
> 2. Cuts and thrusts are not to be given too strongly; should men appear to be losing their temper, their play is to be stopped at once.

---

[395] Ibid. Pages 360-361.

3. No two cuts or thrusts are to be made on the same lunge.

4. The opponents should not both strike at once; should this happen the cut or thrust given in the third position to be considered effective. But should both parties lunge, the hit to count to neither.

5. The act of crossing (and touching) the blades is a guarantee that both parties are ready. Any hit given before this is done, is not to be considered effective. The opponents should always engage out of distance.

6. A disarm to count as a hit to the party effecting it.

7. A hit is only considered effective when given with that part of the stick which represents the edge, or with the point.

8. In stick-play, no hit is to be made at the inside of the leg unless the players wear leg padding, a blow in that part being highly dangerous.

9. When playing with the practice-sword it is necessary to wear full padding, that is, helmet, double-jacket, gauntlet, body-pad, and leg-pad.

10. Players are strongly recommended to fence for a fixed, number of hits, say 3, 5, or 7; this increases the interest in the play, and tends to make the men more careful in their fencing.[396]

These rules show a development in the approach to the activity. While Angelo had mandated a fencing mask, but allowed his students to wear no other protective gear to prove their hardiness, Hutton wrote that it was "necessary to wear full padding". Furthermore, it is interesting to see that a disarm counted as a point against the person who managed to perform such a technical and difficult action – this was clearly part of the growing trend among fencers to look down on disarming techniques as too difficult and too dangerous to be worth attempting.

---

[396] Alfred Hutton. *Bayonet-Fencing and Sword-Practice*. London: William Clowes and Sons, 1882.

Slightly over a decade later, Alfred Hutton wrote the chapter for singlestick in *The Encyclopaedia of Sport*, describing the sport as it had been played earlier in the 19th century. In his 1882 treatise, his very first rule was that no one should play without wearing helmets; in his encyclopaedia entry in 1898, he noted that this safety requirement had not always been common:

> Masks, it is clear, were not in general use, but occasionally a sort of demi-mask was employed, which covered the face up to the eyebrows, leaving the upper part of the head exposed.[397]

In the encyclopaedia, he reiterated his eighth rule that strikes to the inside of the leg should be forbidden, due to the possible damage and consequences of such hits:

> In all well-regulated schools of arms the blow at the inside of the leg is strictly forbidden, on account of its serious consequences.[398]

Towards the end of the 19th century, the concept of health and safety was becoming more integral to the sport of singlestick. Dangerous techniques were banned, masks and helmets became mandatory, and protective gear in general became strongly advised. It little resembled the country fair styles of singlestick from the previous centuries.

3.8   1890: *Broad-Sword and Single-Stick*

In 1890, R.G. Allanson-Winn published his book *Broad-Sword and Single-Stick*, having asked his friend C. Phillipps-Wolley to write the section about singlestick for him.[399] This book was then reprinted several times across the following thirty years. It contains separate chapters about singlestick and cudgelling – two different disciplines, with different methods of performance.

---

[397] Hedley Peek and F.G. Aflalo. *The Encyclopaedia of Sport*. Vol. II, London: Lawrence and Bullen, 1898. Page 360.
[398] Ibid. Page 361.
[399] R.G. Allanson-Winn and C. Phillipps-Wolley. *Broad-Sword and Single-Stick*. London: G. Bell and Sons, 1911. Page: preface.

A contemporary, J.M. Waite, published *Lessons in Sabre, Singlestick, Sabre & Bayonet* in 1880. In his opinion, singlestick was simply a light training tool for the sabre or broadsword, just as a foil was the light training tool for the smallsword. The singlestick was to be used in exactly the same fashion as the sabre.[400]

However, according to Phillipps-Wolley, there were various different schools of thought on this issue at the end of the 19th century in Britain:

> There are to-day in England several distinct schools of single-stick, the English navy having, I believe, a school of its own; but all these different schools are separated from one another merely by sets of rules, directing, for the most part, where you may and where you may not hit your adversary.[401]

Furthermore, Allanson-Winn provides some compelling reasons why a novice fencer should not be given a singlestick, but rather the proper sabre, contrary to the common practice of giving novices a foil rather than a proper smallsword:

> Though stick-play is invaluable as an aid to work with the sword, it may be remarked that there are two reasons, and those important ones, why the single-stick should not be first placed in the hands of the beginner, and why it should never altogether usurp the place of the more lethal weapon. The reasons are—
>
> (a.) The stick is very light, and short smart hits can be made, which are impossible with a sword.
>
> (b.) The hit with the stick is really a hit, and there need be no draw, which, as already explained, is so important in sword-play.
>
> To these may be added a third reason. With the stick there is always the temptation not to cut with the true edge, and it is very hard to detect faults in this direction—faults which are hard to cure, and which may quite spoil good swordsmanship.[402]

---

[400] J.M. Waite. *Lessons in Sabre, Singlestick, Sabre & Bayonet, and Sword Feats.* London: Weldon and Co., 1880. Page x.
[401] R.G. Allanson-Winn and C. Phillipps-Wolley, 1911. Page 55.
[402] Ibid. Page 32.

He continues to show why he believes the singlestick to be a very practical weapon for people to learn as a last-ditch weapon of self-defence:

> Single-stick really combines both styles of fencing [point and edge]. In it the player is taught to use the point whenever he can do so most effectively; but he is also reminded that his sword has an edge, which may on occasion do him good service. It seems, then, to me, that single-stick is the most thoroughly practical form of sword-play for use in those "tight places" where men care nothing for rules, but only want to make the most out of that weapon which the chance of the moment has put into their hands.[403]

However, using the singlestick does have some quite serious disadvantages in terms of likely behaviour and conduct, which need to be addressed by instructors:

> The only sound objection to single-stick being that the sticks used are so light as not to properly represent the sabre.

> This is a grave objection to the game, when the game is regarded as representing real business; but for all that, the lessons learnt with the stick are invaluable to the swordsman. The true way to meet the difficulty would be to supplement stick-play by a course with broad-swords, such as are in use in different London gymnasiums, with blunt edges and rounded points.[404]

Another valuable aspect of the practice of singlestick is that it teaches individuals to be tough and to deal with minor inconveniences, without receiving grievous injuries:

> There is just enough sting in the ash-plant's kiss, when it catches you on the softer parts of your thigh, your funny bone, or your wrist, to keep you wide awake, and remind you of the good old rule of "grin and bear it;" but the ash-plant leaves no marks which are likely to offend the eyes of squeamish clients or female relations.[405]

---

[403] Ibid. Pages 51-52.
[404] Ibid. Page 52.
[405] Ibid. Page 54.

He also provides some interesting information about how to select and store singlesticks, so that they are safe for use and survive intact for as long as possible in the school's storage area:

> The sticks themselves should be ash-plants, about forty inches in length and as thick as a man's thumb, without knots and unpeeled.
>
> If you want them to last any time it is as well to keep a trough of water in the gymnasium, and leave your ash-plants to soak in it until they are wanted. If you omit to do this, two eager players, in half an hour's loose play, will destroy half a dozen sticks, which adds considerably to the cost of the amusement.
>
> The old English sword hilt was a mere cross-piece; but in play it has always been customary to protect the fingers with a basket. This may be either of wicker or of buffalo hide. The latter is infinitely the best, as wearing much longer, affording a better protection to the fingers, and not scraping the skin off the knuckles as the wicker-baskets too often do. The basket has a hole on either side; one close to the rim, and the other about a couple of inches from the edge. In putting your basket on, put your stick through the former first, as otherwise you will not be able to get a grip of your stick or any room for the play of your wrist.[406]

Phillipps-Wolley has an interesting point of view on the earlier method of protecting the head with the left elbow. Earlier in the century, one of the traditional methods of playing at singlestick was to wrap a handkerchief around the left thigh, hold it in the left hand and raise the left arm as high as possible. The left hand would rest at rib-height, and the left elbow would come up to head-height, to provide protection for the head.

> A [wood]cut on p. 57 by Mr. Graham Simpson represents the way to acknowledge a hit, and a [wood]cut by the same artist on p. 61 illustrates, as far as we know it, the less careful method of our forefathers. The use of the elbow to shield the head, though common in the contests on the village greens, was in its way no doubt more foolish than our pads; for though a sturdy yokel might take a severe blow from a cudgel on his bare arm, without

---

[406] Ibid. Page 59.

wincing, the toughest arm in England would have had no chance against a sabre.[407]

Effectively, this method used the left arm as ablative armour. Phillipps-Wolley points out the obvious problem with this method if the game of singlestick is to be used to represent combat with sharp weapons. However, the traditional English game of singlestick where this method was implemented was often a game unto its own end rather than training for the use of the sabre. It is therefore very important to realise that sometimes the "singlestick" was used to describe a weapon, sometimes used to describe a game with little military application, and sometimes used to describe the activity of practising for military purposes with a lighter cutting weapon. As noted above, "there are to-day in England several distinct schools of single-stick ... separated from one another merely by sets of rules",[408] so it would be a mistake to assume that everyone practised and understood singlestick in the same way across the whole country.

In his excellent textbook *The English Master of Arms*, J.D. Aylward offers the suggestion that "all that remained of the [English] tradition [of play with edged weapons] in 1795 was combat with the single-stick, which had become so curiously conventionalised that knowledge of it was rather more dangerous than protective."[409] The latter part of his statement may mirror the opinion of Phillipps-Wolley, that the style of civilian singlestick with the left elbow in the air, holding a handkerchief wrapped around the thigh, was a poor method of learning how to fight with a cutting weapon. Aylward later states that "generally, practice was conducted with single-sticks, leading in the end to a highly-conventionalised and peculiar play in which the left forearm was used to parry blows, and no hit counted unless placed on the head",[410] so it seems safe to assume that this is what he meant by "curiously conventionalised".

---

[407] Ibid. Page 60.
[408] Ibid. Page 55.
[409] J.D. Aylward, 1956. Page 213.
[410] Ibid. Page 250.

Phillipps-Wolley had a very practical point of view with regard to the use of the singlestick as a method of self-defence. One common problem suffered by students of any martial art, who indulge in gentle and friendly training and sparring without any rougher or less "civilised" play, and by those who do not attempt any test outwith their comfort zone, is that eventually the student will face an opponent who fights differently. For example, students of fencing (or some forms of eastern martial arts) where grappling is not allowed, will find themselves struggling against an opponent who wants to close to grapple. Likewise, students of grappling arts where striking is prohibited may find some difficulties when facing an opponent who strikes with knees and elbows during the grappling process. In this treatise, there is some good advice about dealing with an "excitable player" who tries to rush in close:

> In passing, let me say that if a man will try to overwhelm you with rushes, the best thing you can do is to straighten your stick, thrust, and don't let the stick run through the basket. This has a wonderfully soothing effect upon an excitable player.[411]

A thrust with a stiff weapon does indeed have certain "soothing effects" on opponents who enjoy rushing in to close quarters. Later rulesets for singlestick, such as the Calpe rules, forbade thrusting because of the risks that come from thrusting with a rigid weapon; here, the risks are embraced and emphasised as one of the advantages of the weapon, so that the individual can stop someone who intends to close the distance and grapple. This is a very practical point of view to take on the matter.

It would be wrong to assume that a system involving such practical points of view might be a system that is less sophisticated or technical. One of the hallmarks of unskilled fighters is that they use many actions to achieve what a single skilful technique can achieve. Phillipps-Wolley encourages readers to develop this skill and to choose the most appropriate response for any situation:

---

[411] R.G. Allanson-Winn and C. Phillipps-Wolley, 1911. Page 64.

Time is the very essence of single-stick, and the chief object of the player should be to make his attack in the fewest possible motions.[412]

The book provides a description of the various singlestick competitions in which people could test themselves against others. It seems there were not very many such competitions in London at the end of the 19th century:

> Unfortunately the stick-player will not find many opportunities of displaying his skill in public. As far as the present writer knows, there are only two prizes offered annually in London for single-stick, and neither of these attract much attention. One of them is given at the Military Tournament at Islington, in June, and one at the German Gymnasium, in December. The former of these prizes is open only to soldiers, militia-men, or volunteers, the latter to any member of a respectable athletic club, who is prepared to pay 2s. 6d. for his entrance fee. The attendance of spectators at both shows is very poor, which is to be regretted, as the interest of the public in any game generally goes a long way towards insuring improvement in the play.[413]

Both competitions played the bouts in the confines of a ring 14 feet (~4.27 metres) in diameter. This required players to work in a relatively small area, without the ability to move around very much – although the author noted that players went outside the ring quite regularly, and the judges never really seemed to mind.[414]

The rules were very simple for the two different competitions:

> At the Military Tournament the play is for the best out of three hits, i.e. the man who scores the first two points wins.

> At the German Gymnasium the competitor who first scores five wins the bout.

> This is better than at the Tournament, although it will seem to some that even this is hardly a sufficient test of the merits of

---

[412] Ibid. Page 65.
[413] Ibid. Page 81.
[414] Ibid. Page 82.

each player. The bouts seem too short, but probably this is unavoidable; that which is to be regretted and might be remedied, being that no points are given for "form:" the result is that, in many cases, the anxiety to score the necessary points as soon as possible results in very ugly and unscientific rushes, in which no guards are attempted and from which the most reckless and rapid hitter comes out the winner. This, of course, is the same for every one, and therefore perfectly fair, but it does not tend to elevate the style of play. (...)

In order to facilitate the scoring they have a very good plan at the Military Tournament of chalking the competitors' sticks. This precaution ensures a mark upon the jacket every time the ash-plant hits it; but even this is not always sufficient, for it is quite possible for a true guard to be opposed to a hard cut with a pliant stick, with the result that the attacker's stick whips over and leaves a mark which ought not to be scored, for had the weapons been of steel this could not have happened. This, however, is a point which would generally be detected by one of the three judges in the ring.[415]

The kind of behaviour shown in these tournaments and mentioned here, with unscientific play and aggressive rushing, is perhaps one of the reasons why earlier in his treatise he spoke about using a stout thrust to "soothe an excitable player". Not only was such behaviour likely to occur in a self-defence situation, but it was also the sort of behaviour that players would have to deal with in the formal competitions that they chose to enter.

Later in the book, Allanson-Winn provides a chapter about the cudgel, slightly different to the singlestick. He describes the weapon and game as such:

Any thick stick under two feet long, such as a watchman's staff or a policeman's truncheon, may be fairly called a cudgel, and it is not so long ago that cudgel-play formed one of the chief attractions at country fairs in many parts of England.

A stage was erected, and the young fellows of the neighbourhood were wont to try conclusions with their friends or those celebrities

---

[415] Ibid. Pages 82-83.

from more distant parts of the country who were anxious to lower their colours.

> The game was at times pretty rough, and the object of each combatant was to break the skin on the scalp or forehead of his antagonist, so as to cause blood to flow. As soon as the little red stream was seen to trickle down the face of one or other the battle was at an end, and the man who was successful in drawing first blood was declared the victor.[416]

This is quite a different method of play from the singlestick competitions at the Military Tournament and the German Gymnasium. Phillipps-Wolley had suggested that cudgel-play was a "less careful method" and that even "the toughest arm in England would have had no chance against a sabre". Clearly he felt that the old method for cudgel-play was not very sensible for training soldiers who would need to fight with and against sharp swords. However, this description of cudgel-play illustrates the fashion for fighting with a stick for recreational purposes, and it was not supposed to be a military training system.

One final interesting piece of information is that sometimes the combatants stood very close together when playing with cudgel:

> I have never been fortunate enough to witness a bout with the cudgels, but those who have been more lucky say that the combatants stood very close to each other, making all the hits nearly straight on to the top of their adversaries' heads, and guarding the returns and attacks with their cudgels and with their left arms.[417]

In summary, by the time of Allanson-Winn and Phillipps-Wolley in 1890, singlestick was used more for training troops to fight with the broadsword or sabre, and cudgel was regarded as a civilian game played by "forefathers" in country fairs. The terms "singlestick" and "cudgel" were understood to mean different weapons and different activities. Even so, within the activity of "singlestick", every school in England had a different set of rules;

---

[416] Ibid. Page 100.
[417] Ibid. Page 101.

there was no unified method or ruleset by which everyone could play.

3.9   1896: Cassell's Rules

In 1896, Cassell's *Complete Book of Sports and Pastimes: Being a Compendium of Out-Door and In-Door Amusements* was published. This book included a section on "Broad-Sword and Single-Stick", which described a method to conduct such play. Unlike the Calpe Rules, which followed less than 40 years later, this method of singlestick allowed for (and indeed emphasised the importance of) including thrusts in the practice:

> It is no uncommon thing for men to play at stick and bar thrusting, but it is a thoroughly bad plan, for those who pursue it are certain to get too close, hit wildly, and counter. It is true they may plead the ancient custom on their side; in the old English back-sword and cudgel play there was no thrusting, not was upper-cutting generally thought fair, though the rules differed in different counties. First blood from the head decided the bout.[418]

The rules are expressed more simply than Hutton's rules, although they are very similar. Cassell's rules are as follows:

> 1. The cut and thrust must not be given too strongly, so as to cause irritation and anger.
>
> 2. Each cut or thrust to be acknowledged by the person touched, passing the stick into the left hand, the opponent recovering to an engaging guard.
>
> 3. The combat to be renewed out of distance, the parties coming within it cautiously.
>
> 4. No two cuts or thrusts to be made upon the same longe. In case of a mutual hit, the cut giving in third position to be reckoned only.

---

[418] *Cassell's Complete Book of Sports and Pastimes: Being a Compendium of Out-Door and In-Door Amusements.* London: Cassell and Company, 1896. Page 161.

5. All cuts being made from a defensive position, such must be returned to as soon as the cut or thrust is delivered.

6. No practice to be allowed without masks; and as the stick is the substitute for the sword, the cut can only be considered effective when given with that part which corresponds with the edge, nor should any movement of attacks or defence be attempted with the stick which would not be risked in a combat with swords.[419]

Although Hutton was a Captain in the Army, it is interesting that his rules did not specify explicitly that techniques had to be realistic, while the Cassell rules note that players should not attempt "any movement of attacks or defence be attempted with the stick which would not be risked in a combat with swords."

3.10 1904: Singlestick in the Olympics

In 1904, the Olympic Games were held in St. Louis in America. The sport of fencing was not very well attended, with only three nations sending competitors: Germany sent a single fencer, Cuba sent two, and the USA sent eight fencers.[420]

One of the fencing events at these Games was men's singlestick, the first and only time this has been included in the Olympic games. This particular event was held on Thursday the 8th of September 1904, and only three fencers participated.[421] All three fencers were from the USA, and although the gold medallist (Albertson Van Zo Post) was recorded in the IOC database as being a Cuban national,[422] he was in fact a member of the New York Fencing Club and represented the USA at the Games.[423]

---

[419] Ibid. Page 162.
[420] "Fencing at the 1904 Summer Olympics." *Wikipedia*, accessed 11th July 2014. http://en.wikipedia.org/wiki/ Fencing_at_the_1904_Summer_Olympics
[421] "Fencing at the 1904 Summer Olympics – Men's Singlestick." *Wikipedia*, accessed 11th July 2014. http://en.wikipedia.org/wiki/ Fencing_at_the_1904_Summer_Olympics_-_Men%27s_singlestick
[422] Ibid.
[423] Maxime Chouinard. "Singlestick... Or is it? Stick sports in America, an investigation." *I Don't Do Longsword*, 23rd December 2013, accessed 20th July

174

However, this event has caused much confusion: it was not actually British style singlestick that was played at the 1904 Olympic Games, but instead it was the French game of La Canne. [424] According to some excellent research by Maxime Chouinard, it appears that "singlestick" came to America with Antoine J. Corbesier, [425] who taught at the New York Fencing Club, [426] and this "singlestick" was in fact Canne Royale.

In the USA, in the late 19th and early 20th century, "any combat sport with a stick was called singlestick, even kendo."[427] Even into the later 20th century, activities described as "singlestick" were probably La Canne: the President Theodore Roosevelt was a famous player of "singlestick", but it was definitely not British style singlestick that he practised. It seems that while singlestick in British sources tended to mean a somewhat specific activity with a specific type of weapon (although, as described by Walker, Waite, Allanson-Winn and Phillipps-Wolley, the precise activity may differ from school to school and context to context), American sources tended to use the term in reference to something other than British style singlestick, often French cane systems such as La Canne or Canne Royale.[428]

It would be wrong to assume that every mention of "singlestick" in American sources refers to La Canne, and that British style singlestick was never played in America. It is important to be aware that in America the situation not the same as it was in Britain. The nomenclature was different, and that people were not as concerned about using precise terminology as we are today.[429] Some sensitivity to context is important when reading historical

---

2014.   http://hemamisfits.wordpress.com/2013/12/23/singlestick-or-is-it-stick-sports-in-america-an-investigation/
[424] Ibid.
[425] Ibid.
[426] "Differences between military and civilian saber styles?" *Schola* Forum, 2013, accessed 11th July 2014.
http://www.fioredeiliberi.org/phpBB3/viewtopic.php?f=3&t=20644
[427] Ibid.
[428] Maxime Chouinard. "Singlestick... Or is it?"
http://hemamisfits.wordpress.com/2013/12/23/singlestick-or-is-it-stick-sports-in-america-an-investigation/
[429] Ibid.

sources and sources from other parts of the world. As with most things, jumping to conclusions is rarely fruitful.

It is important to keep this problem in mind when looking for sources about singlestick. For example, there is an interesting snippet about singlestick in the book *White-Jacket* by Herman Melville:

> Among other diversions at present licensed by authority in the Neversink, were those of single-stick, sparring, hammer-and-anvil, and head-bumping. All these were under the direct patronage of the Captain, otherwise—seeing the consequences they sometimes led to—they would undoubtedly have been strictly prohibited. It is a curious coincidence, that when a navy captain does not happen to be an admirer of the Fistiana his crew seldom amuse themselves in that way.
>
> Single-stick, as every one knows, is a delightful pastime, which consists in two men standing a few feet apart, and rapping each other over the head with long poles. There is a good deal of fun in it, so long as you are not hit; but a hit—in the judgment of discreet persons—spoils the sport completely. When this pastime is practiced by connoisseurs ashore, they wear heavy, wired helmets, to break the force of the blows. But the only helmets of our tars were those with which nature had furnished them. They played with great gun-rammers.[430]

However, Melville notes in his preface that:

> In the year 1843 I shipped as "ordinary seaman" on board of a United States frigate then lying in a harbor of the Pacific Ocean. After remaining in this frigate for more than a year, I was discharged from the service upon the vessel's arrival home. My man-of-war experiences and observations have been incorporated in the present volume.[431]

As this discusses the sport on an American ship, and since the seamen fought with "long poles" rather than short sticks with baskets, it was probably not British style singlestick that Melville

---

[430] Herman Melville. *White-Jacket: or the World in a Man-of-War*. New York: United States Book Company, 1892. Chapter 66: Fun in a Man-of-War.
[431] Ibid. Preface.

describes. Most likely it was some form of French cane play, but described as "singlestick".

3.11 1931: Calpe Rules

The British garrison at Gibraltar continued to practise singlestick between the two World Wars, and in 1931 produced a set of rules to govern the practice of the discipline. The classical name for Gibraltar is Calpe, so they became known as the "Calpe Rules". These rules, along with some contextual information, were printed on pamphlets that are unfortunately difficult to acquire today.

This first excerpt includes the introduction, which describes the general method and mindset for playing at singlestick:

> 1. The Calpe Rules aim at making the singlestick the cutting equivalent of the epee. The use of the point in sabre tends to restrict play with the cutting edge, to encourage the stop thrust in preference to the time hit with the edge. Furthermore, the modern basket hilted stick is dangerous as a thrusting weapon. With the old hide hilt, the stick passed through a leather tube in the hilt so that in the case of a strong thrust, the hilt would slide forward along the stick. As the stick itself is now gripped directly by the hand (within the basket hilt), this no longer happens. Hence the Calpe Singlestick Rule which treats the use of the point as dangerous play and penalises it by counting it as a hit against the offender, even when he offended purely by negligence in leaving his point where it was accidentally run on to.

> 2. A sound fencing motto is *Toucher sans l'etre*. "To hit without being hit," is the foundation of sound play. To evolve play on that basis these rules have been framed.

> 3. The joy of fencing lies in the art itself.

> 4. The discussion of judges not only interrupt play and waste time, but interfere with full enjoyment. Just as in verbal debate, no man is fully pleased with an argument he has put forward if his opponent does not admit its force or if he knows it is based on a fallacy, even so no hit is satisfactory to the fencer to whom it is

adjudged, if he does not believe it good, or if it does not convince his adversary.

5. By making essential elements of each hit, first its acknowledgement by the recipient and then its acceptance by the striker, and by cutting out the talkers, minimum waste of time and maximum enjoyment are made possible.

6. Hearty loud acknowledgements add enormously to the pleasure of both players and make their play enjoyable to watch.[432]

It seems that teaching sensible fencing skills was an important part of the practice, as well as making the game enjoyable for the participants and the audience.

This second excerpt describes the rules of singlestick match:

1. Judges. There shall be no judges and no referee.

2. Ground. Unlimited, preferably out of doors and not very even, but without any deep holes or large loose stones.

3. Dress. Vest, shorts, gym shoes, sabre (or bayonet) mask, any glove. An elbow pad is good; knee pad may be desired

4. Play. Is started by both players engaging sticks, thus showing they are both ready. After any stoppage of play it is restarted in the same manner.

This ceremonial engagement of sticks is not to be a prelude to an indecently precipitous surprise attack. There should be time to come peacefully back to an "on guard," or resting position before having to face an onslaught.

5. Hard hitting, using the point, or holding the point in line are forbidden.

6. Hits. A *hit* is a cut cleanly delivered with the stick on any part of the opponent without its force having been broken by his stick

---

[432] R.A. Hay. *Singlestick: The Calpe Method and Rules*. Gibraltar, January 1931.

or guard hilt. A bayonet glove used instead of a guard-hilt will be regarded as one.

7. Acknowledgements. All *hits will* **at once be audibly acknowledged** by their recipient, whether he is fully satisfied or in any doubt. If the other player is not satisfied that the touch acknowledged was a good *hit* as defined by Rule 6 it is for him to say so, **he must disclaim it**; it will then be deemed not to have arrived at all.

NO BLOW THAT IS NOT ACKNOWLEDGED IS A HIT.

8. Claiming hits is forbidden. If an apparent hit is not acknowledged, it must have been too indifferent or too light for the recipient to feel; he is right in not acknowledging what he is satisfied is not a *hit*.

9. Stoppage of play. The recipient of a *hit* will stop as soon as he can after feeling it. If before he succeeds in stopping **he** delivers a *hit*, both *hits* count, even though one arrived very late; this constitutes a *double-hit*; should either *hit*, however, be disclaimed, as not satisfying Rule 6, the other only will be scored. It is "not done" to make a double hit intentionally.

With this exception: acknowledgement stops play.

10. Scoring. Every *hit* acknowledged that satisfies the other player will be scored, unless too hard or made with the point. If either player becomes unintentionally impaled on the point, a *hit* will be scored against his adversary. No *hit* will be scored that does not satisfy both players.[433]

One of the features of this rule set is that hits do not count unless the recipient acknowledges them. If there is no verbal acknowledgement, there is no point. Once the opponent acknowledges the hit, the person who scored has the opportunity to disclaim the hit if it was not clean or good enough. This creates an environment of mutual respect and honesty.

Another feature is that of the thrust: if the point makes contact with the other player, even accidentally, then a point is scored

---

[433] R.A. Hay, 1931.

against the person who made the thrust. This is clearly a nod to health and safety, to ensure that the fencers did not receive a stiff thrust with an inflexible weapon.

Yet feature is that of the preferred terrain: outdoors and uneven. Fencers would have to be aware of the terrain and therefore of their footwork, more so than in normal fencing bouts. This would better simulate the sort of terrain that the soldiers and sailors would have beneath their feet if they ever engaged in close-quarters combat with swords.

3.12 The Boarding of the Altmark

Following on neatly from the previous thought is that sometimes the British Navy did engage in close-quarters combat, in terms of boarding actions. Obviously this was more common in the age of sail, at battles such as Trafalgar, and had become less common in the 20th century. Nonetheless, it could still happen, and according to Lieutenant Commander Locker Madden: "the last boarding party of blue jackets in action with cutlasses was in HMS Cossack's boarding of the German prison ship Altmark in 1939."[434]

Madden was an important figure in the revival of singlestick in the 1980s and will be discussed later in this chapter. I believe it is important to address his statement about the boarding of the Altmark, because in some ways it is incorrect and has helped to perpetuate a myth about the use of cutlasses, and therefore singlestick practice as a preparation for using cutlasses at sea.

There are some problems with Madden's account. The Royal Navy did perform a boarding action against the Altmark, but not in 1939. It actually took place on the 16th of February 1940. Ed Rogers notes that the Royal Navy withdrew the cutlass from service in 1936,[435] so it would have been unlikely that the crew would have had cutlasses ready for a boarding action.

---

[434] Locker Madden. "Cudgels & Singlestick." 1986.
[435] Ed Rogers. *Advanced Fencing Techniques: Discussions with Bert Bracewell*. Ramsbury: The Crowood Press, 2013. Page 150.

An article in *The Evening Independent* newspaper published on the 17th of February 1940 (the day after the incident) included some information from the German captain of the Altmark. He stated that the British boarding party "fired at close range", and that there were "indications that the British used daggers in boarding the ship." There were no mentions of cutlasses.[436]

An article in The Strait Times, published on the 19th of February 1940, included some further details. Apparently "the officer in charge of the [boarding] party leaped eight feet from H.M.S. Cossack to the Altmark, waving a revolver and shouting: 'Come on, follow me!'" In other parts of the article, it notes that the British fired upon the Germans, rather than falling upon them with cutlasses.[437]

The *Wikipedia* article on the boarding action states that this was the "last recorded Royal Naval action with cutlass", but does not provide any citation to substantiate this claim.[438]

An article by David Bober on the *Naval Matters* blog also states that the incident was "last recorded use of the cutlass in a boarding action by the Royal Navy." [439] However like the *Wikipedia* page, he does not cite any sources to support his assertion. His article was published online on the 16th of February 2014, while the *Wikipedia* article was first contributed in 2005, so it might be likely that Bober's assertion is based on the *Wikipedia* article, but without showing where he received his information.

Jim McLoughlin and David Gibb published a book called *One Common Enemy* in 2006. The book records McLoughlin's experiences as a sailor in the Second World War. One experience

---

[436] "Britain Orders Altmark Captured Off Norway." *The Evening Independent*. Vol. 33, no. 90, St. Petersburg, FL, 17th February 1940. Page 14.

[437] "Bravery of Men of Cossack." *The Straits Times*. Final edition, 19th February 1940. Page 9.

[438] "Altmark Incident." *Wikipedia*, accessed 21st July 2014.
http://en.wikipedia.org/wiki/Altmark_Incident

[439] David Bober. "'The Navy's here!' HMS Cossack frees prisoners from the Altmark, 16 February 1940." *Naval Matters*, 16th February 2014, accessed 21st July 2014.
http://navalmatters.wordpress.com/2014/02/16/the-navys-here-hms-cossack-frees-prisoners-from-the-altmark-16-february-1940/

was as a crewmember on the HMS Valiant during the Altmark incident. He relates that the boarding party was put together with sailors from various Royal Navy ships in the area; one such sailor was Tom Cox from the HMS Valiant, who was armed only with a cutlass when he boarded the Altmark. Upon his return, he "climbed back on board our ship with his cutlass clenched between his teeth ... this extraordinary sight left a lasting impression on the teenage seamen like me."[440]

Wat Tyler contributed an article to the *WW2 People's War* archives, noting that his grandfather George Earnest Jewitt took part in the boarding action, armed with a pick axe handle,[441] not a cutlass.

In 2003, the HMS Cossack Association published a brief article in the *Daily Mail* to provide a final answer to the question:

> QUESTION: When were swords last used in combat by the British armed forces?
>
> Further to previous answers, over the years there has been some soul-searching about the story of cutlasses being used during the boarding of the German ship Altmark in Norwegian waters to rescue 300 PoWs in February 1940.
>
> It's a lovely idea but is thought to have been a bit of embroidery by over-enthusiastic newspaper reporters after the destroyer HMS Cossack returned with the rescued prisoners.
>
> Some cutlasses were locked in a case and held aboard the Cossack for ceremonial purposes but the consensus of opinion is that bayonets were carried in the raid, not cutlasses.
>
> The bayonet in 1940 was about 18 inches long and had a hilt like a sword.

---

[440] Jim McLoughlin and David Gibb. *One True Enemy*. Kent Town: Wakefield Press, 2012.

[441] Wat Tyler. "The Last Boarding Action of the Royal Navy." *WW2 People's War*, 6th November 2003, accessed 21st July 2014.
http://www.bbc.co.uk/history/ww2peopleswar/stories/53/a1979553.shtml

Four Germans died in the conflict, one of whom fell overboard, and five were wounded – none by cutlasses.

Peter Harrison, Secretary,
HMS Cossack Association.[442]

It would seem that the boarding party used an assortment of weapons, including revolvers, rifles, bayonets, and miscellaneous hand weapons. However, it would be inaccurate to state that it was a boarding action with cutlasses – or indeed that it was the last boarding action by the Royal Navy.

It would appear that this story has relatively little bearing upon the history of singlestick as a preparation for close quarters combat, although articles by Lieutenant Commander Locker Madden and others have suggested a greater link than probably exists. However, it was worth addressing the story, as it has helped to spread a myth about the role of singlestick as a preparation for using the cutlass for boarding actions as late as the Second World War.

3.13 Post-war Singlestick

The practice of singlestick continued after the Second World War, albeit in a rather low-key fashion. Edinburgh and Birmingham were the two main locations in Britain where the practice survived. It died out in Birmingham, but in Edinburgh the tradition passed down to the people who began the current historical fencing movement in Scotland, which has ensured the survival of the discipline to the current day and hopefully beyond.

1940s – Colonel Hay

Colonel R.A. Hay was an officer in the British Army during the 20th century, and he was a great singlestick enthusiast.[443] In 1949 and

---

[442] "When were swords last used in combat by the British armed forces?" *Daily Mail*. 20th June 2003.
[443] Ed Rogers, 2013. Page 150.

1950 he published articles in *The Sword* (the journal of the British Fencing organisation), describing the history of the singlestick.

He wrote that in the final decade of the 19th century, the practice of singlestick was "much in evidence in the Army" and that it was also "practised at public schools which employed Army Gymnastic Staff instructors."[444] However, he noted that in the early 20th century, the First World War "seems to have almost killed the singlestick" as an activity. After 1918 "the Royal Navy, Army and R.A.F. practised sabre instead, and instructors versed in singlestick were no longer produced by them",[445] and so the practice fell out of fashion with the armed forces.

Even so, up until 1929, Royal Navy ships were equipped with singlesticks,[446] so the practice must have continued in at least some small fashion. Indeed, apparently the captain of one ship was reputed to use singlestick sparring in the late 1920s as a method of unofficial punishment, giving "offenders a chance – a small chance – of self-protection and retaliation."[447]

At some point between the two World Wars, apparently "some unofficial activity with the singlestick started in the Army."[448] The style of play was lighter than that of previous singlestick games, and "a method evolved of hitting quickly, but lightly, without hurting and of ensuring adequate control of the stick."[449] By 1928, apparently most of the junior officers stationed in the south end of Gibraltar participated in singlestick and enjoyed its practice in the evenings; this led to an unofficial publication of a "privately printed leaflet" entitled *Singlestick: The Calpe Method and Rules*, which was apparently distributed widely.[450] Colonel Hay says nothing about the authorship of this leaflet, but Ed Rogers notes that the Colonel "wrote a pamphlet explaining its rules and

---

[444] R.A. Hay. "Singlestick – I. History." *The Sword* (Winter 1949): 150-153. Page 153.
[445] Ibid.
[446] R.A. Hay. "Singlestick – II. History." *The Sword* (Spring 1950): 37-40. Page 37.
[447] Ibid.
[448] Ibid.
[449] Ibid. Page 38.
[450] Ibid.

conventions" and was likely the author or at least part of the team behind it, and was one of the driving forces behind the development of the rules included in that pamphlet.[451]

After 1944, Colonel Hay returned to Edinburgh, and taught the Calpe method of singlestick at Edinburgh University.[452] Fencers from Edinburgh sometimes enjoyed playing at singlestick with fencers from the Birmingham Fencing Club,[453] where it was still practised.

Captain Hutton had made a study of singlestick and other historical weapons in the late 19th century and into the first decade of the 20th century. His sparring partner was a man called T. Hill, a Corporal in the 1st (King's) Dragoon Guards. When Corporal Hill was discharged from the Army, he joined the Birmingham Fencing Club as an instructor, and taught all the weapons found in an Army gymnasium, including singlestick and bayonet.[454] The practice of singlestick must have survived until at least a while after Colonel Hay returned to Edinburgh, into the 1940 or 1950s, as the two clubs competed against each other in this discipline.

At the same time as Colonel Hay taught singlestick at Edinburgh University, Colonel Ronald Campbell also taught singlestick in Edinburgh to some boys' clubs.[455] Colonel Hay suggested that singlestick may see a revival, because of the "cheapness and simplicity" of the sport,[456] but unfortunately it faded away and no revival was seen.

1960s – Professor Bert Bracewell

In the early 1950s, Herbert Thomas Bracewell (more commonly known as "Bert" Bracewell) began learning to fence at the age of

---

[451] Ed Rogers, 2013. Page 150.
[452] R.A. Hay, 1950. Page 39.
[453] Ibid.
[454] REX. "Correspondence." *The Sword* (Spring 1950): 40. Page 40.
[455] R.A. Hay, 1950. Page 39.
[456] Ibid.

17. The following year, he started National Service with the RAF and pursued his passion for fencing. In 1966, he moved to Edinburgh and in 1967 became a Professor in the British Academy of Fencing (a qualified master in all three modern disciplines).[457]

In the 1960s, Professor Bracewell took lessons in singlestick from Colonel Hay, who in turn took lessons in épée from the Professor. This meant that the tradition of singlestick survived, and continued to be taught by Professor Bracewell, even if the large scale revival that Colonel Hay had hoped for never quite came to be.

1980s – Royal Navy Revival

In 1982, the Royal Navy revived the practice of singlestick in a competitive fashion, at least for a few years.[458] In 1986, Lieutenant Commander Locker Madden wrote an article entitled Cudgels & Singlestick, in which he described a little of the history of the weapons, and provided some insight into their revival.

By 1986, the Navy had held five singlestick competitions, governed by the Calpe rules, and in 1985 they had held what was claimed to be the "first recorded cudgel competition since Elizabethan times".[459] Apparently the events attracted a not-insignificant number of attendees, with around 50 competitors from across the UK, and in 1985 a Dutch contingent of competitors arrived to participate.[460]

In the early years of the first decade of the 21st century, Louie Pastore, a historical fencing enthusiast from Greenock in Scotland, conducted significant research into the history of singlestick, and managed to find some information about the 1980s revival. Furthermore, he found that Lieutenant Commander Madden was one of the driving forces behind this revival.

---

[457] Ed Rogers, 2013. Pages 149-150.
[458] Locker Madden, 1986.
[459] Ibid.
[460] Ibid.

Pastore put together a rough timeline with some help from Madden. This timeline suggested that the revival in 1982 began when Madden discovered some singlesticks in the Navy stores.[461] It then suggested that in 1984, Madden created an amended version of the Calpe rules for the Navy competitions. In one of these competitions, Madden won the title of "Champion of Singlestick & Cudgels", which he maintained at least until 2003,[462] although it seems that the revival fell apart and no further competitions were held after the end of the decade.

Lieutenant Commander Locker Madden appears to have been an important and influential figure in the 1980s Royal Navy revival of singlestick, but unfortunately very little written material has been produced about this period, and so it is difficult to find more information about it. The little that we do know is mainly thanks to the investigative efforts of Louie Pastore.

1990s – Dawn Duellists Society

In the 1990s, Professor Bracewell taught singlestick to Paul Macdonald, Guy Windsor and Milo Thurston while they studied at Edinburgh University. Around 1994, Paul and Guy set up the Dawn Duellists Society to study historical fencing disciplines,[463] and from this group the singlestick teachings they passed down from Professor Bracewell have spread to other historical fencing groups across the United Kingdom.

My own introduction to singlestick and Scottish broadsword in general came from Paul Macdonald at the Celtic Exchange event hosted in Glasgow in 2009.

---

[461] "UK Singlestick 1900's to 2003." *Singlestick Yahoo Group*, 2003, accessed 21st July 2014. https://groups.yahoo.com/neo/groups/Singlestick/conversations/topics/997

[462] "Living Tradition ALIVE!" *Singlestick Yahoo Group*, 2003, accessed 21st July 2014. https://groups.yahoo.com/neo/groups/Singlestick/ conversations/topics/964

[463] My thanks to Phil Crawley for his input with regard to the history of historical fencing in Scotland.

In the 1980s, Gordon Love learned both classical fencing and singlestick from Professor Bracewell. Since 2010, he has been teaching singlestick to children through the "Fencing is Fun" programme offered by his PaFF organisation. He estimates that in the last four years, at least 3000 children have experienced the discipline through this programme.

Although Gordon and his activities are rarely in the spotlight, he has been making huge strides in preserving this tradition and passing it to the younger generation.

3.14 Master-at-Arms Badge for Boy Scouts

During the course of the 20th century, the Scouting Association offered the "Master at Arms" merit badge for its members to achieve. A pamphlet for the badge was published in 1925. Achieving this badge required that:

> A Scout must attain proficiency in two out of the following subjects:—
>
> Single-Stick, Quarterstaff Fencing, Boxing, Ju-Jitsu, Gymnastics, and Wrestling.[464]

The pamphlet described the weapon and equipment required for the practice of singlestick:

> Singlesticks are made of young ash plants. The guard for the hand is of wicker basket-work or leather. Put a rubber or leather washer over the stick close up to basket. If sticks are kept in water they will not be so liable to break. Never fence with a broken stick. Always wear a stout jacket with a high collar, a helmet with strung wire mask, and a sporran or apron. Use a strap or gauntlet to protect the wrist. Hold the stick with the

---

[464] *Master-at-Arms Badge for Boy Scouts*. Glasgow: James Brown & Son, 1925. Page 5.

thumb along it, not grasped round it. The thumb will represent the back of the blade, and the middle knuckles the edge. All cuts are made with the edge, do not slap the stick sideways. Guards or parries are also made with the edge and not with the side or back of blade.[465]

It also described how to conduct a sparring match against an opponent:

When you are having a bout of "loose play" you both try to outwit the other. Use your brains and vary your guard. Draw an attack by appearing to expose yourself, them parry and riposte. Feint at one part and attack another. Try various plans but never let your play degenerate into merely slashing about or hitting sticks aimlessly.

In sword or "sabre" fencing the arm is held straight when on guard and parries are made by slightly bending the elbow and giving at sort of forward spiral push to opponent's blade. Cuts and points both count. Hits count anywhere above hips.[466]

However, by later in the century, an emphasis on health and safety had overtaken the Scouting Association, and the merit badge became somewhat easier (and albeit safer) to achieve:

To gain this badge, Scouts must complete the requirements below:

Attend regular training sessions in a chosen activity (fencing, shooting or archery) and demonstrate an improvement in skill. Training should be for at least five sessions.

Know the safety rules associated with the activity and demonstrate their use.

Take part in the chosen activity at an officially supervised contest and discuss performance with the instructor.

---

[465] Ibid.
[466] Ibid. Page 8.

Notes

Reference must be made to the activity rules in Policy, Organisation and Rules relating to shooting and archery.[467]

It is unfortunate that this badge has become so easily achieved and so far removed from its original intention. However, nothing in the modern merit badge prevents Scouts from learning singlestick, or any of the original disciplines from a historical fencing club, so this might be an interesting opportunity for singlestick practitioners to reach out to the local community and work with a local Scouting group.

[467] "Master at Arms Activity Badge." *The Scouting Association*, accessed 11th July 2014. http://members.scouts.org.uk/supportresources/ 576/master-at-arms-activity-badge

Chapter 4: *The Art of Defence on Foot (1804)*

I have transcribed the text from an 1804 copy of Roworth's *The Art of Defence on Foot*, and present it within this chapter. I believe that this choice helps to improve the value of this book as a study guide for beginners; there is no need to buy a separate book, or to decide which manual to attempt to recreate, as the necessary information is presented here in one package.

Roworth's text is very accessible and is clearly written. The illustrations help to show what the different guard positions should look like. Although it was written by an Englishman, I believe it provides a reasonable example of what Scottish broadsword may have looked like at various times in history. A new student to the discipline does not need to read several different sources to gain a broad point of view, nor will he need to compare and contrast between authors and descriptions, as with disciplines such as Liechtenauer's longsword; Roworth's text is relatively complete and comprehensive. It is therefore an excellent source to use at the beginning of one's study of Scottish broadsword.

This transcription is as close to the original text as possible, with a few pertinent exceptions. I chose to render the long 's' character simply as a normal 's', to facilitate easy reading. In a similar fashion, to improve readability, when a word is spread over two pages and is broken by a hyphen, I have chosen to render the full word on the first of the two pages, so that it is not split between two pages in my transcription.

Whenever the original text moves to a new page, I have indicated that with [n], where 'n' is the page number in the original text.

The original text used an asterisk character '*' to indicate a footnote, with the footnote appearing in a slightly smaller font at the bottom of the page. Footnotes in the original text did not leave white space between paragraphs, but instead took just a single new line. To represent this in my transcription, I have made the font size of the transcribed footnotes smaller than the rest of the text, and they follow the main part of the text for the original page. If the footnote continues across two pages of the original text, I have reproduced it as exactly as possible: I give the footnote text from the first page, then indicate the move to the next page, provide the main text of that page, then provide the continued footnote at the bottom of that new page. So an example layout could be:

[n]

First paragraph of text.

Second paragraph of text.*

Third paragraph of text.

* Footnote.
Second paragraph of footnote.
Third paragraph of footnote

[n+1]

First paragraph of text.

Second paragraph of text.

third paragraph of footnote continued.

This might be a little confusing, but it does provide the most accurate representation of the original text. Luckily there are not very many footnotes that are split across two pages!

The illustrations have been drawn from Roworth's 1798 treatise. Our organisation possesses a physical copy of the earlier book, and so we could scan those illustrations without falling foul of copyright law. Unfortunately it was not possible for us to obtain a copy of the 1804 illustrations for inclusion in this work. While it might seem strange to use the 1798 illustrations alongside the 1804 text, rather than producing a straight copy of the 1798 treatise, there was a good reason. The 1804 book contains additional information not found in the 1798 version. This made it worth transcribing the 1804 treatise to gain the greatest value from the text, while inserting the 1798 illustrations where images occurred in the 1804 book.

For some of the illustrations, I have included a footnote of my own in order to discuss the difference between the 1798 image provided and that 1804 image that is not included. Such footnotes will be marked with "Keith's note:" to show that they are my input and not just part of the transcribed text.

Finally, I have endeavoured to reproduce the spellings, punctuations and capitalisations as faithfully as possible.

I hope that readers will find this short treatise on fencing with the broadsword and sabre to be of interest and value.

THE

ART OF DEFENCE ON FOOT,

WITH THE

BROAD SWORD AND SABRE:

ADAPTED ALSO FOR

THE SPADROON, OR CUT AND THRUST SWORD.

IMPROVED, AND AUGMENTED WITH

THE TEN LESSONS

OF

MR. JOHN TAYLOR,

Late Broadsword Master to the Light Horse Volunteers of London
and Westminster.

ILLUSTRATED WITH PLATES

By R. K. PORTER, Esq.

LONDON:

PRINTED FOR T. EGERTON, AT THE MILITARY LIBRARY,
NEAR WHITEHALL.

1804.

CONTENTS.

PART I.

PRACTICE at the TARGET.

Note: the illustrations in this transcription are drawn from the 1798 edition and from Thomas Rowlandson's 1798 posters for Hungarian and Highland Broadsword. When preparing this transcription, unfortunately, the illustrations from the 1804 edition were not available for inclusion in this book.

PART II.

PRACTICE with ANTAGONIST.

-----

[3]

APPLICATION of the POINT.

APPENDIX.

THE

ART OF DEFENCE

WITH THE

BROAD SWORD AND SABRE.

The *following treatise is divided into Two Parts. The FIRST containing a Mode of Practice at a Target**, which may frequently afford exercise or amusement when it may not be possible, at the instant, to find another person equally desirous of improvement in the science. In this part is described the method of directing the edge, and recovering to a guard from any cut which may

* The target for this purpose will be found at the beginning of the book, from whence it may be taken and fixed against a wall or partition, as directed in p. 11.

have either missed or cut through its object, without suffering your body to remain exposed, or straining your wrist.

It is not, however, necessary for learners to occupy a great length of time with the first part, before they proceed to practise with an antagonist: it will be sufficient if they make themselves acquainted with the direction of the several cuts and the numbers by which they are distinguished. The mode of recovering to guard by whirling up the blade, and the turns of the wrist requisite for that purpose, may be acquired at convenient intervals, by practising with either a sabre, broad sword, cut and thrust sword, or hanger; and gentlemen will by that means become accustomed to the weight of the weapon, and accurate in carrying a true edge; whereas if they practice only with a stick, the weight of the sword will render it so unwieldy when they are compelled to draw it on a real occasion, as to frustrate almost every offensive movement made against an antagonist possessed of either science or agility.

[7]

The SECOND PART treats of the *Practice with an Antagonist*; by attention to which gentlemen may improve each other very fast, provided they act, and communicate their remarks, as directed under the head of GENERAL OBSERVATIONS, p. 31, with that candour which every one has a right to expect in this kind of friendly contest and amusement.

I would not however venture to recommend the practice with a friend for the sake of improvement with naked swords; since although not attended with danger in the cavalry exercise, yet as the situation of persons engaged on foot does not confine them to one or two particular cuts at commencing the attack, but admits of more various and complicated movements, an error in regard to the parades might prove fatal.

In this treatise the broad sword and sabre are generally mentioned, yet the instructions will be found equally applicable to the hanger and spadroon, or light cut and thrust sword. The deviations which

[8]

may prove necessary for the latter are noticed under the head of REMARKS on the SPADROON.

In the APPENDIX are some hints which may be found useful when opposing a person armed with a small sword, or with a musquet and bayonet. The variations from the general principles of the system, when contending with sticks only, are also noticed in that part.

9

PART I.

PRACTICE at the TARGET.

Of HOLDING the SWORD or SABRE.

The broad sword and sabre must be held with the fingers clenched around the gripe, sufficiently fast to prevent the blade wavering, the thumb being either placed on the back or towards the left, as most convenient. At the instant of parrying or attacking, it will be requisite to grasp it with strength, but that exertion of the muscles is so natural, as not to need much insisting on. The chief object is to keep the grip encircled as much as possible with the fore finger and thumb, whatever may be the position of the blade, relaxing or contracting the other fingers according to its direction. Placing the thumb upon the back

of the gripe is the mode always adopted by small-swordsmen and spadroon players; but the hilts of broad swords and sabres are frequently made too short and confined to permit it, and the curve of the sabre blade renders it unmanageable and unsteady in that matter. In practising with light sticks, and in using the spadroon or cut and thrust sword, the placing the thumb in that position will be found to give a celerity and sharpness to the cut; but the weight of the blade of either a broad sword or sabre will, in some instances, prove too great to be thus acted upon, and will frequently require that the gripe be completely encircled with the forefinger and thumb, in which manner I would advise holding the sword when practicing the cuts at the Target.

11

POSITION.

THE first object of the learner should be to attain a firm yet flexible position. For this purpose he must learn to support the most part, if not the whole, of his weight on his *left* leg, in order that the right, which is to be advanced, may be either retired from a cut, or thrown rapidly forward on a longe. It is therefore necessary to commence the practice in the following manner:

Fix the sheet, on which the six cuts are described, flat to the wall, the center of it about one inch below the height of your shoulder. Leading to the perpendicular line down the center, mark a line with chalk on the floor. At the distance of about ten feet from the figure place your left hell so as just to touch the line, the left knee bent, to throw the weight of the body on that leg, the right foot advanced about 14 or 16 inches towards the target; the toe pointing to the perpendicular line. The left shoulder must be thrown back, and

the body kept as much in a line as possible, in order to expose no more of it than necessary to your supposed antagonist. The left hand may be raised to the height of the left ear, in order to preserve the balance of the body; or may be fixed arm with the inside of it on the left hip bone, as may be found most convenient.

From the above position, practice slipping the right foot back till the middle of it becomes opposite the left heel, in order to retire the right knee from your adversary's reach when necessary, which is easily and quickly done, if you rest no more weight than directed on that foot.

LONGEING

Is the stepping forth with the right foot from the position described in the preceding page, in order to effect a cut or thrust.

In beginning this practice, make the first trial without attempting a cut at the same time, till you can longe straight

[13]

upon the line on the floor, keeping your left foot firm, and recover yourself with ease.

At the instant of longeing, the left hand should drop on the left thigh; from whence it should be thrown up smartly to the left as you recover, which will assist in regaining your position.

Although an extensive longe is doubtless advantageous to those who can make it easily, yet it will not be found on a real occasion so necessary as a quick recover. For which reason it will be imprudent in gentlemen to accustom themselves to step farther out than their strength or activity naturally admit. Care must always be taken to place the right foot flat on the ground, and not to make so violent an extension, as to pitch on the heel of that foot.* The proper extent is to bring the left knee straight, and the right knee perpendicular to the instep.

* It should be considered that in real contest the difference of the ground, and many other circumstances, concur to render any unnecessary extension hazardous; especially to such persons as have used themselves to practise on an even floor, perhaps with slippers chalked at the bottom.

[14]

After practising the longe until you are enabled to step well forward and recover without difficulty, the next object is to execute the cuts in such a manner as not to expose yourself to a counter or retort, by suffering your arm to sway improperly with the motion of your sword.

To prevent accidents; by the sword escaping from the hand, it will be necessary to have a leather sword knot, which should be soft and pliable, and not so tight as to confine the motion of the wrist.

Before you draw the sword, pass your hand through the loop, and give it a couple of turns inwards, which will render it sufficiently secure.

As all attacks should be receded by a defensive posture, and concluded by a return to one, it may be necessary to commence with the following guards, from whence the cuts are chiefly made. I shall reserve the description of the others until I treat on the practice with an antagonist.

[15]

MEDIUM GUARD.

This position rather merits the appellation of *prepare to guard*, as it affords hardly any protection without some change of position, should only be adopted (if at all) when you are in doubt on which side your adversary means to join, and before his weapon is within reach of yours. It consists in presenting your sword perpendicular, with the shell opposite the bottom of the target, the point upwards, and the edge opposite the line down the middle.

It must be observed as an invariable rule, that the ward-iron should be exactly over the middle knuckles, either when holding a guard or making a cut, by which means the direction of the knuckles will always govern the edge of the weapon.

[16]

INSIDE GUARD.

From the medium guard, by a turn of the wrist, bring the hilt of the sword opposite A, the finger nails upwards, the blade sloping sufficiently across the target to point to C, the arm nearly straight from the shoulder to the wrist, but not stiff. See Plate III.

In this position the edge of the sword is to receive the blow from an antagonist, and the bevel of the blade next to the edge should be opposite to the dotted line from A to C. If you turn the edge too much to the left, to will find a difficulty in striking, or be exposed to a cut on the outside of the wrist.

This guard secures the face and front of the body from cuts I. and V.

[17]

OUTSIDE GUARD.

From the last described position, by a motion of the wrist turn your knuckles outward till the hilt arrives opposite B, the blade at the same instant crossing the target till the point is directed to D: the bevel of the edge opposite the dotted line from B to D, and the finger nails downwards. See plate VI.

Having observed the relative situation of these two guards, practice the change from one to the other and back again, till you are able to execute it with such agility and precision, as to render it impossible for an adversary to disengage his weapon from one side and cut at the other without being opposed by the edge of your sword.

In this parade, the action of the wrist should always precede that of the shoulder; and be so immediately followed by it, as not to present an

[18]

opening to your adversary by holding a crooked wrist; an error to which beginners are very liable, especially on the inside guard.

INTRODUCTORY REMARKS on the SIX CUTS.

The following method of making the six cuts, though not practiced or taught as a necessary part of the science of broad sword in England, till lately introduced into the cavalry exercise, will be found with some advantages. For instance; when first engaging, many persons are apt to retire out of distance as you aim the first or second stroke, if they have sufficient space for that purpose, and unless such cut be made on a principle of expeditiously recovering your weapon, the loss of time will afford your antagonist an opportunity of cutting or thrusting before you regain your defensive posture. Others practice a mode of slipping a cut by withdrawing the arm; in which if they

[19]

succeed, they are almost certain of throwing in a cut before you can recover from a forcible stroke, except you have accustomed yourself to this manner of executing the six cuts.

Secondly. The strain, from the weight of your sword and force of the blow, may so far disable your wrist, as to render you incapable either of a vigorous attack or of a quick and firm parade.

On which account a person, who cannot perform the cuts upon the principle here recommended, must not attempt to strike with rapidity or force, until he perceive an absolute certainty of every blow reaching his antagonist unless parried by his weapon.

This disadvantage is obviated by the following method of practice, in addition to which, facility of execution and flexibility of wrist are obtained.

20

In making cuts I. and II. the point nearly describes a circle, from the commencement of the cut to the return to the guard;– To make this easily from the motion of the wrist and preserve the arm in its proper direction is of much importance, and can only be attained *by beginning gradually, and observing how far you can conduct the blade in making the cut in the requisite direction, without straining the wrist, or disordering your position*. For instance, in making cut I. you will find that you cannot proceed farther than to bring your point a little below fig. 4, without some change of position; this change must be effected by turning the wrist, till you can give freedom to the blade to complete the remainder of the circle, which brings the point up to the front of your position. Every unnecessary width of motion (which would be a sure consequence of bending the arm) must be avoided. Therefore, having brought your point from fig. 1 to fig. 4 in the first attempt, pause and observe the position necessary to be taken by the wrist, as described in the directions for making cut I.

A similar obstruction will be found in making cut II. as soon as your point sinks below fig. 3, which must be surmounted in the same manner, by observing the directions given for the third motion of cut II.

These difficulties may be easily removed by attention and practice; and when the learner has attained the mode of executing the two first cuts, he will find little trouble in acquiring the others, as they are performed on the same principle.

It is however to be observed that cuts I. and II. cannot be well performed with the ancient close or basket hilt upon this principle, as independent cuts; although the six cuts when combined may be made with it.

Direction of the Six Cuts.

There are but six directions in which a cut can be properly and safely made with a broad sword or sabre; four of which are diagonal and two horizontal. Some persons may perhaps here mention a seventh, viz. perpendicular; but, in practice, that cut will be found to partake so much of the diagonal direction, and of course be so easily parried either by the inside or outside guard, or if aimed at the head by the hanging guard, or the St. George, that I shall not trouble the reader farther with it, than by observing, that whatever guard he resorts to against the upper cuts, if it be correctly held, will form a sufficient obstacle to the perpendicular stroke; and proceed to describe the six cuts above mentioned.

CUT I. is made downwards from right to left of your own position.

CUT II. downwards from left to right.

[23]

CUT III. upwards from right to left.

CUT IV. upwards from left to right.

CUT V. horizontally from right to left.

CUT VI. horizontally from left to right.

Each cut being named according to that figure on the target from which it is commenced.

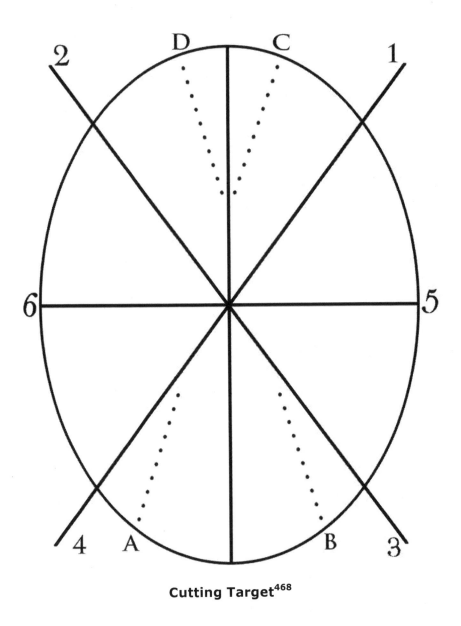

Cutting Target[468]

---

[468] Keith's note: the target illustration is not actually included in the 1804 edition; at least, not in the copy from which this transcription has been made. I have chosen to include it here, copied form the 1798 edition, because it is useful, and following sections of text refer to the positions and points on the diagram.

METHODS of PRACTISING the SIX CUTS at the TARGET.

Having placed yourself opposite the target as before directed, adopt the outside guard, and from thence commence CUT I. in the following manner:

Motion 1. Turn your hand to A, the point of your sword to fig. 1.

Motion 2. Conduct the point from fig. 1. To fig. 4. taking care that the edge leads and the arm remains steady.*

Motion 3. Turn the wrist so as to bring the thumb downwards, the back of the hand and flat of the blade opposite yourself, and recover to the outside guard by bringing

* The learner, I trust, will excuse my repeating the caution given in p. 20, that he must *begin gradually*. If he attempts to make the cuts *rapidly and with force*, before he attains the *proper turn* of the wrist by which the weapon is to be recovered, he will be liable to unpleasant accidents.

up the blade with a sweep clear of the inside (or front) of your position.

CUT II.

Motion 1. From the inside guard, turn your knuckles towards B, the point of your sword to fig. 2.

Motion 2. Conduct the point of the sword from 2 to 3.

Motion 3. Turn the inside of the wrist upwards, which will drop the point of the sword outwards to the rear, relax the three fingers nearest the pommel, and recover to the outside guard by raising the blade with a sweep clear of the right shoulder.

[26]

Having ascertained the changes in the wrist necessary to recover your blade in these two cuts, practise them until you are able to perform each as one motion without any pause, and to recover from either cut to the inside or outside guard as occasion may require.

CUT III.

Motion 1. By turning the upper part of the wrist and back of the hand downwards from the inside guard, drop the point outwards to the right till the edge of the blade is opposite the diagonal line from 3 to 2, at the same instant raising the wrist with a straight arm as high as the shoulder.

Motion 2. By the contraction of the fingers and motion of the wrist conduct the point up the line from 3 to 2.

[27]

Motion 3. When arrived at fig. 2. turn the back of the hand up, and drop the hand so as to bring the blade into the position of the outside guard.

CUT IV.

Motion 1. From the outside guard by a turn of the wrist, drop the point to the left, till the edge becomes opposite the diagonal line from 4 to 1, raising your hand to the height of your shoulder, the arm extended and straight.

Motion 2. By the spring of the wrist conduct the point along the line from 4 to 1.

Motion 3. Turn the inside of the wrist rather upwards, and sinking the arm, come to the inside guard.

[28]

CUT V.

Motion 1. Turn the back of the hand downward from the inside guard, thereby dropping the point of the sword to the right till it becomes opposite fig. 5.

Motion 2. By inclining the wrist inward, and keeping the nails upward, the point will be conducted across the target to fig. 6.

Motion 3. Raise the point from fig. 6. to C, and come to the inside guard.

CUT VI.

Is the reverse of cut V. and is performed with the nails downward.

Motion 1. Drop the point to the left till opposite fig. 6.

[29]

Motion 2. By inclining the wrist outwards make the cut across the target to fig. 5.

Motion 3. Raise the point to D, and recover to the outside guard.

The preceding guards are not mentioned as the only positions to which it will be necessary to recover, after making these cuts, but as the most eligible in the first stage of practice.

COMBINING the SIX CUTS.

The learner may now proceed to combine the six cuts, that they may all be performed without pausing, which will be found extremely useful in an attack, especially if an antagonist breaks ground and continues to retire, as is frequently the case at the onset; it may also prove advantageous in an engagement at night; since if properly performed, the blade will necessarily cross your own position in such a manner as to afford considerable security from the stroke of your adversary,

[30]

and by the reiterated attack will compel him to remain almost entirely on the defensive, or subject him to a certainty of receiving your edge on his sword arm, particularly if he does not know the direction of those cuts which so rapidly succeed the one he may have at first escaped or parried.

The difference between executing the six cuts singly as before described and when combined consists in not resorting to any particular guard after each cut, but continuing your attack from cut I. till you have made II. III. IV. V. and VI. in doing which the point proceeds from the conclusion of one cut to the commencement of the next, according to the dotted lines on the plate.

Be cautious not to lift your arm towards the figure at which the cut begins, as that would leave your body unprotected.

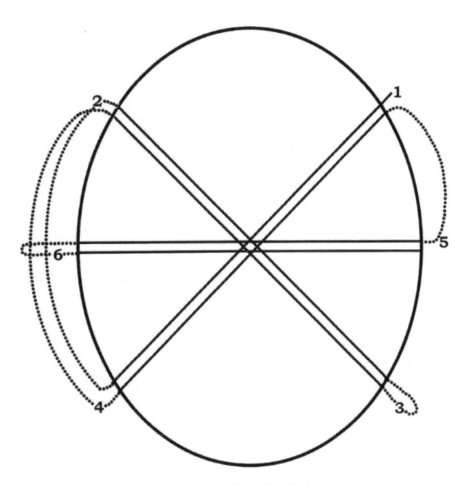

Combining the Six Cuts

213

31

PART II.

PRACTICE with ANTAGONIST.

GENERAL OBSERVATIONS.

In commencing your practice with an antagonist, for the sake of improvement, begin slowly: the one taking the defensive part entirely; the other attacking, and mentioning the number of the cut he means to make; each carefully observing the motion of his opponent, and informing him what part appears to become exposed by the changes from one position to another; where any defect of that kind appears, repeat your practice, till by the correctness or celerity thus acquired, you become more perfect. Then change situations, and let the assailant act on the defensive. By making observations coolly in this manner, you will acquire

more skill and precision in one lesson, than in playing twenty at random; and will likewise avoid unpleasant accidents.

Next proceed to attack and defend without naming what cuts you intend; in doing which endeavour first to become correct in making cuts I. and II. and opposing them by the inside and outside guards. Then add III. and IV. Afterwards V. and VI. increasing the celerity of your attack by degrees, and opposing each cut according to the following table.

Cut I.	Parried by *Inside Guard*,	described in page 50
Cut II.	*Outside Guard*	described in page 55
Cut III.	(if made by disengaging from the outside,)	
	Inside Half-hanger	described in page 60
Cut III.	(if made by disengaging from the inside,)	
	Half-circle guard	described in page 52

Cut IV.	Outside half-hanger	described in page 60
Cut V.	Inside guard	described in page 50
Or, if made low, by the Inside half-hanger		described in page 60
Cut VI.	Outside guard	described in page 55
	Or Outside half-hanger	described in page 60
	Cuts made directly at the head are opposed by the St. George	described in page 61

The whole of the six cuts may be warded by the hanging guard, the hand or blade being moved a

[33]

little to right or left, and raised or lowered accordingly, but observe, if already engaged on an *inside guard*, it will be useless to attempt taking the hanging guard against Cut V. or III. unless your antagonist makes a feint at the outside before he delivers his cut.

I have before remarked that it will be unsafe in friendly practice to make use of broad swords or sabres, and shall now take the liberty of cautioning learners, who wish to attain the science of real defence, also against the false mode of defending themselves with a basket so large as that which cudgel players generally use, and on which they receive two thirds of the blows aimed at them, since that will be accustoming themselves to a protection which they cannot have on a real occasion.

The baskets for this purpose should therefore be made narrow, and as small as possible without hurting the hand: and as gentlemen should always endeavour to defend themselves rather with the fort* of the sword than the hilt, they ought not to practise

* The *fort* of the sword is that half of the blade next to the hilt; the half nearest the point in is denominated the *feeble*.

stopping the blow with the sides, or any other part of the basket except where the hilt of a sword would equally project.

By marking a narrow line with chalk down the supposed edge of the stick, accuracy in carrying the edge of the sword may be acquired.

In Part I. the *mode of recovering to guard* has been considered under the idea of the cuts not meeting with sufficient resistance either from the blade or body of your antagonist to impede their course: but in practising with an opponent, it is not to be understood that the recovery to guard must be *always* made on that principle: From cuts I. and II. when parried, the blade naturally rebounds up the line in which it fell, till the point rises high enough to form an inside or outside guard. From cuts V. and VI. the point must be raised in a similar manner, if the cut is opposed by the blade of your antagonist. In making cuts III. and IV. it should be a rule, never to apply above four inches of the point, in order that it may free

itself, and mount to the inside or outside guard: if that be prevented by your antagonist's blade cross above yours, you must withdraw your blade from your attempt to make cut III. under the half-circle guard, and from attempting cut IV. under the hanging guard.

After making a cut be careful always to recover to that guard which brings your *edge* opposed to your antagonist's blade.

If at any time you should be compelled to oppose a weak parade to your adversary, by your wrist being in a constrained position, quit that posture as soon as possible, either by directing a cut at him, or springing back at the instant you change.

To attain security from a counter stroke whilst attacking, it is requisite that in every cut made by you, the fort of your sword should be direct in some degree towards your antagonist's weapon; so that although the point of your sword may effect the cut, yet the fort shall at the same instant be opposed to any blow he may then delivery. For example:

[36]

In making cut I. the hilt being carried to the left of your position, as much as when on the inside guard, at the instant the point commences the cut, occasions your blade to form a cross on that of your antagonist, and thereby affords a certainty of protection, unless he can change his position in considerably less time than you can make the cut. Cuts I. and II. should therefore in general be made with the hand lower than the shoulder, and III. and IV. with it raised above the height of the shoulder.

On this principle it is that the ARM *should never* be lifted towards the side at which you intend a cut, since by that motion both hilt and blade would be entirely removed from between yourself and antagonist, and consequently you must become exposed to the same cut you aim at him.

Experience will soon direct to how great a degree it is requisite thus to cross your adversary's blade. By extending the principle to an unnecessary extreme, you may indeed frequently prevent your own blow taking effect, by encountering

[37]

your antagonist's sword only; and on the other hand, by not sufficiently observing it, may become exposed yourself by every cut you attempt.

In some situations it will undoubtedly be proper to cut *from* your antagonist's blade, instead of *towards* it; for instance, in making a cut over and within his guard, or under and within his guard; in such cases this attack may be safely risked, because you have previously forced his sword far enough from the line to prevent a counter stroke or retort before your recover takes place.

DISTANCE.

Want of attention to preserve the proper distance is an error to which beginners are very liable. No invariable positive space can be recommended, as almost every situation must depend on the height, strength and activity of your opponent. The most general principle that can be laid down is, that your left knee should be about six or eight inches beyond the reach of your antagonist's

[38]

point upon the most extensive longe he can exert. But it is difficult to prove your distance by this method in real contest; in that case you may judge more easily from the point of your sword just reaching his shell when both your arts are straight, and neither inclining the body improperly forwards. If you permit him to advance nearer, he may throw in a cut or thrust too rapidly for your parade, especially if he first deceive you by a feint. To avoid this, some persons accustom themselves to spring back, frequently dropping their point to their antagonist's face, when contending with one of an impetuous and forward temper; a mode which will undoubtedly be found very useful, if the ground on which they are engaged should afford sufficient room.– Others adopt a circular step (called Traversing) to right or left, and thereby effect their purpose in less length. But experience and practice will best determine which to make use of, according to the circumstances and situation in which you may chance to contend.

-----

[39]

The ADVANCE

Is to gain ground upon an adversary when at too great a distance to reach him by a longe, or by pressing forwards to compel him to retreat into worse ground or a more disadvantageous situation: it is effected by stepping forward with the right foot about one third of your longe, at the same time transferring the weigh of your body from the left leg to the right, that you may be enabled to slip the left foot along the ground to within six inches of the right heel; then step forward again with the right foot, and draw up the left as before (still preserving the position of body erect, and being careful to oppose a proper guard) till your object be attained.

-----

[40]

The RETREAT

Is used to gain a more advantageous situation that may be behind you, or to avoid any inconvenience you may sustain from an adversary of superior strength or impetuous temper pressing too closely upon you. In this situation the left leg must lead, and the weight must be thrown in the first motion on the right, lifting the left foot from the ground to avoid any unseen obstacle in the rear, then planting it firmly about sixteen or eighteen inches backward, and drawing the right to within ten. After this raise the left foot, and planting it as before, draw the right after it, continuing your retreat as occasion may require.

41

TRAVERSING.

There are two modes of traversing, viz. *backward* and *forward*; either of which may be adopted according to the ground or other circumstances in which you may engage, and will be found useful, if in retiring from an adversary you are obstructed by a ditch or other impediment. Traversing is preferred by many to retiring, because it has not so much the appearance of suffering a defeat.

The FORE TRAVERSE

Is performed in a large circle, the center of which is the middle of the *line of defence*,* on which line you and your adversary engage; such

* A straight line supposed to be drawn through the center of your own body, and that of your adversary.

is the line P, Q, **C**, H, G, in the opposite page, and the circle formed by the traverse will be P, A, C, E, G, I, L, N: For the right foot being at Q and the left at P, the traverse is begun by stepping about with the left foot from P to A, and the right foot immediately after from Q to B; and then the line A, B, **C**, K, I, will be the line of defence; at the next step remove the left foot from A to C, then the right from B, to B; which will make the line C, D, **C**, M, L, the line of defence. In the same manner continue till you have obviated your difficulty, or drawn your adversary into the bad ground, carefully attending to your guard, and not stepping so far as to disorder the erect position of your body.

The BACK TRAVERSE

Is the counter-part of that already described; and is commenced by moving the *right* foot first: for instance: Standing in the line of defence P, Q, **C**, H, G, remove the right from Q to O, the left from P to N, which renders the line N, O, **C**,

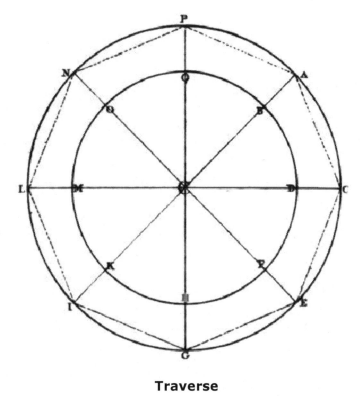

Traverse

[43]

F, E, the line of defence: Thus stepping back, the right foot moving first, you may traverse the whole or such part of the circle as may be requisite.

This practice may at times prove exceedingly useful, especially if you should be at first engaged with the sun directly in your face, as a person who performs it readily, by traversing half the circle, brings his opponent into the place he has just quitted, and by a vigorous attack at that instant may redouble the embarrassment.

44

DISENGAGING

Consists in quitting that side of your antagonist's blade on which you are opposed by his guard, in order to effect a cut or thrust where an opportunity may present. It is performed either by raising the point of your sword towards yourself so as just sufficiently to clear the blade of your opponent, or by dropping the point below his hilt. The change in either way should be made very quickly, and in the instant of passing your adversary's weapon, the edge of your blade should be turned to meet any cut that he may direct at you become liable to be disabled, from the ward-iron not protection the hand.

The disengage to effect a cut is generally performed over the wrist; that with intention of thrusting, under it. To cut III. or IV. under the wrist, it is sometimes best to disengage below it.

FORCING your ADVERSARY's BLADE.

If at any time your antagonist appears languid and weak on his guard, and barely covers his body on the side he is opposed; by stepping well forward and striking your fort smartly on his blade, you may be enabled to deliver a cut without risk even at the part he intends to secure, taking care to direct your bade in such a manner that the plate or cross bar of your hilt shall prevent his sword coming forward, and sufficiently bearing your hand to the site opposite that at which your point is directed, to prevent an interchanged cut.

This should be performed partly by the sudden extension of the arm, and partly by the spring of the wrist.

TIMING

Is the exact and critical throwing in a cut or thrust upon any opening that may occur as your antagonist changes his position. For instance, if he changes from an inside to an outside guard, or from outside to inside, in a negligent manner, his wrist becomes exposed, and frequently part of his sword arm above the elbow. The same opportunity presents itself, if in his feints he should suffer his sword to sway his arm, instead of making them lightly from his wrist, or should not recover quickly from a cut which you have parried.

The SLIP

Is performed by withdrawing that part at which your antagonist directs his cut; in order that his weapon being deprived of the expected resistance may sway his arm from the defensive posture, and thereby afford an opening for a cut. It will

[47]

not however often effect this purpose against a person who can execute the cuts on the principle recommended in this work, as the recover is so very expeditious; but may prove an excellent deception against an impetuous antagonist, especially if he be ignorant of the science.*

It will therefore be proper for the learner to accustom himself sometimes to recover from the longe with his right hand drawn quickly up to the breast, the edge of his sword turned to the left or right, according to the direction of the cut he means to slip. If the cut he intends to avoid be made at the inside of the sword arm, the edge should be turned to the left as in the inside guard, the point raised perpendicular to the hilt, and the return

* It has been frequently asserted, that a bold active man, unacquainted with the art, by rushing forward with repeated attacks, will perplex a good swordsman, and, if not defeat him, reduce the contest to an equal hazard: but this can only happen if such swordsman has never reflected on the measures fit to be adopted in an engagement of that nature. For instance, if a swordsman slips a cut attempted by one of that description, instead of parrying it, he may effect a cut before the ignorant can possibly recover, and with such force as totally to deprive his antagonist of that vigour and audacity on which alone he could defend.

[48]

from this position should be cut II. Should the attack be made at the outside of his arm, the edge should be turned outwards, and the hilt held a little below the right shoulder, returning cut I. the instant his adversary's blade passes.

Some are so partial to this manoeuvre of slipping an adversary's cut, that by practice they become enabled to slip a cut even when directed at their body. But this, unless exceedingly well executed, becomes hazardous, on account of its disordering their position, especially if an adversary should longe farther than expected, and cut low; added to which, by throwing their body from the line of defence, the antagonist may be induced to thrust upon them in that unguarded position, and will thereby obtain a decided advantage.

In circumstances where the withdrawal the hand up to the breast is not sufficient, the slipping a cut on the inside if effected by drawing the right foot backward and sideways to the right of the line, letting your adversary's sword pass a little out of reach, then stepping into the former position,

Spadroon Guard[469]

---

[469] Keith's note: the 1804 edition has an illustration of a fencer slipping back, parrying an incoming thrust. This 1798 illustration is of the same parry, but without the slip, unfortunately.

return cut II. or VI. at his outside, which becomes exposed by his weapon not meeting the resistance expected.

To an outside cut the slip is performed by drawing the right leg with the whole body backwards and sideways a small degree out of the line towards the left, contracting the arm a little, the sword still in the line, and under an outside guard; let your antagonist's point pass, and returning your right foot to its former place, make cut I. at the inside of the arm, or II. at the head. I have mentioned this method of performing the outside slip, as it is attempted by some, but not with the intention of recommending it, as the hazard is much greater than the probable advantage.

On the hanging guard the slip may be practised with great safety, by stepping the foot quite out of and at right angles with the line of defence, the whole body being this brought well beyond it to the right; and the guard remaining still opposed to your antagonist to protect you from his

cut, in case he should longe farther than you expect.

INSIDE GUARD.

Turn your hilt to the left, the finger nails upwards, as in Plate III. the pommel directed towards the inside of your chest, the point opposite your antagonist's left eye, or elevated from one to four inches above it. Should he bear against your blade to force it out of the line, raise your point, so as to withdraw your feeble from his bearing; or disengage quickly and cut at the outside of his arm.

Cuts I. and V. are warded by this position, the latter however requires a trifling inclination of the hand downwards.

In parrying cut I. at the cheek, it will be found adviseable to carry the wrist rather more to the left, as in Plate IV. raising the point nearly perpendicular, to prevent you from being deceived by a

Inside Guard[470]

[51]

feint:– If you suffer your point to remain low, an offer may be made at your cheek, and the cut delivered over your guard at the head.

Although when standing on an inside or outside guard the right foot is advanced, yet when parrying a cut with either of these guards it is deemed most eligible to slip back that foot to the left; lest instead of cut I. or II. at the upper part, your antagonist may be tempted to cut at the leg of thigh. See Plate XII.

---

[470] Keith's note: the illustration of the inside guard in the 1804 edition shows just a single fencer; the 1798 illustration presented here shows a pair of fencers engaging upon the inside guard.

Cut V. is frequently made too low to be parried by the inside guard, which is intended only to ward the inside cuts above the wrist. The next consideration therefore will be the method of parrying the inside cuts below the wrist.

-----

[52]

HALF CIRCLE GUARD.

This guard is adapted to ward cuts III. or V. made at the inside below the wrist, and is formed by swiftly dropping your point to the right, as in the first motion of cut III. till it becomes opposite your antagonist's body, carrying your hand to the left of your line of defence, and directing the edge of your weapon towards your antagonist's sword, instead of his body or arm. The general rule for the height of your hand is to hold it in a line with the left eye, but that must depend in a great degree on the attack made by your antagonist; otherwise if he sinks his fort low enough to strike it across your feeble, he will probably beat your blade sufficiently out of the line to effect his cut.*

Finding his attack parried by the half circle, your opponent may endeavour to double his cut

* For this reason if cut III. or V. be made at you by disengaging from the outside guard, it will be best to parry them with an inside half-hanger. See page 60.

228

Spadroon Guard

[53]

(as he recovers) on the upper part or outside of your arm: this you may prevent by raising your point to an inside guard, and thereby meeting his blade with yours as he endeavours to cut or disengage over your wrist. If he disengages by throwing his point wide, and thereby escapes your inside guard, parry by an outside guard.

This position (or at least one differing only in holding the hilt lower and the blade more horizontal) is by many termed the SPADROON GUARD; it is not however to be considered as a chief position of defence with that weapon, being weak and very liable to be forced. It should therefore only be adopted for the purpose of parrying a low cut or thrust at the inside, and not as a guard on which to engage or wait for an antagonist, except by a player who may be skilful enough to use it as a lurch,* in order to induce his antagonist to throw at some part which he intends to withdraw from

* When standing on the Spadroon Guard, it is usual to bring the left arm across the chest, and place the left hand on the right arm between the elbow and the shoulder, in order to steady it.

[54]

his cut, that he may seize the opening afforded by such attack.

When on this guard, you should always remember, that if your antagonist succeed in making a forcible beat on your blade, especially on the back of it, he will in all probability disarm you. Therefore, instead of receiving his blow in that position, slip it by withdrawing your weapon at the instant, and return cut II. at the outside of his sword arm.

Caution however will be requisite, that you do not withdraw your sword instead of parrying a blow aimed at yourself. The difference will depend on the distance you are from your antagonist, and on his advancing or remaining stationary. Always quit this position as soon as possible for the inside or outside guard, in doing which spring back that your antagonist may not throw in a cut by timing your change of position.

Outside Guard[471]

The Consequence of not shifting the LEG.

Publish'd Sep.1, 1798 by H.Angelo N.º13 Carwer Street May Fair.

Cut at the Right Knee[472]

---

[471] Keith's note: the illustration of the outside guard in the 1804 edition shows just a single fencer; the 1798 illustration presented here shows a pair of fencers engaging upon the outside guard.

[472] Keith's note: this image is taken from Thomas Rowlandson's posters for *Hungarian and Highland Broadsword*, illustrating Henry Angelo's system. The 1804 edition of Roworth's treatise includes an illustration very similar to this, showing a cut to the knee.

231

OUTSIDE GUARD.

Turn your knuckles to the outside, the finger nails downwards, carrying the hand about 6 or 8 inches to the right of the line of defence, so as to protect the outside of your position, and direct your point to the right eye of your antagonist. (See Plate VI.) Should he endeavour to force your blade out of the position, gain his feeble by withdrawing and raising your point,* or disengage and cut on the other side.

This guard secures against cut II. and by sinking the hand in a small degree against cut VI. In parrying cut II. at the right cheek, be careful to turn the hand well outwards, and raise the point as in Plate VII.

* If your adversary's point has crossed above the back of your blade so as threaten the inside of your position, adopt the hanging guard, by throwing up your wrist quickly as possible, and bear his blade off to the inside; should you attempt to parry by the outside guard after his point has crossed your blade in such a degree as to come withinside your guard, you will only add to the force of his cut. See *cut V. over and within the guard*, p. 81.

56

HANGING GUARD.*

This may be taken from either the inside or the outside guard, by dropping the point of your sword till it is directed towards your antagonist's body, a little above his right hip, raising the hand as high as your head, and looking your adversary in the face under the shell of your sword.

* The hanging guard possesses several advantages and is at the same time liable to some objections. I shall mention the principal of each, and leave the learner to exercise his own discretion in what circumstances to adopt it.
Among the advantages to be derived from the hanging guard, the most important will be found in the protection it affords by covering so large a

portion of the body, as the whole of the blade is appropriated to that purpose, especially in the direction in which the first and most natural blows are made; while from the oblique position of the weapon, a blow, however forcible, slides down it without endangering the hand. For these reasons, it seems well calculated to parry off any sudden attack in the dark, especially if it should be made against a person armed only with a stick.

The hanging guard is also well adapted to prevent an antagonist from thrusting at the body beneath the wrist, and to obviate those feints which might otherwise be made, by shifting his point from side to side under your wrist on either the inside or outside guard.

Another material advantage is, that it requires a very trifling

[57]

This guard admits of two positions, according to the cuts it may be used to oppose, which may be denominated an inside hanging guard, and outside hanging guard.

The inside (or *prime*) hanging guard, is formed by bending the elbow, till the back of the wrist is brought opposite the forehead over the left eye, and is intended to protect against cuts I. III. and V. when made at the inside; the left of the head being covered from attack by the hilt; but if the cut be made direct at the head, it is most prudent to adopt the St. George's guard, especially as the hilts now used have no basket, and very little shell.

If the antagonist cuts II. IV. or VI. at your

motion of the wrist to meet with your blade any cut whatever that may be made.

The constrained position of the hand, and weight of the weapon, will at first be found tiresome on this guard, but practice will soon overcome that defect, and enable a person to deliver a blow with amazing rapidity and force from it, as may be observed in the practice of the French Spadroon players, many of whom place their chief dependence on the protection offered by their guard in seconde, which only differs from this guard in the wrist not being held quite so high.

outside, you must meet his edge by carrying the weapon to the right of your position.

The outside (or *seconde*) hanging guard differs from the former, in having the arm perfectly straight, the blade being carried to the right, so as to protect against cuts II. IV. and VI.

When in this position, the adversary's sword must be kept by your blade sufficiently to the outside to prevent any cut or thrust being made at that part.

If your antagonist disengages from the *seconde* hanging guard to make cut I. III. or V. you must oppose them by the *prime hanging guard*, which is formed by inclining your wrist to the left till the back of the hand is in a line above the left eye, the point rather lowered, to prevent cut III. being made under it.

Although the *prime hanging guard* will be found very useful for parrying cuts III. and V. when made by disengaging from an outside guard;

yet it cannot be used to parry those cuts when the are made by disengaging from an inside guard: in such case the half circle guards must be adopted.

It will be necessary by practice to obtain a degree of firmness and celerity in changing from the *prime* to the *seconde* hanging guard, since a cut made at either of those guards occasions the assailant's sword to rebound with swiftness, and enables him without much hazard to strike at the other side; and although it is against the rules of broad sword play in schools or friendly contests, to make two cuts on one longe, yet in an engagement for life this is not likely to be attended to.

60

HALF-HANGING GUARD.

When parrying a thrust or cut directed low, it will be unsafe to hold the hand high enough to view your adversary under the hilt; because such position would enable him to apply the fort of his blade against your feeble, and thereby render your resistance inadequate to the force of his attack.

To obviate this disadvantage the *Inside* and *Outside half-Hanging Guards* must be resorted to, which differ from the preceding only in your hand not being raised so high, but held low enough to view your opponent over your hilt. The right foot is to be slipped back, and the point of your sword dropped sufficiently close to your own position, to prevent your antagonist forcing in his cut or thrust, by encountering your sword with the fort of his own weapon. See Plates IX. and X.

Hanging Guard

St. George's Guard

61

St. GEORGE's GUARD

Is intended to ward a blow at the top of the head, if your adversary disengages from the outside for that purpose; it differs from the hanging guard only in raising the hand somewhat higher, drawing back the right arm, and bringing the point nearer yourself. In this position, the fort of your blade, which is to receive the blow, will be at least 3 or 4 inches above your head. The ward-iron of the hilt must be turned well up to protect the knuckles. It will be proper to slip the right foot back to the left heel at the same instant. (See Plate XI.)

Some persons, instead of keep the sword advanced before them, raise the hand till the blade crossed above the head in an horizontal direction from right to left.

This latter position is seldom used, and can hardly ever be necessary, except to protect the

[62]

head from a blow made by an antagonist behind, (for which purpose it is adopted in the cavalry exercise) or to withdraw your weapon from one in front who endeavours to seize it, and is unarmed himself.

Against a blow made by a person in front, however near, the first described position will be found preferable, raising your sword hand and point, according to circumstances.

It must be observed that the St. George's guard is not intended to lie under, but only to stop a blow at the head, when your antagonist advances so closely upon you, that the hanging guard is not sufficiently secure. The best way in general of changing from the St. George (unless when you immediately return a cut or thrust from it) is to adopt the hanging guard, taking care to direct your point towards the ribs of your antagonist, and to keep your body well in a line. From

[63]

this position, there is less danger in taking another than if you change directly from the St. George to the inside or outside guard.

Having acquired the preceding guards, the next articles to attended to are *bearing*, *battering*, the *feints* and *disarms*.

-----

[64]

BEARING

Is generally practised by longeing forward briskly on the outside guard, opposing the fort of your blade to that of your antagonist, and from thence slipping your fort towards his feeble,* by which means you may press his sword out of the line; this (unless he takes to the hanging guard) leaves his head, neck and breast exposed to your edge, and from this position a *cut over and within his guard* may be made, but must be executed with celerity.

Bearing on an inside guard is sometimes practised, but it not so safe, as the opponent may easily drop his point, and springing back make cut III. at your arm.

Upon the hanging guard *bearing* cannot be used to advantage, since in bearing on an antagonist's blade to obtain an opening at the outside of his

* In attempting this, be careful not to slip your sword too far down, lest your antagonist disengage and cut withinside.

238

position, you expose your own head and inside, and by slipping from your bearing he will in all probability effect a cut.

BATTERING

Is striking on your antagonist's sword to obtain an opening, and requires the same degree of caution as bearing, lest your antagonist slip his blade from your stroke, and make a cut on the contrary side. It can seldom be attended with success against any but the outside and spadroon guards, when used to force an opening on the side at which you batter; but sometimes by inducing an adversary to resist that attack, you may disengage and cut on the contrary side.

66

Of FEINTS.

A feint is an offer at a cut or thrust without striking home. There are two sorts, *single feints* and *double feints*. The single feint is made by disengaging from that side on which you are opposed by your adversary's guard, and making a slight motion at the other, you then return to the first and deliver the cut. For instance, if engaged on the outside guard, you will disengage over the point, and dropping your point on the inside of your adversary's blade about six inches, return to the outside, and deliver cut II. at his arm, or VI. at his ribs. If you find him prepared to parry those cuts (II and VI.) you will only make an offer as before, which constitutes it a double feint, and deliver your cut at the head or inside of his position.

But as cutting at the inside against an antagonist who is tolerably perfect in his guards, especially from feints, is attended with the danger of a counter-stroke, I would recommend when you intend a double feint to commence it by a disengage from the inside.

[67]

The purpose of feints being only to induce your adversary to guard a part at which you do not design to strike, the feints, whether single or double, may be directed at any other parts as well as those mentioned. Great caution is necessary, that in making your feints you do not uncover yourself so much as to receive a time thrust or cut. The feint should also be directed at a part from whence you can quickly recover your weapon to effect the cut you intend.

DISARMING.

There are various methods of disarming attempted, but the safest and most likely to succeed is, after parrying an inside cut to change quickly to the outside, and longeing forward to bear your adversary's blade out of the line to the outside, then step with your left foot up to his right heel, seize his shell with your left hand, quit your bearing on his blade, and present your point to his breast.

[68]

A disarm on the hanging guard may be effected by making cut III. at the feeble of your antagonist's blade, traversing at the same time to the left and gliding the edge of your sword strongly against the back of your opponent's. It will however require some caution, lest he should turn his wrist at the instant you attempt it, and make a cut at the inside.

Those disarms which are to be effected by wrenching from an inside guard to a seconde hanging guard, or from an outside guard to a half circle will not often succeed, except with very light swords. With such, they must be commenced by turning the knuckles rather more up than usual on those guards, and swiftly reversing them as you wrench the adversary's blade down, directing your point rather in a diagonal line across his body, than permitting it to form a circle. These latter disarms are only applicable if the antagonist presents his blade and arm nearly horizontal; and in that case, if they do not succeed in wrenching the sword out of his hand, will prove useful to obtain an opening for a cut or thrust.

[69]

The method of avoiding them is by disengaging under your adversary's hilt at the instant he endeavours to cross your blade. If this disengage be well timed, he may probably throw his own sword from his hand, by not meeting the resistance he expected.

APPLICATION of the POINT.

The weight of the broad sword will not permit the same number of thrusts that may be made with the small sword. All that can be safely introduced among the cuts of the former are four, viz. *Carte*, *Tierce*, *Low Carte*, and *Seconde* which is a low tierce: these should be thrust with the hilt high enough to ward any blow your adversary may be likely to make, and to retard a disengagement over your wrist at the instant of longeing.

CARTE is thrust at the inside of the upper part of the body, with the nails upward, and the edge of the sword turned rather upward to the left

[70]

and well opposed towards your antagonist's weapon by keeping your pommel opposite your left temple at the time of longeing.*

LOW CARTE is thrust at the inside of the lower half of your antagonist's body, with the same precaution of opposing your edge towards your adversary's blade.

241

TIERCE is a thrust at the upper part of your antagonist's body, over his arm, with your nails downward, the edge of your sword turned to the right and opposed towards his blade.

SECONDE differs from tierce in being thrust below the sword arm.

In thrusting *Carte* and *Low Carte* be careful to form a good opposition toward your antagonist's weapon by carrying your wrist to the *left*. In

* If when thrust at the inside of your antagonist you are apprehensive of his cutting downwards, you must turn your wrist as in the half circle guard, that your ward-iron may be upwards. In thrusting at the outside, turn the wrist as in the hanging guard.

[71]

thrusting *Tierce* and *Seconde* the opposition to his blade must be formed by bearing your wrist to the *right*.*

In thrusting with the SABRE the safest thrusts are those already recommended, since the convex *edge* of the sabre, when opposed to your antagonist's blade, affords protection from a counter cut or thrust. Yet the advantage that may sometimes be attained by the curve of the sabre enabling you to deceive your adversary's guard deserves consideration. For instance–

Engage on an outside guard, your edge opposed to mine: thrust at me, *turning your nails upwards* as you longe, thus forms the thrust called *Carte*

* Although in using the small sword, there are other thrusts, which are made with the back of the blade opposed to the weapon of the antagonist, yet they cannot be executed with a broad sword, without great hazard of receiving a cut on the arm at the time of longeing; since if your antagonist springs back, his body will be out of the reach of your thrust, and your arm become exposed to his edge. This is not the case with the small sword, which being much lighter, the thrust and recovery to guard are executed with more celerity, and when opposing another small sword without danger from the edge of your antagonist.

242

over the Arm, and brings the hollow back of your sabre against my weapon, and thereby enabled you to direct the point 6 or 8 inches more toward my left than you otherwise could, and to effect either a thrust, or a sawing cut at my face or neck. Observe, that as you deliver this thrust, your opposition to my blade must be formed by carrying your wrist to the *right* of the line of defence.

If I parry this thrust, of carte over the arm, by an outside guard; the instant your point passes the outside of my position, I may cut II. at the outside of your sword arm; this you must parry by an outside guard, or a *seconde* hanging guard: or if I drop my point over your blade, and cut at your cheek, you must parry by a *prime* hanging guard.

Some after parrying carte over the arm by an outside guard, whirl the blade round with a half circle parade, and return low carte: this may be easily effected against a person who is slow in recovering from his longe.

Advantages similar to that in thrusting carte

over the arm may be obtained with a sabre by reversing the wrist on the other thrusts: these may be better understood by taking the sabre in your hand, and observing the effect produced on the direction of the point by turning your nails up and down, than by the most accurate description. However, do not be too partial to this mode of obtaining an opening, but recollect, that in making a thrust on this principle, the ward-iron of your hilt will not be on the side where you want the protection, and that if your thrust be parried, the position of your arm exposes you to the edge of your antagonist as you recover.

As thrusting is not the principal object of the broad sword, I shall not trouble the reader farther on this than to recommend his acquiring by practice a facility of making the before mentioned in good position, directing the point with accuracy, and recovering to his guard with expedition; for which purpose it will be necessary to practise at a target with the sword, sometimes thrusting only, at others cutting half way, and finishing with a thrust, for instance,

[74]

Cut I. half way, then turn up the nails and thrust carte, or low carte.

Cut II. about one third of the line, then turn down the nails and thrust tierce, or seconde.

Cut III. part of the line and thrust carte or low carte.

Cut IV. half way and thrust seconde.

By this practice the learner may not only attain accuracy in directing his point, but also a celerity in returning either a cut or thrust after having parried; otherwise if he accustoms himself to find a support from his point always hitting the target, he will not acquire a proper method of recovering to guard.

-----

[75]

Of parrying Thrusts made above the Wrist.

These thrusts may be parried by an inside or outside guard, striking your fort with an abrupt beat on your adversary's feeble, and retaining your point in the line of defence, presented to his face. In doing this it will be proper to sink your hilt rather lower than when opposing a cut, and to keep the arm somewhat more flexible.

Of parrying Thrusts made below the Wrist.

The most usual method of parrying thrusts made below the wrist, with a broad sword, is to beat the opponent's blade to the outside, by dropping the point to a *seconde*, or outside half-hanging guard, whether those thrusts be made by disengaging from an outside or inside guard.

In performing this parade, observe to retain a sufficient command of your sword to be able to change quickly to an inside (or *prime*) half-hanging

[76]

guard by carrying your wrist to the left, if necessary; otherwise your antagonist may deceive you by a feint, and deliver his thrust at the inside.

This mode of parrying, first with a *seconde*, and then changing to a *prime* half-hanging guard if your antagonist disengage to attack the inside of your position, seems peculiarly adapted to the broad sword, as the situation of the hand at the same time affords great security from a cut as well as a thrust.

In some circumstances, especially in an attack at night, your safety must depend greatly on not losing the feel of your antagonist's blade; you should therefore learn to parry the lower thrusts by following your antagonist's weapon with your own blade,– with a *seconde* parade if he disengages from an inside guard; and with either a *prime* or a *half-circle* parade, if he disengages from an outside guard.*

* The *Seconde Parade* is the same as the Outside Half-hanger. The *Prime Parade* is similar to the Inside Half-hanger; but in parrying a *thrust* with the *prime*, the antagonist's sword is opposed by the *back* of your blade; in warding a cut with the *Inside Half-hanger*, it is opposed by your *edge*.

77

Of following your Antagonist's Blade from the inside to parry with a SECONDE.

As your antagonist drops his point from the inside guard, to thrust below your wrist, you must follow his blade by the *seconde* or outside half-hanger. Having parried his thrust, you may turn up your nails and return cut V. under his blade, or you may return a thrust in seconde.

If he completes the circle with his point by continuing the motion till he brings it over your hilt to thrust at the inside, you must parry by changing from the outside to the inside half-hanger.

Of following your Antagonist's Sword with the PRIME PARADE.

At the instant the antagonist sinks his point from your outside guard in order to thrust under your wrist, drop your point over his blade,

and striking the *back* of your blade on his weapon, draw your hand to within a foot of your forehead, in a line with your left temple, so as to bring his thrust clear of the inside of your position. To effect this you must bend your elbow; then having brought his blade past your body, extend your arm to a hanging guard, turning the back of your hand opposite your forehead. This should be practised till you can perform it with readiness as one motion.

The *prime thrust* may be frequently delivered with safety after forming this parade. It differs from the thrust in *seconde* in being directed at the inside instead of the outside, and the opposition to your antagonist's blade being formed by bearing your wrist to the *left* of the line of defence instead of to the *right*.

If you intend to return a thrust after having parried by the *prime*, it will be safest either to oppose your antagonist's blade with your left hand as you thrust, or to step out of the line to the right as you parry, which gives you an opportunity of thrusting at the inside of your antagonist.

[79]

If your antagonist should only make a half thrust and disengage to the outside, you must oppose any cut or thrust he may there attempt, by carrying your hand to the right as in the *seconde* hanging guard.

Of following your Antagonist's Sword by the HALF CIRCLE PARADE.

This is to be effected by dropping you point over your adversary's blade as he quits your outside guard to thrust under your hilt, and striking with the *edge* of your sword against his blade, to beat his thrust past the inside. In performing this, the arm must be extended and inclined to the left till the wrist becomes opposite the left temple, the back of the hand downwards, and the point directed towards your antagonist's hip. When by this parade you have beat his blade out of the line to the left, you may either return a thrust in low carte, or turn the nails down and cut VI. beneath his blade as he recovers, springing back as you cut.

[80]

if in performing the half-circle parade, you miss the feel of your adversary's blade, by his raising his point over your hilt to thrust at your outside, you must instantly carry your hand about six inches to the right or outside of your line of defence, the inside of the wrist still upwards, and oppose his thrust with the back of your blade;* then whirl your point up in a circular direction outwards, and thus bring it round to the *seconde* hanging guard, without sinking your wrist as you turn it.†

Observe to keep the gripe encircled with your forefinger and thumb, or you will be liable to lose your sword. Hold your head well back, and incline your body on the left hip. This parade may be practised alone with your sword, till you can perform it rapidly and without any pause.

If in whirling your blade up, you beat your antagonist's

* This forms the Parade called *Quinte* or *Octave*, by small swordsmen.

† Instead of parrying in the above mode, first with *half-circle* and then with *octave*, it will sometimes be preferable to continue the motion of your point till it describes the whole circle, which may be repeated without stopping if there should be occasion.

[81]

weapon out of the line; then, instead of dropping your point to form a *seconde*, make cut II. at his head or arm.

ROUND PARADES.

These cannot be well performed with a very heavy sword, yet will prove useful to a person armed with a spadroon or light cut and thrust sword.

Engage on an inside guard:– Your antagonist disengages to thrust tierce or carte over the arm; follow his blade by describing a small circle with your point, keeping your wrist on the line of the inside guard; this will bring his blade to the position from which he disengaged.– Observe this circle is began by sinking your point from *left to right*.

On an outside guard:– Your opponent disengages to thrust carte; follow his blade with a small circle began by dropping your point from the *right to the left*, keeping your wrist on the outside guard:

this also brings his blade up to the position from which he disengaged.

N.B. The motion of your wrist and the circle described by your point must not be greater than may be sufficient to enable you to preserve or regain the feel of your antagonist's weapon; for which reason, when you intend to use these parades against a thrust, you must engage with your point directed towards the upper part of your antagonist's breast.

CIRCLE PARADE.

This is formed by describing a circle of about three feet diameter with your point, keeping your wrist the height of your shoulder, on the line of either an inside or outside guard, your weight resting on the left leg, and holding your head back. This parade is extremely serviceable for regaining the feel of an adversary's blade, especially when engaged in the dark, and will be found useful against a person who may endeavour to embarrass you by a multiplicity of feints.

[83]

It may now be necessary to notice such cuts as deviating from the principles of the system become exceptions to every general rule, and therefore demand particular attention.

Of this description are those cuts in which we abandon that *general principle of security of cutting towards an antagonist's blade in order to prevent a counter stroke or time thrust*. Under this head may be classed the three following cuts, in which security if to be attained by first throwing an adversary's blade out of line.

Cut V. under the Sword.

If on the inside guard your antagonist lowers his point and presents his arm and blade in a line nearly horizontal, so that you can cross about 8 inches of his feeble with your fort, drop your blade smartly across his, and wrench his sword to the outside under your blade, then turn your wrist

[84]

and cut V. beneath his blade and recover to an outside guard.

(In order to be able to perform this cut with safety and effect, it will be necessary frequently to practise alone with a sword, dropping the point from an inside guard to a *seconde* hanging guard, then turning up the nails cut V. and recover to an outside guard.)

If your antagonist be aware of your design, he will probably withdraw his blade or disengage under your wrist: in which case you must spring back on a hanging guard the instant you lose the feel of it, presenting your point at his ribs, or seek his sword by the circle parade.

The parade to this cut is formed by raising the point and dropping your hilt low to an inside guard, upon feeling your point borne out of the line, in which case the person who attempts the cut must also recover to an inside guard.

[85]

Cut VI. under the Sword.

When you are on the outside guard and your antagonist presents his point low, as before described, drop your blade smartly across his as if to make cut III. wrench his blade to the left, and then quitting it, turn the wrist and cut VI. under his sword across the body, recovering to the inside guard or to a hanging guard.

Unless this be well executed it is somewhat dangerous, especially if your antagonist suspect your design, and withdraw his blade or disengage; should he do that, you may spring back on the half circle guard the instant you lose the feel of it; or regain his sword by the circle parade.

This, as well as the preceding cut, will require practising alone with a sword, first dropping the point as in the half circle parade, and then making cut VI. and recovering to an inside or a hanging guard.

[86]

The parade to cut VI. thus given beneath the sword, must be made by raising your point and dropping the hilt low to an outside guard, on the instant you are borne out of the line. When the cut is thus stopped, the person who attempts it must also take an outside guard.

Although it is not to be supposed that in an attack at first a skilful antagonist will be very likely to present his blade and arm in the horizontal direction described in the two preceding lessons; nevertheless the method here recommended will prove useful, as a practice for improvement, in order to attain a celerity in returning a cut after having parried a thrust either by the *half circle* or *seconde* hanging guard.

-----

[87]

Cut V. over and within the Sword.

If at any time on the outside guard your antagonist holds his wrist too low, bear his blade a little out of the line, and turning the back of your blade to the back of his, cut V. above his sword across the neck, retreating as you cut.*

This must be parried by raising the hand quickly to a prime hanging guard.

Your antagonist having parried your cut by the hanging guard, your feeble will become opposed to his fort: unless you withdraw it very quickly, he may whirl your blade outwards, and make cut V. at your face, or thrust carte over the arm: if he attempts either, parry by the hanging guard, and return a thrust in seconde as he recovers.

* A similar cut to this may sometimes be effected against an inside guard, but as that is the strongest guard which can be held, will not often succeed.

[88]

The CUT at the ADVANCED LEG or THIGH.

This cut can seldom be made without considerable danger to the person who attempts it against a swordsman, as it must be always attended with an inclination of the body, and the head being thus brought forward, becomes exposed, even when the leg or thigh at which the stroke is directed, is removed out of distance.

It should never be attempted without previously diverting your antagonist's blade by a feint at the upper part of his position: and may afford variety of play to gentlemen in friendly assaults for mutual diversion, and will so far be necessary in order to attain the parade against it. The cut at the leg is generally preceded by a feint at the head; but this feint brings the antagonist to a St. George's Guard, on which almost every one retires the leg, in which case you must advance considerably to effect your cut.

The Consequence of not shifting the LEG.

Publish'd Sept.r 1. 1798. by H. Angelo N.º 11. Curzon Street. May-Fair.

Cut at the Right Knee[473]

[89]

In Plate XII. the assailant is supposed to have made a feint at the inside of his antagonist, who has parried to the feint, and again returned to the outside guard, but has neglected to withdraw his leg.

This cut will always be extremely hazardous with the sword in real contest, unless your antagonist advances his right foot by standing much too wide upon guard. Otherwise, in striking at his leg, your head and sword arm must become exposed even to a person wholly ignorant of the science; and his attention not being occupied by endeavouring to parry, his blow at the head would

---

[473] Keith's note: this image is taken from Thomas Rowlandson's posters for *Hungarian and Highland Broadsword*, illustrating Henry Angelo's system. The 1804 edition of Roworth's treatise includes an illustration very similar to this, showing a cut to the knee.

253

probably prove fatal, even though he received a cut on the leg at the same instant.

I must however observe that in attempting it a considerable degree of safety may be attained by raising the hand, as in the hanging guard, when cutting at the outside of the leg, and sinking the body behind the protection of the hilt; and, when cutting at the inside turning the wrist in the position of the spadroon guard. But to effect this requires a very great degree of practice and agility.

[90]

Having mentioned the dangers to which this attempt is liable, I shall now describe the method of executing it in the safest manner according to the opinion of an able writer on this science, without fear of its begin adopted rashly in a real contest.

"The first method is to parry an inside cut, and instead of returning an outside, step a little forwarder, sinking your body at the same time you transfer your weight from the left to the right leg, bring the point underneath your adversary's sword, and cutting swiftly at the calf of his leg, spring back as from a longe under cover of a St. George or hanging guard. This throw should never be used against a master of *timing*, for if he slip his right leg instead of parrying, he may cut you either on the head or arm.

"The second way of going down to the leg is by much the safest of the two, and is done by sinking the body very low at half sword under a St. George's guard, make a feint to the leg, recover to a St. George, feint to the leg again, then stopping

The Advantage of Shifting the LEG.

Published as the Act directs by H.Angelo, Curzon Street May 7th & September 1798.

Slipping a Cut at the Knee[474]

[91]

fully with a St. George go swiftly down to the leg, and spring off as before."

A very trifling reflection on the openings afforded to your adversary's point as well as his edge, by this manoeuvre, which the author stiles the *safest*, will certainly prevent its being too hastily adopted.

---

[474] Keith's note: this image is taken from Thomas Rowlandson's posters for *Hungarian and Highland Broadsword*, illustrating Henry Angelo's system. The 1804 edition of Roworth's treatise includes an illustration very similar to this, showing a fencer slipping to defend against a cut to his knee.

Parade against the Cuts at the Leg or Thigh.

If you are upon the inside or outside guard. At the instant your antagonist drops his wrist to make the cut, slip the right foot back to the left heel, and meet the inside of his sword arm with cut I, III, or V, if he cuts at the inside of your leg or thigh. Make cut II, IV, or VI, if he strikes at the outside. (See Plate XIII.)

Should you have any reason to suspect the offer at your leg to be only a feint, present your point opposite to the face of your antagonist, drawing in the sword arm a little on either an inside or outside guard, (according to which side your adversary may threaten) and retiring the leg. His intention may

[92]

generally be discovered by his inclining the head and body forward if he means to cut; and retaining them when only making a feint.

Some persons when they suspect the offer at the leg to be only a feint, present the point to the antagonist's face, and *extend* the sword arm, in order to prevent his advancing too close to be avoided by slipping the leg. This method must, however, be used with caution against a swordsman; for when you thus present your blade and arm horizontal, if your antagonist should strike his fort smartly against your feeble, he may beat your blade upwards and deliver a low thrust.

If you are upon the hanging guard, and your antagonist has advanced too near to be avoided by slipping the leg, drop your point so as to meet his edge with yours, retiring the leg in the manner above directed, and as soon as you have parried, make cut I. or II.

-----

[93]

BROAD SWORD SALUTE.

The modes of Saluting are various at different academies, according to the fancy of the teachers:– the following is taught by Mr. Taylor.

Draw swords – Inside guard – Take off your hat with left hand, and poise the sword to a very high inside guard; turn your face and edge to the left and then to the right – Drop your point and raise your hilt to the inside half-hanger, at the same time putting on your hat – Raise your point with a circle to the left, and bring the right hand across the chest so as to place the hilt of your sword in the left hand, the pommel between the two middle fingers – Extend the left hand to the rear, the back of the blade falling on the left shoulder, and advance the rear foot, presenting your right hand to your antagonist – Shake hands – Recover, seize the gripe of your sword with right hand, and come to outside guard.

-----

[94]

THE TEN LESSONS
TAUGHT BY
MR. JOHN TAYLOR,
Late Broad Sword Master to the Light Horse Volunteers of London and Westminster.

LESSON I.

Cut at my head – Guard your own.
Cut at my leg outside – Guard your head.

257

Cut at my head – Guard your own.
Feint at my leg – Guard your head.
Cut at my leg – Guard your head.

III.

Cut at my head – Guard your own.
Feint at my leg – Guard your head.
Cut at my leg – Guard your head.
Cut at my ribs.

[95]

IV.

Cut at my head – Guard your own.
Feint at my leg – Shift your own.
Cut at my head – Guard your own.

V.

Stand on outside guard; drop your point to the right, turning the inside of your wrist upwards – Parry my cut at your face with a high Inside guard.
Cut at my thigh outside – Guard your head.
Cut at my head – Guard your own.

VI.

Stand on an inside guard –
Feint outside at my face, and cut III. at my wrist.
Parry the thrust in carte with inside guard.
Cut at my head – Guard your own.
Cut at my head.

VII.

Cut at my head – Guard your own.
Cut at my arm outside – Guard your head.
Cut at my head – Guard your arm outside.
Cut at my head – Guard your own.
Cut at my ribs – Guard your head.
Cut at my head – Guard your ribs.

VIII.

Stand on outside guard –
Feint at my face inside, and cut at my arm outside – Guard your head.
Cut at my head – Guard your own.

IX.

Stand on an outside guard –
Feint inside, and cut at my arm outside – Guard your head.
Cut III. at my wrist – and parry carte with inside guard.

[97]

Cut at my head – Guard your own.
Thrust seconde – Guard your head.
Thrust seconde again – Guard your head.
Cut at my head.

X.

Cut at my head – Guard your face.
Cut at my arm outside – Guard your belly.
Cut at my face – Guard your head.
Cut at my breast – Guard your arm outside.
Cut at my belly – Guard your breast.

The following Lesson is intended for PRACTICE WITH THE SWORD, *upon the Principle on which the* EXERCISE AT THE TARGET *has been recommended in* PART I. *of this Work, and may be performed in Line, proper Caution having been first taken to open the Files sufficiently.*

Line, Half-face
Carry swords
Guard
Cut I. at head and recover to St. George's guard

II. at right cheek	-	Outside guard
III. at left cheek	-	Inside guard
IV. at right side	-	Outside half-hanger
V. at belly	-	inside half-hanger
VI. at knee	-	Shift-St. George
III. at wrist	-	Half-circle guard

Guard – Slope swords, Front.

* It will be proper to allow more space between each than may *at first* seem absolutely necessary; because the cuts are to be made on a longe, and learners are very apt to move the left foot, when stepping forward, or to shift their ground as they recover to guard.

This lesson is intended to impress on the mind the guard applicable to each cut, rather than to point out the succession in which cuts will follow each other when in contest.

[99]

REMARKS on the SPADROON.

The spadroon being much lighter than the broad sword, and made both to cut and thrust, is therefore a weapon well adapted to those gentlemen who are masters both of the small and broad sword, and unite according to circumstances the defensive and offensive movements of the two. In thrusting, the spadroon has an advantage over the broad sword, on account of the celerity with which that fatal movement may be executed, but in cutting it is much weaker in its effect.

The chief defensive position of the spadroon among the French, resembles the *seconde* hanging guard, except that the blade is held more horizontal, the point is directed at the antagonist's body about two inches below the arm-pit, and the wrist held on a level with the shoulder, instead of raising it high enough to view your adversary under the shell.

[100]

From this guard, by dropping the point to the inside or outside of your position, as in the *prime* or *seconde* hanging guard, you may parry any cut or thrust made below the neck. Cuts at the head are parried by the *St. George*, those made at the cheek and neck by raising the hilt to a *prime* or *seconde* hanging guard, as with the broad sword.

Much practice will be necessary to enable you to hold the sword in the position above described, without constraint or wavering, and to attain the *firmness* requisite for parrying, and a sufficient degree of *celerity* in striking or thrusting.

The left hand should be placed with the palm flat on the left hip bone, in order to preserve the balance. The center of gravity must be thrown on the left leg, and the feet placed as directed for the broad sword.

Although the above guard in *seconde* is that on which the most eminent French master place the chief dependence, and in which they principally instruct their scholars; yet the guards mentioned in

[101]

the preceding work for the broad sword, will be found equally useful, especially to those who cannot retain their arm a sufficient length of time in that posture.

In adopting the inside and outside guards to parry a thrust, remember to sink the hand rather lower than when opposing a cut at the arm, and keep your point presented to your adversary's face.

The *cuts* with the spadroon are made on a principle similar to those of the broad sword, except in the following instances. The weapon being lighter and the blade held more horizontal, the disengaging may be effected with a smaller circle described by the point, and the attack made more rapidly.

The mode of recovering from cuts I. and II. when you chance to miss the object at which your cut is directed, may be rather more in front than with the broad sword or sabre, instead of the blade swinging so much round to the outside or inside of your position, as is necessary with those weapons.

[102]

To facilitate this method of recovering, cuts I. and II. with the spadroon may be made with a circular direction; whereas the weight of the sabre renders it difficult to apply the edge unless the cut be made in a more direct line.

One cut *withinside* the arm seems indeed peculiar to the spadroon, since few have sufficient strength in the arm to effect it with the broad sword. It is thus performed; your antagonist being on the hanging guard, feint a thrust in seconde, and if he attempts to parry it with his feeble, turn your nails up without disengaging, and raising your point cut at the inside of his sword arm. This cut, if performed with spirit, is generally sure to disable; and is rendered safe, by your antagonist's feeble being occupied in a vain attempt to bear out your fort, which is brought against his feeble by your longeing forward as you raise your point. If he sinks his hand to parry with his fort, spring off with a cut at the upper part of his arm, on the outside.

The most eligible thrusts to be made with the

spadroon are those already recommended, p. 69, for the broad sword.– Those who wish to become perfect masters of the spadroon should however be acquainted also with the system of the small sword, on which there are already so many treatises published, that it is unnecessary to swell this work with further remarks on the subject.– That published by Mr. Angelo, intitled the School of Fencing, is indeed so clear and comprehensive, that it cannot be too much recommended to those who are desirous of attaining a just idea of that art, and yet may not be able to attend regularly to lessons from a fencing master.

In retiring from a superior force, the mode taught by the French of flourishing the weapon is stiled *a la debandade*, and consists in brandishing it in front of your position from right to left, turning the wrist up and down so as to lead with a true edge, the point described the figure ∞, the wrist held level with the shoulder. By this method an antagonist may be prevented advancing too fast upon you, as he must first stop the motion of your blade before he can safely attack, and the

next step you retreat again sets your weapon at liberty.

The practising this figure alone with the sword, will tend much to supple the wrist, and to give you a proper command of your weapon. It should be performed sometimes in the manner of cut I. and II. combined; at others as cut III. and IV. only in a direction more horizontal.

105

APPENDIX.

Opposing the Small Sword.

In contending with a broad sword against a small sword, your first object should be to disable your antagonist's sword arm is possible, keeping your body well back, and springing off at the instant he longes, far enough to remove your body from his thrust, cut at his arm. Be cautious not to make wide motions or to strike with too much exertion; and recover to your guard with your point well opposed to his face.

When you parry a thrust by the inside or outside guard, remember to sink the hilt lower than when opposed a cut.

If your antagonist disengages from an inside

guard, and thrusts below your wrist, follow his blade by dropping your point to the outside half-hanger, and having parried his thrust to the outside of your position, turn your wrist, and before he recovers from his longe cut V. beneath his blade. If from the outside guard he lowers his point to thrust beneath the hilt, parry with the half circle or prime parade, and cut VI. under his blade.

Should your antagonist be so near when on the above longe as not to allow sufficient sweep to give cuts V. and VI. with force; in that case, instead of striking, draw your sword swiftly across his body, retreating or traversing at the instant.

Observe that after parrying a thrust made at you with a small sword, your chief advantage lies in returning a cut without longeing forward, because your antagonist will always endeavour to recover from his longe with his point directed towards your body. This renders it necessary to confine your attack particularly to his sword arm, except when you may be able to beat his sword

[107]

first out of the line; otherwise if you longe eagerly to effect a cut at his head or body, you will rush on his point. If you have an opportunity of striking on the back of his blade, as he recovers from a longe, you may probably disarm him.

Opposing the Spadroon.

To oppose this weapon, you must be master of the parades against the thrusts (described p. 75 to 82,) since thrusting is a principal object with the spadroon. Should your antagonist's weapon be much shorter than your own, be always ready to spring off from an attempt to inclose, otherwise he will get within your point, and the length of your sword will prove a material disadvantage.

Many persons use the spadroon in a manner very similar to that already described for the broad sword, against those the guards and cautions before mentioned will be sufficient. I shall therefore only observe that in contending with such as depend on the guard in *seconde*, it will be best to

[108]

engage them with the hand in the position of the inside guard, the fort of your blade crossing above your antagonist's feeble, and your point about eight inches to the right of your line of defence, threatening the inside of his position.* At the same time sink on your knees, keeping your body well poised, and your left hand on your hip, but do not rest too much weight on your right foot, lest you should be unable to withdraw it, or to spring off, when necessary.

If your antagonist endeavours to thrust under your hilt, parry by sinking your hand on an outside guard. If he disengages under your hilt, your hand is already on an inside guard, and you have

265

only to raise your point to the left. If he disengages over your point, he must expose the inside of his position and sword arm.

* Your point would otherwise be opposed to your adversary's hilt, and both weapons in parallel lines, by which you would lose your principle of defence, which must always depend in a great measure on the cross your weapon forms to that of your antagonist.

[109]

In attacking the spadroon when held in *seconde*, the easiest cut to effect will be on the outside of the sword arm, first making a light feint at the head or inside of the face, but be careful not to make wide motions.

Another cut may be effected by attacking the feeble of his blade briskly with your fort, and beating it *downwards to the outside of his position*, then turn your wrist and cut VI. at his ribs, recovering to an inside guard.

The mode of commencing with a cut and finishing with a thrust (p. 73, 74,) will be found useful against this guard of the spadroon. If your antagonist holds his thumb on the back of the gripe, when on this guard of seconde, you may disarm him by making cut III. at the feeble of his blade. In perform this keep out of distance of a longe.

It will not be prudent to attempt beating the spadroon to the outside of your position, because your antagonist can easily slip from that beat and thrust at your inside; neither would I recommend

[110]

the broad sword hanging guard to be opposed to the spadroon, except merely to stop a cut, unless you are in considerable practice, and much accustomed to that guard; for the spadroon is so much lighter and swifter in its motions, that by repeated feints your arm will tire, and your antagonist soon gain an advantage from your not being able to answer his motions with sufficient celerity.*

* The hanging guard, with a long heavy sword, will not afford you so much real protection against the point of a determined adversary, as it may, at first view of the position be thought to do. This advantage arises from the ease with which he may attack your feeble and beat it out of the line of defence, by which he gains an opening to thrust carte, or low carte. To avoid this attack, you may raise your point with a circular motion over his blade at the instant he strikes at your feeble; and having thus slipped from his stroke, return a thrust in seconde, or a cut at his outside; should your blade be too heavy to effect this, spring off. If you are aware of his intention time enough, the best method of resisting his attack will be to drop your point and incline your hand towards the *prime* hanging guard, meeting his blow with your edge. In performing this do not make your motion too wide, nor bent your arm unnecessarily, lest your antagonist effect a cut at the outside of your arm.

[111]

Opposing the Musquet and Bayonet.

It will be in general best to parry the bayonet to the outside by dropping the blade across the barrel of the musquet, as in the outside half hanging guard, the back of your fort close behind the elbow of the bayonet. The purchase thus obtained will assist your stepping forward with the left foot to seize the barrel with the left hand, which being once effected, places your adversary's life in your power.

If you parry with the inside half hanger, the fort of your sword should be directed to the hollow of the elbow of your antagonist's bayonet, and you must step obliquely to the right with the right foot, advancing your left hand under the arch formed by your right arm to seize your antagonist's weapon.

In this method it is to be observed that although your parade may not have weight enough to beat the bayonet far out of the line of defence, yet by stepping about with your left or right foot, according to which parade you use, you change the line of defence, while your blade prevents your antagonist from withdrawing his weapon, or following your motion with his point.

Another method by which the thrust of a bayonet may be parried, is by opposing the fort of the bayonet with that o your sword on an inside guard, and beating the bayonet towards the left of the line of defence, seize it with your left hand. But in performing this, unless you are very quick, your adversary may deceive you by disengaging under the hilt of your sword.

Engaging with Sticks.

As it may happen that a gentleman may be compelled to defend himself with a common walking stick, against a ruffian who may presume on his skill in cudgel playing, the following hints may prove useful, in pointing out such deviations from the general system of broad sword as are requisite to be known in that case.

In a contest with sticks, if you parry with an inside or outside guard, you must endeavour to meet your antagonist's blow with your fort, rather more to the left or right of the line of defence, according to which side you are protecting than with a sword. By these means the recoil of the sticks will prevent the blow sliding down to your knuckles, and in proportion as you can stop your antagonist's blow wide of the line of defence, you obtain a greater opening to return it.

The hanging guard is however the most usual, and often the safest, as it affords more protection to the head and face, at which blows with a stick are generally directed. The only difference in holding this guard with a stick instead of a sword consists in directing the point about six inches towards the outside of your antagonist's right hip, instead of opposite his side; because the point of a stick is held stationary like the point of a sword, will not prevent his advancing; but on the contrary may be seized with his left hand.

Among cudgel players the blows from this position

[114]

are effected by a turn of the wrist differing from that used with the broad sword, the *large* knuckles of the hand (instead of the *middle* ones) being directed towards the object at which the blow is discharged, and turned downwards at the instant of making it. If the opponent springs off from a blow made in this manner, the general consequence to the assailant, is a strain of the wrist, or the loss of his stick Another material disadvantage in this mode of striking is, that unless they engage very close they cannot reach to his their antagonist.

When contending with a person who endeavours to advance for this purpose, receive his blows on your hanging guard, and return a thrust beneath his arm either at his face, right side, or belly, griping your stick very firm that your thrust may be of sufficient force; recover quickly to a hanging guard.

If you stand on guard with a stick previous to your antagonist making his attack, it is impossible to avoid presenting your knuckles as an object for

[115]

his cut, without some change of position, and the more correctly you are on guard (that is the less opening you leave at your head or body) the more probable will it become that he should select your hand as the part at which to direct his blow. To avoid giving him this opportunity, you must change repeatedly from the inside to the outside and hanging guards, threatening his face with your point in each motion, which will occupy his attention, and prevent his making such choice: or if you do not choose thus to become the assailant, but with that your antagonist should make the first attack, adopt the following:

Stand on a wide outside guard, your right foot advanced rather more than usual; this presents an opening at your head and inside; the instant he moves to seize this advantage, shut up the opening by dropping your point and raising your hand to an inside hanging guard, at the same time drawing back the right foot; which in all probability will remove you so far that his blow will fall to the ground, or sway his arm so much as to leave him exposed to your return.

[116]

Observe, that the hanging guard for the above purpose is not to be taken by raising the point first with a sweep and then dropping it; but by *instantly dropping the point, and raising the hand to the left*, and will require practice to execute it with strength and celerity.

Cudgel players seldom pay much attention to protecting the outside of their right arm or ribs. It will not however be safe to strike at their outside, except in returning a blow which you have just parried. If you commence an attack at that part, you will most probably receive a cut in the face at the same instant. The best method therefore is to receive and return a few blows on the hanging guard, and alternately intermix your play with cutting at the wrist and elbow, and thrusting, thus keeping them at a greater distance than they have been accustomed to; and if you can by this mode of attack induce them to defend their ribs, feint at their outside and throw at the head.

Very few cudgel players accustom themselves to longe at the time of striking, therefore if you can keep them at a proper distance, you will be out of their reach while they are within yours.

Should your antagonist succeed in rushing close up to you, notwithstanding all your endeavours to keep him at a proper distance, you may easily disarm him at the instant he closes.

If he advances on a hanging guard, oppose him with the same guard; lower your body by suddenly bending your knees, and pass your left hand under your right wrist, seize his stick, advance your left foot and knee behind his right, and dart the pommel of your stick in his face, striking up his right foot at the same instead.

Or as your opponent advances, you may thrust your left arm into the upper angle formed by the cross of your weapons, twine your arm around his, by passing your hand under his wrist and over his arm, and bear it downwards. Use your pommel and left foot as before.

If he advances on an outside guard, lay hold of

his stick with your left hand, and pull it downwards over your own, at the same time dropping your point and raising your weapon forcibly to the position of the seconde hanging guard.

There are other methods of disarming by advancing the left hand and foot, but these are the easiest and most readily executed, as they require only a previous reflection on the position, to enable a person to adopt them whenever there may be occasion.

FINIS.

Printed by C. Roworth, Bell-yard, Fleet-street.

Chapter 5: Salient Points for Study

It is not enough simply to read textbooks about fencing; to understand and learn properly, one must practise the steps, cuts and parries, preferably with a partner. Ideally you should train with a skilled and experienced teacher who can help to correct your mistakes and coach you to achieve excellence. Unfortunately, this is not always possible. Since many people who study historical Scottish swordsmanship do not have ready access to a fencing master from whom they can learn, the purpose of this chapter is to highlight some useful pieces of advice, so that readers have some idea of what is important to focus upon while practising.

The author of this book learned a lot of lessons the hard way; hopefully this chapter will help readers to avoid many of these mistakes, and it will facilitate successful, fun and healthy study of the historical source material.

5.1   Learning How to Strike

What could be simpler than performing a strike? It seems like such a basic thing to do, but in fact it is very complicated to do this correctly.

There is a huge difference between merely hitting toward someone and actually striking them properly. There are all kinds of mechanics involved in every motion; with some mechanics you can keep yourself safe even as you move forward to strike, and with other mechanics you can open yourself to all sorts of counter-hits, pain and injury.

One of the most important elements of Roworth's treatise is that he describes the striking mechanics explicitly. For example, he describes cut 1 as follows:

Motion 1. Turn your hand to A, the point of your sword to fig. 1.

Motion 2. Conduct the point from fig. 1. To fig. 4. taking care that the edge leads and the arm remains steady.*

Motion 3. Turn the wrist so as to bring the thumb downwards, the back of the hand and flat of the blade opposite yourself, and recover to the outside guard by bringing up the blade with a sweep clear of the inside (or front) of your position.

* The learner, I trust, will excuse my repeating the caution given in p. 20, that he must begin gradually. If he attempts to make the cuts rapidly and with force, before he attains the proper turn of the wrist by which the weapon is to be recovered, he will be liable to unpleasant accidents.[475]

Begin by assuming an outside guard. By studying the target in the treatise (reproduced below), it becomes clear that motion 1 requires the hand to move across the centre-line. Not towards the centre-line, nor onto the centre-line, but across the centre-line.

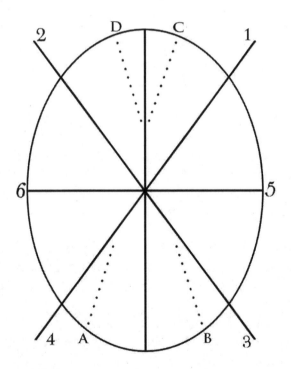

---

[475] Charles Roworth, 1804. Pages 24-25.

This motion also puts the point of the sword up high, ready to descend. Motion 2 brings the blade through the target, but only after the hand has crossed the centre-line to provide opposition and ensure your safety. Motion 3 describes how to recover your sword after the cut, returning to a useful guard position so that you may escape safely.

All three elements are of critical importance: enter safely, cut properly, and exit safely. Ignoring any one part of these instructions, taking a "shortcut", or using striking mechanics from other martial arts will result in an imperfect performance of the technique. With a sharp sword, this might mean you would not actually cut your opponent. In sparring, it might mean that you leave yourself vulnerable to receive a painful hit that could injure you.

Guy Windsor provides a very insightful piece of advice with regard to reconstructing historical martial arts:

> Execute all instructions *exactly* as written. This is the hard part. Any previous experience is likely to colour your interpretation. When you hear yourself saying "but surely he means *this*, not *that*," stop, go for a walk, and don't pick up the book again until you are ready to take it at face value.[476]

This is immensely importance advice. While you are learning a martial art from a historical source, even if you are a skilled martial artist yourself, you must do it "by the book". If you assume that you know better, then you will take shortcuts and will invariably make mistakes in performance and understanding that will set you back by months, if not longer.

I had a black belt in karate and some years of experience teaching longsword when I began to study Roworth's treatise. I assumed that I could develop a rough overview of the source material and then be able to perform well – I was wrong. Because I did not follow the information about striking mechanics, step by step, and because I did not follow Roworth's advice about starting slowly

---

[476] Guy Windsor. "Getting Started in Historical Swordsmanship." Brian Price, 2005. Page 32.

and carefully, I ended up damaging my wrist and giving myself an injury that took more than a year to heal. Had I followed the book and performed all instructions exactly as written, then I would have avoided this injury, and I would be almost a year ahead of where I am now in terms of understanding, training and performance.

If you follow the instructions given in the treatise, you will learn to strike properly with correct mechanics, gradually developing strength and stamina so that you will not damage your wrist. After that, you should learn how to strike with varying degrees of force: sometimes you need to strike softly and with immense control; sometimes you need the ability to hit hard and impart significant force.

Another piece of advice about mechanics that is not obvious in Roworth's treatise, but is necessary for correct performance of the strikes, is that your cuts should always move forwards with the blade. There are no "drawing cuts" where you pull the hilt back towards you to introduce a sawing or slicing motion; all the cuts are performed by slinging or pushing the blade in a forward direction. While this may be obvious for cuts 1, 2 and 4, it is not always obvious for cut 3, which is often very difficult to perform comfortably. Nonetheless, you must practise cut 3 as an action going forward, so that your arm ends up extended forward, angled up and to your inside, but not drawn back to your shoulder. Cut 3 does not end up in the spadroon guard or half-circle guard; it goes forward and takes threat to the opponent. This may be awkward, and it may be more comfortable to practise this cut as a drawing action, but that is not the correct way to perform this technique. Take your time, build the musculature and control of your arm to be able to perform this technique, and gradually build your ability to perform it swiftly and with power. As with everything, it is important to build the fundamentals before developing attributes such as speed and power.

The Highlanders could win duels and encounters by showing their skill and control of the situation, leaving their opponents with no doubt as to who was the better swordsman. It was not always important to kill, and indeed sometimes that was the wrong option; wounding was sometimes the better choice, or even managing to demonstrate skill without even drawing blood, as in this encounter between Serjeant Donald Macleod and Captain Macdonald:

> They met accordingly, without seconds, unaccompanied, and all alone, at a place appointed, nearly midway between the two armies. Macdonald pulled out a large canteen, willed with whiskey; and, before he should begin his attack on our hero, Donald, offered to drink with him. "No, the Devil a drop," said Donald, and calmly stood on his defence. Macdonald began; assailing Macleod with great fury, but with little skill. The Serjeant did not think that his life, or limb, was any object: he cut off his purse, and immediately demanded a parley.– "I have cut off your purse," said he, "is there any thing more I must cut off before you give up?" Macdonald acknowledged himself inferior in prowess to our Serjeant, and leaving his purse, in token of his inferiority, went back, with a very bad grace, to Marr's camp.[477]

However, the Highlanders were also known for the devastation that they could cause with their sword blows. James Browne described the aftermath of the Battle of Killiecrankie, and although his book was written 145 years later, his description is similar to many of the eye-witness accounts of the battle:

> On the morning after the battle – for night had thrown its sable curtain over the horrors of the scene, before the extent of the carnage could be ascertained – the field of battle and the ground between it and the river, extending as far as the pass, presented an appalling spectacle in the vast numbers of the dead which strewed the field, and whose mutilated bodies attested the savage and unrelenting ferocity with which Mackay's men had been hewn down by the Highlanders. Here might be seen a skull which had been struck off above the ears by a stroke from the broad-sword – there a head lying near the trunk from which it had been severed – here an arm or a limb – there a corpse laid open from the head to the brisket; while interspersed among these lifeless trunks, *dejectaque membra*, were to be seen broken pikes, small-swords and muskets, which had been snapt asunder by the athletic blows of the Lochaber axe and broad-sword.†

---

[477] William Thomson, 1791. Pages 39-40.

† In allusion to this battle, the author of the memoirs of Viscount Dundee, says, "Then the Highlanders fired, threw down their fusils, rushed in upon the enemy with sword, target, and pistol, who did not maintain their ground two minutes after the Highlanders were amongst them; and I dare be bold to say, that were scarce over such strokes given in Europe as were given that day by the Highlanders. Many of General Mackay's officers and soldiers were cut down through the skull and neck to the very breast; others had skulls cut off above their ears like night-caps; some soldiers had both their bodies and cross-belts cut through at one blow; pikes and smallswords were cut like willows; and whoever doubts of this, may consult the witnesses of the tragedy."[478]

It would be wrong to assume that you must always hit hard; it would be just as wrong to believe that you must always hit gently.

In the beginning, while you have relatively little protective gear other than a fencing mask, practising gently with your partners is a good idea. However, as you start to wear more safety equipment, such as forearm and elbow guards or a padded jacket, for example, you can increase the level of force with which you throw your strikes – within reason, of course. It is useful to practise striking with a higher level of force, so that your partners can learn to defend themselves against stronger attacks, but you should not increase your level of force until you have mastered the basics, and even then preferably under the specific instruction of a skilled and experienced teacher.

As you are developing the control of your body and of your sword to be able to land strikes with different (and planned) levels of force, you should also ensure that your cutting mechanics are correct. Edge alignment is immensely important; acceleration and body structure are more important than simply swinging and hitting hard. Not everyone has a sharp sword with which to practise cutting, nor the legal environment to allow such practice. Nonetheless, it is important to use good and correct cutting mechanics even with blunt replica swords, and edge alignment is always something worth working on to improve. Listen for a sharp

[478] James Browne. *History of the Highlands and of the Highland Clans*. Vol. II, part 1. Glasgow: A Fullarton & Co, 1834. Page 167.

"whooshing" sound when you make your cut through the air, to indicate that your edge is correctly aligned. If your cut produces a flat sound, as if you are displacing a lot of air, then it means you are striking with your flat and need to improve the alignment of your cut.

To summarise: first of all, when learning to strike, follow what the text says. Do not deviate, take shortcuts, or assume that you know better. Learn to control your strength and blade, but also learn to impart force effectively. Learn to work with edge alignment, and develop correct cutting mechanics.

Always start slowly, correctly and precisely. Ensure that your fundamentals are correct before worrying about speed and power. If you follow this advice, you will have a higher chance of developing correct historical fencing technique without injuring yourself. Correctness and precision are the virtues that you need to associate with your fencing; speed and strength are very useful attributes, but without correctness and precision, you will be wasting your time and that of your instructor and training partners.

5.2   Stance, Posture and Footwork

Students usually regard these concepts as boring and of little consequence. On the contrary, they are immensely important, and it is worth spending some time learning to do these properly.

Footwork can be the key to controlling a fight, striking your opponent without receiving any hits in return – obviously a very desirable state of affairs. Pay attention to Roworth's description of traversing backward, forward, and to the sides. The correct method of stepping is not just whatever comes naturally, it is worth reading his description of the mechanics and angles of the steps, and working to implement them in your practice.

Your stance and posture can be the difference between effective, comfortable fencing and messy, uncontrolled fencing that causes long-term damage to your joints.

Again, the best advice is to follow the information written in Roworth's treatise. Where you are told to place your weight on your back leg, do so. Yes, in modern fencing, people hold their weight in the middle between their legs, or even have their weight entirely over their front foot, ready for explosive forward actions. Yes, in other martial arts, people stand differently. That is irrelevant. In Roworth's method, the weight is held on the back leg, because this facilitates the kind of actions and movements found in his system. Follow the instructions and everything will fall into place.

Even if it seems incredibly boring, spend some time and attention looking at your stance and posture. Develop your balance and poise. Undertake appropriate exercises in flexibility so that you can hold your position or lunge as required. Improve your explosiveness, so that you can lunge and recover more swiftly. Obviously, the best way to do this is to consult a professional physical trainer or physiotherapist, but even asking your instructor for some basic suggestions will give you something to work on.

One of the most important things to develop is the necessary balance, flexibility and musculature to keep your knee directly above your ankle when you lunge. Many practitioners allow their leading knee to "collapse" inwards, placing a lot of stress upon the joint, which can lead to long-term damage. Training yourself to keep your knee directly above your heel when you lunge will be tiring and painful at first, but over time it will become natural. If you make this effort, you will enjoy a greater longevity of the knees than if you accept poor stance without corrective action.[479]

One method to help you keep your balance upon the lunge, and to keep control of the front knee, is to make short and controlled lunges rather than long, uncontrolled advances. Roworth cautions against excessively long lunges and recommends shorter, more controlled movements:

> Although an extensive longe is doubtless advantageous to those who can make it easily, yet it will not be found on a real occasion so necessary as a quick recover. For which reason it will be imprudent in gentlemen to accustom themselves to step farther out than their strength or activity naturally admit. Care must always be taken to place the right foot flat on the ground, and not to make so violent an extension, as to pitch on the heel of that foot.* The proper extent is to bring the left knee straight, and the right knee perpendicular to the instep.
>
> * It should be considered that in real contest the difference of the ground, and many other circumstances, concur to render any unnecessary extension hazardous; especially to such persons as have used themselves to practise on an even floor, perhaps with slippers chalked at the bottom.[480]

One of the objectives of lunging in modern Olympic fencing is to cover a large amount of distance very quickly. Roworth's lunge has a different objective, simply to carry the attack forward in a controlled fashion, ready for a controlled and swift withdrawal afterwards. By keeping the lunge controlled and not attempting to cover too much distance with the motion, you will have more

[479] Keith Farrell and Alex Bourdas. *German Longsword Study Guide*. Glasgow: Fallen Rook Publishing, 2013. Pages 27-28.
[480] Charles Roworth, 1804. Page 13.

success in training your stance and posture (and in looking after your knee) while remaining true to the system.

In terms of general posture, it is a good idea to take corrective action to reduce muscular imbalances,[481] such as anterior pelvic tilt (incorrect alignment of the pelvis)[482] and upper crossed syndrome (slouched shoulder posture)[483] amongst others. Again, it is worth consulting a professional to see what you should do to correct your posture and improve how you hold your body. It may take some amount of time and effort, but it is never a bad investment to improve your body and its carriage.

Your posture during fencing is also important. You need to remain balanced otherwise you risk falling over. That is an obvious example; a less obvious example is that you could go over on your ankle if you are not properly balanced, or your opponent may catch you flat footed and unable to move to a place of safety. If you decide to attack your opponent's leg and you lean forward too far, then you expose yourself to a counter-strike and will make it more difficult to recover safely to a guard position afterwards.

One final reason why it is important to work on your deportment is that the masters who wrote the textbooks we study thought that it was important. For example, in 1805, Thomas Mathewson wrote about the benefits that come from fencing with a good and careful upright posture:

---

[481] Alex Bourdas. "Muscular imbalances in the hip, part 2." *Encased in Steel*, 2013, accessed 2nd October 2014. http://historical-academy.co.uk/blog/2013/07/12/muscular-imbalances-in-the-hip-part-2/

[482] Alex Bourdas. "Muscular imbalances in the hip, part 1." *Encased in Steel*, 2013, accessed 2nd October 2014. http://historical-academy.co.uk/blog/2013/07/05/muscular-imbalances-in-the-hip-part-1/

[483] Alex Bourdas. "Upper Crossed Syndrome." *Encased in Steel*, 2013, accessed 2nd October 2014. http://historical-academy.co.uk/blog/2013/ 08/02/upper-crossed-syndrome/

It is the cultivation of this art that unfetters the body, strengthens it and makes it upright; it is it that gives a becoming deportment and an easy carriage, activity and agility, grace and dignity; it is it that opportunely awes petulance, softens and polishes savageness and rudeness, and animates proper confidence; it is it which in teaching us to conquer ourselves, that we may be able to conquer others, imprints respect, and gives true valour, good nature and politeness; in fine, which makes a man fit for society.[484]

It is beyond both the scope of this book and my qualifications to suggest physical exercises, so I shall not presume to give such advice. The best thing to do is to speak to a professional physiotherapist for further advice. Alternatively, you could read more about the issue online for yourself, but beware of websites giving poor, incorrect or out-of-date advice.

Whether or not you take steps to improve your general posture, you must ensure that you read the treatise and follow its instructions with regard to footwork, stance and posture. Do your best to reconstruct these fundamentals in the correct style, and be careful with your front knee when you lunge.

5.3   The Concepts of Line and Opposition

Roworth calls the centre-line the "line of defence", and defines it as: "a straight line supposed to be drawn through the center of your own body, and that of your adversary."[485]

If you yield the centre-line to your opponent then you give him an opportunity to thrust straight along it into you. Likewise, if you control the centre-line with your sword, then you have a good opportunity to thrust into your opponent.

When you make your strikes, following Roworth's advice, your hand needs to cross the centre-line when making cuts. This provides some amount of protection and "opposition" against your

---

[484] Paul Wagner and Mark Rector, 2004. Page 225.
[485] Charles Roworth, 1804. Page 41.

opponent's blade. It does not mean that you must make big, wide, sweeping motions; it means that you need to make small and subtle motions to position your hand on one side of the centre-line or the other, so that you benefit from the greatest amount of protection from your sword.

Two terms are very important to understand: "inside" and "outside". For a right-handed swordsman, the "outside" is anything to the right of your sword, and the "inside" is anything to the left of your sword. It is simple to remember this: you keep your organs inside your body, and when you stand in a fencing stance, your stomach faces to the left, so your insides are on your inside. If your opponent stands facing you, and you thrust "inside" his guard, you will thrust him in his insides; if you thrust "outside" his guard, you might catch him on his right shoulder or on the right arm: the outside parts of his body.

Wherever the sword moves, the concepts of inside and outside follow.

In the outside guard, with your sword held at your right hand side, your outside line should be "closed": it should not be possible for your opponent to hit you outside your guard. However, your entire body will be "open" inside your guard, which is not a problem: you may expect and plan for an attack towards your inside, since your outside is completely covered and defended by your sword.

In a similar fashion, when you move your sword across your body into the inside guard, then your opponent should not be able to hit the inside of your body because your inside line should be "closed". However, your entire body will be "open" outside your guard; it would be relatively easy to hit you on the outside of your right forearm, elbow and shoulder.

It is important to become familiar with the idea of "closing a line" and recognising when your opponent is "closed" or "open". If your opponent holds an outside guard, but you can still see and target his sword arm outside his guard, then his line is not quite closed: you can snipe his arm because he did not ensure his defence properly. Likewise, if he takes a hanging guard in prime (point sloping down to his left) but he does not lift his hilt high enough to defend his head, then he has not quite covered himself properly and so you may be able to hit him on the head even though he thought he was protecting himself.

A useful exercise is to practise in front of a mirror. Hold your guards and look to see if you are closing a line properly with your position. If you can still see part of your body above your hanging guard, outside your outside guard, or inside your inside guard, then you should improve your position so that you cover yourself correctly.

Another useful exercise is to work with a training partner who should be armed with a light thrusting weapon such as a smallsword or fencing foil. With your broadsword, assume your guard positions, and see if your partner is able to make a swift thrust and land a touch on the lines that are supposed to be closed, without you moving your sword any further to effect a parry. So, if you stand in an outside guard, your training partner should try to thrust into your arm or body outside your sword. If you close your lines correctly then this should be a very boring exercise and your training partner should not have any opportunity to land a thrust. If you leave yourself open, then he should have plenty of opportunity to stab you! Of course, make sure you are wearing appropriate protective gear for such an exercise, most definitely a fencing mask.

Commonly, the inside and outside are further subdivided into the "high line" and the "low line" on each side. The high line is anything higher than your sword hilt and the low line is anything below your hilt. With the broadsword, most actions (especially cuts) will be made to the high line; attacking the low line is very dangerous, because the action of doing so exposes your high line (particularly your head and sword arm) to a counter-cut by your opponent. In smallsword and other thrusting disciplines, the attacking the low line with a technique such as the flanconade can be of more value than similar techniques with broadsword.

The concept of "opposition" is relatively simple: whenever you make an offensive action such as a thrust or a cut, you "oppose" the fort (or stronger half) of your blade to the feeble (or weaker half) of your opponent's blade. This gives you some amount of control over the situation and some cover as you enter with a strike or thrust.

For example, if your opponent stands in the medium guard, his blade on the centre-line without actually closing any lines, you have a good opportunity to thrust or cut at him. However, if you simply thrust at him from your right, from the outside guard, without doing anything to provide opposition, he may make a thrust along the centre-line back at you and you will both suffer a double hit. However, from that same outside guard position, if you make your thrust by turning your hand into the inside guard going forwards, then your fort will make contact with his feeble as your point lands on his chest. This will prevent him from making a simple straight thrust along the centre-line and provides you with some measure of protection.

The concept of opposition is very important in thrusting-centric disciplines such as smallsword, and is also important with cutting weapons like the broadsword. If you do not cover yourself, if you do not close a line as you move forward, then you are open and liable to be hit. The striking mechanics of Roworth's system are designed to provide opposition as you cut, so it is valuable to spend time practising the mechanics exactly as described in the treatise.

A good exercise to practise the concept of opposition is to stand with a training partner, both of you engaging in the outside guard. It does not matter if your blades cross or not. Your partner gives you the signal to strike by moving from his outside guard to a medium guard; you react to the signal by thrusting in opposition: extend your arm with point towards his chest, turn your hilt towards his blade so that your fort comes towards his feeble, and lunge to land the thrust. You can do the same exercise from the inside guard by turning your hand to the outside guard as you thrust, providing opposition and cover.

Then, to develop the exercise (because broadsword is not primarily about thrusting), you should make a cut instead of a thrust. When engaging upon the outside guard, when your partner moves to the medium guard, perform a cut 1 exactly as described by Roworth: bring your hilt across the centre-line towards your opponent's blade, use your fingers to carry the blade forward in the cut, and lunge. This set of mechanics will oppose your fort to his feeble, and will give you some cover as you lunge with the cut. In a similar fashion, engage upon the inside guard, and perform a cut 2 when your opponent moves to the medium guard.

These exercises help to show why the medium guard is a useless position for defence, described as a "prepare to guard" position by Roworth due to its lack of protection.[486] It is very easy to take advantage of an opponent who uses the medium guard to engage. While simple, these exercises will help you to develop an understanding of opposition and its value in fencing with the broadsword.

You may find in the beginning that it is difficult to create opposition with your cuts when sparring, or that performing the techniques as described by Roworth might result in lighter, weaker hits. This is probably going to be the case, and in the early days of sparring you might find more success by ignoring opposition and by using incorrect striking mechanics. However, if you do let yourself ignore Roworth's advice, then you will plateau quickly, and you will be training bad habits into your muscle

[486] Charles Roworth, 1804. Page 15.

memory. It might be frustrating, it might be boring, but practising the basics as described in the treatise will pay great dividends over time.

5.4 Learning the Slip

When someone attacks to your legs, the appropriate response according to Roworth is to slip your leading leg back to meet your rear leg, rather than trying to lower your sword to make a parry. However, this is a skill that is easy enough to perform in drilling, but can be quite difficult to apply correctly in sparring.

A typical manner of practising the slip, seen in many clubs, is for students to pair up. One person is the attacker and the other is the defender. The attacker makes cuts to the defender's leg, to which the defender must respond by slipping back, perhaps making a simultaneous cut to the attacker's head or arm. However, this often falls into a rhythm, and it does not include enough other context to make the exercise helpful for sparring. People who practise this kind of exercise rarely have much success applying these skills in sparring.

A more sensible way to structure these drills is to simulate a sparring environment. In sparring, you have to be able to respond to attacks at any height, not just to the leg. So, to develop the drill to help make it a little more relevant, the attacker must be able to strike at other targets, not just the leg. A very basic way to simulate this situation is to give the attacker a choice of two attacks: a cut to the head or a cut to the leg. Thus the defender must prepare for any incoming cut, and cannot focus simply on slipping his leg against a low cut.

Gradually, the drill needs to become more and more like sparring. The purpose of the drill is of course to teach the student how to use the slip against a leg cut, but if it is too abstracted and too different to sparring, the skills learned will not be applicable in sparring. The exercise can begin in an abstract, basic fashion, to teach the fundamentals of the motion. However, to become relevant, it is important gradually to add more and more "noise" to the situation so that the student can learn to use the slip in a more realistic situation, until eventually it is quite natural to use the slip in the most realistic situation: sparring itself.[487]

The purpose of slipping the leg is to take it away from a potential strike, so that it remains safe. Therefore, even though it might be more tiring, you need to ensure that you move the entire leg and do not leave the thigh forward. This is a common mistake, when practitioners become a little lazy and do not make the effort to move the whole leg. Eventually laziness will be punished with a heavy and painful blow to the thigh.

It is worth paying attention to this movement, developing the skill to use it in sparring, and developing the discipline to do it properly every time.

---

[487] Sparring might not be the most realistic training that we can do, and there have been many long discussions online about precisely what we try to achieve with sparring, and how to simulate "a real fight". However, real life is complicated, and the most complex method for practising skills under pressure is usually sparring. The intention here is to make the skill useful and relevant for practitioners, not to debate the nature of "a real fight".

5.5 Using Taylor's 10 Lessons

The 10 lessons of John Taylor, included in Roworth's 1804 edition of *The Art of Defence on Foot*, provide a useful framework of exercises to help practitioners learn to use their weapon properly. This section will look at each lesson in turn, describing one possible interpretation of the movements, and suggesting the value and use of each exercise.

If you are not yet familiar with the guards, cuts, parries, thrusts and other terminology from Roworth's treatise, then it will be most helpful to read that before working through this section. Of course, it will be helpful to read this section before trying to work with Taylor's lessons at the end of Roworth's treatise. My suggestion is to read the majority of Roworth's treatise (pages 5 to 92 in the transcription, found in Chapter 4: *The Art of Defence on Foot* (1804) of this book) to learn the necessary terminology first. Then it would be best to read this section before diving straight into Taylor's lessons yourself. Of course, if you already know the techniques and terminology, then you should be able to tackle the lessons yourself without needing this input, although perhaps some of the observations and ideas written here will help you with your practice.

When working through these lessons, it is important to keep two things in mind.

Firstly, if you want your opponent to attack you, then you need to provide the opportunity and opening for him to do so. If you close your line or make a parry too early, or move ahead in the sequence too quickly, then your opponent will not have the opportunity or opening to attack; his attack will be half-hearted or incorrect, and you will lose the chance to learn to defend yourself correctly against a proper, committed attack.

Secondly, if you want your opponent to defend himself, you need to give him a reason to do so. If your attacks are always out of distance and cannot reach him, or if you attack the wrong part of his body, or if your execution is generally sloppy, then you will not provoke the right kind of parry from your partner. You will be hampering his development as a fencer as well as setting yourself up for failure.

It is always a good idea to work through lessons slowly at first, with emphasis on correctness, precision, and general perfection. Speed and power are irrelevant in the beginning. These attributes will develop over time, but if you focus on speed and strength without ensuring the correctness of your fundamentals, then you will struggle to keep yourself safe and you will become an inadequate fencer through your own neglect.

General Notes About the Lessons

With all of these lessons, precision, targeting and correctness are paramount. Each action should be accompanied by the correct footwork (lunging, slipping, recovering to guard) and both stance and posture should be functional and balanced. With enough practice, your stance and posture may even become elegant as you learn how to control your body.

It is pointless to leap ahead too quickly, moving from lesson to lesson because you think you have mastered them. I will not say that it will take months or years to master each lesson, because that is probably not true. It is possible to become skilful and competent in each lesson with a little competent practice. The key phrase, though, is "competent practice": if you skip through each lesson, paying little attention to your stance, posture and footwork, or to the precision of your attacks and parries, then you will gain nothing from the exercise and you may even learn careless bad habits. If you decide to practise one of these lessons, do so in a mature and sensible fashion, and give it the time and effort it deserves.

Once you think you have mastered a lesson, here are some questions to consider about your performance, to decide whether or not you have actually mastered it:

1) do you perform every single parry by meeting your opponent's feeble with the fort of your blade, or do you sometimes take the strike on your basket or on the middle of your blade?

2) if your opponent suddenly chose not to parry, would you land a perfect hit, or would you miss your target?

3) is your footwork "picture perfect", with discernable lunges and perfectly upright slips?

4) can you hear the whistling "whoosh" of your blade moving through the air, indicating good edge alignment? Or are you hearing more of a flat sound, as you force the flat of your blade against air resistance?

5) are you in complete control of your body throughout the exercise, or do you have to swing and pray at certain times in the hope that the swords end up where they are supposed to be?

6) are you able to attack immediately after each defence, so that there is no noticeable delay at all between parry and riposte?

7) are you attacking genuine openings, or are you attacking a parry that your partner has already prepared for you? Likewise, is your partner attacking genuine openings, or is he attacking parries that you have already prepared for him?[488]

8) if a third person watched your performance, would he describe it as "smooth", "effective" and "controlled"? Or would he describe it as "flailing", "desperate", "messy" or "uncontrolled"?

9) does your instructor still have something to say to help you perform the lesson better? If you are in the lucky position of having an instructor, and he doesn't think you have mastered the lesson yet, then there are probably still things that you could work on to improve your performance!

---

[488] Remember, give your training partner an opportunity to make his attacks without closing the line to early, and make sure your attacks give him a reason to parry and close his line.

Running through entire lessons from start to finish in a single long flurry of blows is probably not very helpful. You might find it much more useful to build the sequences gradually.

Start with the first attack and make sure it hits properly. This is "step 1" of the sequence.

Then add the first parry and riposte. This is "step 2" of the sequence. Practise step 1, step 2, step 1, step 2.

Then add the next parry and riposte. This is "step 3" of the sequence. Practise step 1, step 2, step 3, step 1, step 2, step 3...

And so on. Keep adding parry and riposte as the next step, and build each lesson in a stepwise fashion. Keep returning to step 1 and working through the sequence. If you just concentrate on and repeat step 3 or 4, then invariably your first few techniques are going to start feeling less important, you will pay them less attention, and they will not work properly to give reason and correct positioning for the later steps to fall into place comfortably. If you discipline yourself to return to step 1 and work through the lesson stepwise every time, then you will gradually build the fluency with the earlier steps that you need to be able to flow through to the later steps.

In terms of protective gear, you should always wear a fencing mask. This is an immutable rule. However, other protective gear is not always necessary; you can work through the sequences in just a fencing mask and a t-shirt, as long as you work in a friendly fashion with your partner.

Eventually, though, you need to start wearing more protective gear, such as a padded jacket, forearm and elbow guards for the sword arm, shin and knee protection for the leading leg. Without protective gear, you are limited in terms of how fast and hard you can strike each other, and therefore you will not learn how to defend yourself against faster, harder strikes. In order to learn to defend yourself properly (and to give your training partners the opportunity to learn to defend themselves properly), the level of speed and force will need to increase after the fundamental skills have been mastered, and therefore the amount of protective gear will need to increase commensurately.

It is necessary to test your skills under the pressure of greater force. You may find that when working in a friendly fashion with your partners, you can defend your head without a problem. However, you may find that when your opponents start trying to hit you swiftly and with force that you simply don't have enough structure in your parries to keep yourself safe. By increasing the strength and force of the strikes, you can realise your deficiency, and take steps to correct the problems in drilling before they become bigger problems (and potential injuries) in sparring.

Not all practice needs to be hard and fast, but nor should all practice be slow and gentle. Always conduct your activities at an appropriate level of impact and wear the appropriate amount of safety gear – and always wear a fencing mask, accept nothing less from yourself and your training partners.

Lesson 1

>Cut at my head – Guard your own.
>Cut at my leg outside – Guard your head.[489]

Both fencers stand in the outside guard.

The attacker throws cut 1 at the defender's head, on the lunge.

The defender parries this with the hanging guard, taking care to slip back with the front foot just in case, then ripostes with cut 1 on the lunge at the attacker's head.

The attacker parries this with a high inside guard, taking care to slip back with the front foot just in case, then makes a low cut 2 on the lunge at the outside of the defender's thigh or knee.

---

[489] Charles Roworth, 1804. Page 94.

The defender attempts to parry an incoming strike to head with the outside guard (because that is the most likely response), taking care to slip back with the front foot just in case. Because the actual cut 2 is aimed at the leg, rather than the head, the outside guard will not parry the strike. The slip allows the defender to remain safe, even though his parry fails. He then throws cut 1 on the lunge at the attacker's head.

The attacker slips back and parries this with either a hanging guard or a St. George's guard.

Observation: even in this very first lesson, slipping with each parry is an important feature. Both fencers should make a point of lunging with proper extension, but should also pull back properly with a slip on each recovery to guard.

Observation: the strike to the leg is not the first action in the sequence. The first action is instead a cut to the head, followed up by a low strike. It is silly to use low strikes to begin an engagement, but they can be useful later in a sequence.

Observation: both fencers should try to hit with each strike. As described above, make sure that you give your opponent a reason to defend himself when you attack, but also make sure that you give your opponent an opportunity to attack you before you make your parry. If you hurry ahead and close a line before he cuts at you, then the right thing for him to do is to cut at one of your other openings. Follow the sequence as described, take it in turns as described, and ensure that each part of the sequence makes sense and follows logically.

Lesson 2

> Cut at my head – Guard your own.
> Feint at my leg – Guard your head.
> Cut at my leg – Guard your head.[490]

This is similar to lesson 1, with a development halfway through.

Both fencers stand in the outside guard.

The attacker throws cut 1 at the defender's head, on the lunge.

The defender parries this with the hanging guard, taking care to slip back with the front foot just in case, then ripostes with cut 1 on the lunge at the attacker's head.

The attacker parries this with a high inside guard, taking care to slip back with the front foot just in case, then makes a low cut 2 on the lunge at the outside of the defender's thigh or knee.

The defender attempts to parry an incoming strike to head with the outside guard (because that is the most likely response), taking care to slip back with the front foot just in case. Because the actual cut 2 is aimed at the leg, rather than the head, the outside guard will not parry the strike. The slip allows the defender to remain safe, even though his parry fails. He then throws cut 1 on the lunge at the attacker's head.

Development: the attacker stays exactly where he is, without slipping back, and parries this with either a hanging guard or a St. George's guard. He then cuts straight from this parry, making a low cut 1 (without taking any further steps) at the inside of the defender's thigh or knee.

The defender slips back as swiftly as possible, covering the torso with an inside guard in case the attacker targets his torso. The attacker has made a low cut, so the parry does not connect, but

---

[490] Charles Roworth, 1804. Page 94.

the slip keeps the defender safe once more. He throws a cut 2 on the lunge at the attacker's head.

The attacker slips back under cover of a high outside guard or St. George's guard.

Observation: the point where lesson 2 develops from lesson 1 is when the attacker makes his strike to the defender's leg – the first leg cut is not the action that is intended to hit him (although it would be nice if that happened), the second leg cut is the intended hit. By lunging on the first leg cut, then remaining in place during the parry and the second leg cut, the attacker is able to work quickly, forcing the defender to move his leg extremely swiftly to slip out of danger.

Observation: even if the second leg cut hits the defender, he should still make the final cut 2 to the attacker's head, and the attacker should still slip back under cover to defend against this. Not every hit is a killing or disabling blow, and so it is good to practise keeping yourself safe in the event that your cut has not been entirely successful.

Lesson 3

> Cut at my head – Guard your own.
> Feint at my leg – Guard your head.
> Cut at my leg – Guard your head.
> Cut at my ribs.[491]

This is similar to lesson 2, with a development at the end.

Both fencers stand in the outside guard.

The attacker throws cut 1 at the defender's head, on the lunge.

---

[491] Charles Roworth, 1804. Page 94.

The defender parries this with the hanging guard, taking care to slip back with the front foot just in case, then ripostes with cut 1 on the lunge at the attacker's head.

The attacker parries this with a high inside guard, taking care to slip back with the front foot just in case, then makes a low cut 2 on the lunge at the outside of the defender's thigh or knee.

The defender attempts to parry an incoming strike to head with the outside guard (because that is the most likely response), taking care to slip back with the front foot just in case. Because the actual cut 2 is aimed at the leg, rather than the head, the outside guard will not parry the strike. The slip allows the defender to remain safe, even though his parry fails. He then throws cut 1 on the lunge at the attacker's head.

The attacker stays exactly where he is, without slipping back, and parries this with either a hanging guard or a St. George's guard. He then cuts straight from this parry, making a low cut 1 (without taking any further steps) at the inside of the defender's thigh or knee.

The Consequence of not shifting the LEG.

Publish'd Sep.t 1, 1798. by H. Angelo N.º 9. Carvin Street May-Fair.

The defender slips back as swiftly as possible, covering the torso with an inside guard in case the attacker targets his torso. The attacker made a low cut, so the parry does not connect, but the slip keeps the defender safe again. He throws a cut 2 on the lunge at the attacker's head.

Development: The attacker slips back under cover of a high outside guard or St. George's guard. If the outside guard is used, the attacker should then lunge forward with a cut 5 across the inside of the defender's torso. If the St. George's guard was used, then the attacker should lunge forward with a cut 6 into the outside of the defender's ribs.

Observation: In the same fashion as before, even if the second leg cut hits, the defender should make his "afterblow" to the attacker's head. The attacker should defend himself competently, then make another cut into the defender's torso. A fight is not over until the opponent stops fighting, or until the referee calls halt, so it is a useful skill to be able to continue fighting and making further attacks even after landing a hit successfully.

Lesson 4

> Cut at my head – Guard your own.
> Feint at my leg – Shift your own.
> Cut at my head – Guard your own.[492]

This is similar to lesson 2, with a development in the middle.

Both fencers stand in the outside guard.

The attacker throws cut 1 at the defender's head, on the lunge.

The defender parries this with the hanging guard, taking care to slip back with the front foot just in case, then ripostes with cut 1 on the lunge at the attacker's head.

---

[492] Charles Roworth, 1804. Page 95.

The attacker parries this with a high inside guard, taking care to slip back with the front foot just in case, then makes a low cut 2 on the lunge at the outside of the defender's thigh or knee.

The defender attempts to parry an incoming strike to head with the outside guard (because that is the most likely response), taking care to slip back with the front foot just in case. Because the actual cut 2 is aimed at the leg, rather than the head, the outside guard will not parry the strike. The slip allows the defender to remain safe, even though his parry fails.

Development: Rather than throwing another cut 1 on the lunge at the attacker's head, the defender uses this opportunity to make a leg cut himself, making a low cut 1 at the inside of the attacker's thigh or knee.

The attacker cannot stay where he, so he must slip back under cover of a hanging guard. After he evades the defender's leg cut, he throws a cut 1 or cut 2 on the lunge at the defender's head.

The defender slips back under cover of a high inside guard (against cut 1) or high outside guard (against cut 2). He then ripostes with his own cut 1 or 2 on the lunge at the attacker's head.

The attacker slips back and parries in a sensible fashion, opposing the fort of his blade to the incoming feeble of the defender's blade.

Observation: after some practice, it becomes less relevant precisely which guard you use to defend yourself against cuts. As long as you oppose the true edge of your fort to your opponent's feeble, in a comfortable yet structured fashion that closes the attacked line, you will be safe. You could go back and practise these first four lessons with different parries, and it should not make too much difference to your safety as long as you follow these rules. You may find that some ripostes become easier or more difficult from the different positions, and that is useful information to gain from experimentation.

Lesson 5

> Stand on outside guard; drop your point to the right, turning the inside of your wrist upwards – Parry my cut at your face with a high Inside guard.
> Cut at my thigh outside – Guard your head.
> Cut at my head – Guard your own.[493]

This is somewhat different to previous lessons.

Both fencers stand in the outside guard.

The attacker throws cut 1 on the lunge at the defender's head. He prepares to do this by dropping his point down to his right side, rather than moving his point to the inside; in other words, he performs a moulinet, but in a different and less intuitive fashion than before.
The defender parries with a high inside guard, then ripostes instantly, lunging with cut 2 at the attacker's outside cheek.

The attacker slips back, trying to maintain blade contact, lifting his point and pulling his hilt to his inside, forming an inside guard that carries the incoming cut 1 away from the face. If this is successful, he then ripostes with a low cut 2 at the outside of the defender's thigh.

The defender attempts to parry an incoming strike to head with the outside guard (because that is the most likely response), taking care to slip back with the front foot just in case. Because the actual cut 2 is aimed at the leg, rather than the head, the outside guard will not parry the strike. The slip allows the defender to remain safe, even though his parry fails. He then throws cut 1 on the lunge at the attacker's head.

The attacker slips back and parries this with either a hanging guard or a St. George's guard. He ripostes with a cut 1 on the lunge to the defender's head.

---

493 Charles Roworth, 1804. Page 95.

The defender slips back under cover of a high inside guard. He then ripostes with his own cut on the lunge at the attacker's head.

The attacker slips back and parries in a sensible fashion, opposing the fort of his blade to the incoming feeble of the defender's blade.

Observation: this lesson can become messy quickly you allow yourself to make big sweeping motions coming from cuts to the hanging guard and from the hanging guard to new cuts. Motions should remain tight and controlled throughout. If the performance becomes messy, slow it down and work towards correctness and precision again.

Observation: the first part of this exercise can be rather difficult. The defender has to be swift off the mark, making his initial inside guard parry and then shooting out with cut 2 to the attacker's outside cheek. The attacker must then be very swift off the mark to pull his cheek away from danger and to make his own parry. The important part of this parry is to try to maintain blade contact, turning the sword into an inside guard with the point upward. This should be practised carefully and precisely until you understand the motion and can perform it correctly, and only then should the speed be allowed to increase.

Observation: this is an interesting sequence because it starts with a complicated action and then continues with simple actions. If you do try something complicated in sparring, be prepared to continue with simple actions afterwards, or at least be prepared to withdraw quickly if it doesn't work. The more familiar and comfortable you become with pulling back into a hanging guard and riposting immediately, the easier you will find it to keep yourself safe while landing hits on your opponents in sparring.

Lesson 6

> Stand on an inside guard –
> Feint outside at my face, and cut III. at my wrist.
> Parry the thrust in carte with inside guard.
> Cut at my head – Guard your own.
> Cut at my head.[494]

This is a little similar to lesson 5, in that it starts with a complicated action, then finishes with standard, simple actions.

Both fencers stand in the inside guard.

The attacker feints cut 2 on the lunge at the outside of the defender's face. Make sure this is a good strike: the plan is to draw a parry, so it has to look real. If your opponent does not parry, then you should take this opportunity to hit him with your cut 2.

The defender parries with a high outside guard.[495] A hanging guard in seconde would also suffice, but will make the rest of the sequence more difficult for the defender.

The attacker uses this opportunity, having drawn a parry from the defender, to abandon his feint and perform a cut 3 to the inside of the defender's wrist.[496]

The defender then has two options. The simplest is to turn the deceived outside guard into an inside guard. The more complicated option for a more advanced student is to attempt the

---

[494] Charles Roworth, 1804. Page 95.

[495] When practising this sequence, the defender should sometimes make the parry, but sometimes stand still. It is therefore up to the attacker to make a good attack that will hit the defender's head unless the defender makes his parry.

[496] As discussed in chapter 5.1: Learning How to Strike, it is important to perform cut 3 by striking forward with the blade, not drawing the sword backward in a drawing, slicing cut. If you draw the sword back then you may not actually make any contact with your opponent's wrist, and even if you do, you probably won't do any damage to him. If you perform cut 3 correctly by slinging the blade up and forward, then you will make contact and have a better chance of delivering a "proper" cut into him.

half circle guard, whereby the defender dips his point outside to his right, drawing his hilt over to his inside in front of his left shoulder (blade turned slightly up and to the left), allowing his blade to hang downwards in front of him, interposing his blade in the half circle guard between his wrist and the incoming cut 3 from the attacker.[497]

If the student is not technically adept enough yet to be comfortable working with the half circle parry, then an inside guard is eminently adequate and suitable for this defence.

Note: in the 1799 poster *The Guards and Lessons of the Highland Broadsword*, Angelo provides some brief instructions for each of his ten lessons, which are very similar to Taylor's lessons. Although Taylor's sixth lesson differs from Angelo's, the first two lines are similar. Angelo writes that the defender responds to the feint with a high outside guard, then specifies that the cut at the inside of the wrist should be stopped with a half circle parry.

Half Circle Parade

---

[497] This parry with the half circle guard is described on page 52 of Roworth's 1804 treatise.

The defender then performs the "thrust in carte" by turning his point towards the "inside of the upper part of the body, with the nails upward, and the edge of the sword turned rather upward to the left and well opposed towards your antagonist's weapon by keeping your pommel opposite your left temple at the time of longeing."[498]

If the defender parried in the inside guard before making the thrust, then the attacker should drop his hilt and lift his point, coming into an inside guard, so that the defender's thrust in carte is guided safely to the side. Once the thrust is safely parried, the attacker should riposte smartly with a cut 2 on the lunge at the defender's head.

If the defender used the half circle parade before making the thrust, then the attacker should likewise respond by lifting the hilt of his sword to his left shoulder and pushing the blade across the body, finishing in a half circle guard. Once the thrust is safely parried, the attacker should riposte smartly by circling the point of his sword across to his right and upwards, letting the sword fall into a neat cut 2 on the lunge at the defender's head.

The defender should parry in an appropriate fashion, slipping as required, and riposte with an appropriate cut to the attacker's head.

The attacker should recover under guard, opposing his fort to the defender's feeble, then riposte one final time to hit the defender in the head.

Observation: this sequence contains the first example of a thrust in action. Normally, parries against a cut should have the point high directed away from the attacker, creating a better and stronger cross, but making a thrust a less advisable option for riposte. In the half circle guard, defending against the cut to the inside of the wrist, the point of the sword is more or less forward and aimed at the opponent already, so a thrust is a more appropriate riposte from this parry than a cut. A good general

---

[498] Charles Roworth, 1804. Pages 69-70.

lesson is that the riposte should always be a fast and easy motion from the parry; a difficult riposte will usually be too slow and awkward to be effective.

Lesson 7

> Cut at my head – Guard your own.
> Cut at my arm outside – Guard your head.
> Cut at my head – Guard your arm outside.
> Cut at my head – Guard your own.
> Cut at my ribs – Guard your head.
> Cut at my head – Guard your ribs.[499]

This sequence is full of relatively standard actions, but it will require some dexterity and stamina to perform the entire sequence rapidly with precision.

Both fencers stand in the inside guard.

The attacker makes cut 2 on the lunge at the defender's head.

The defender parries with a high outside guard, and ripostes with a vertical cut down onto the crown of the attacker's head.

The attacker parries with a high outside guard, then ripostes with a vertical cut targeted at the outside of the defender's arm.

The defender parries with a lower outside guard (opposing fort to feeble), then ripostes with a cut 1 at the inside of the attacker's face.

The attacker parries with a hanging guard then ripostes with cut 2 on the lunge at the defender's head.

The defender draws back with a high outside guard, then ripostes with a vertical cut at the outside of the attacker's arm.

---

[499] Charles Roworth, 1804. Page 96.

The attacker pulls back his arm in an outside guard, then ripostes with cut 1 at the defender's head.

The defender parries with a hanging guard, then ripostes with cut 1 at the attacker's head.

The attacker parries with a high inside guard, then ripostes with cut 6 at the defender's ribs.

The defender draws back and parries with a low hanging guard in seconde (or an outside half hanger). From this position, he brings his point to his left, circles it upwards then strikes down towards the attacker's head with cut 2 on the lunge.

The attacker parries with a high outside guard, then ripostes with cut 1 at the defender's head.

The defender parries with the hanging guard, then ripostes with cut 6 at the attacker's ribs.

The attacker parries with a low hanging guard in seconde (or an outside half hanger).

Observation: the main benefit of this lesson is to be able to parry and riposte very quickly, sometimes from awkward situations. The ability to parry securely and riposte swiftly cannot be underestimated.

Observation: this is not a simple sequence. Therefore, it is imperative that it is built up gradually. It would be sensible to practise the first few movements by themselves, and gradually build the complexity and length of the sequence over the course of a training session. With roughly 13 steps, each step usually consisting of a parry and a riposte, there are a lot of individual steps to learn; develop the exercise gradually, rather than trying to cram it all in at once!

Observation: this is not a good exercise for beginners as it will be more confusing than helpful. For beginners, work with just the first three lines OR the last three lines. These will be lessons of a manageable length, and will still teach a useful skill (attacking/defending the arm in the first half of the lesson, or attacking/defending the ribs in the second half), without becoming too difficult as one massive sequence.

Observation: if precision, correctness and control are not exercised diligently in the practice of this lesson then very quickly the activity will become pointless. You must insist on good behaviour from your training partners, and work at a speed whereby you can train each movement correctly. If you start flailing or becoming messy, then slow down and work on your precision and correctness again.

Lesson 8

> Stand on outside guard –
> Feint at my face inside, and cut at my arm outside
> – Guard your head.
> Cut at my head – Guard your own.[500]

This sequence is shorter and easier than lesson 7, returning to the concept of feinting.

Both fencers stand in the outside guard.

The attacker feints cut 1 on the lunge at the defender's head, with the intention either to hit or to draw a parry.

The defender attempts to parry in the inside guard.[501]

The attacker should redirect his cut, pulling the blade around to make cut 2 at the outside of the defender's arm.

The defender should parry in the outside guard, then riposte with cut 1 to the attacker's head.

---

[500] Charles Roworth, 1804. Page 96.
[501] But sometimes, deliberately, should not parry, ensuring that the feint must be a real attack and not just a vague waving action.

The attacker should parry with the hanging guard, then riposte with cut 1 to the defender's head.

The defender should likewise parry in the hanging guard and riposte with cut 1 to the attacker's head.

The attacker should recover under the hanging guard or St. George's guard and ensure his own safety.

Observation: this is a relatively useful lesson, beginning with a feint, and finishing with a flurry of hanging guards and descending strikes if the intended action fails.

Lesson 9

> Stand on an outside guard –
> Feint inside, and cut at my arm outside – Guard your head.
> Cut III. at my wrist – and parry carte with inside guard.
> Cut at my head – Guard your own.
> Thrust seconde – Guard your head.
> Thrust seconde again – Guard your head.
> Cut at my head.[502]

This sequence involves a lot of thrusting as a riposte after a parry.

Both fencers stand in the outside guard.

The attacker feints cut 1 on the lunge at the defender's head, with the intention either to hit or to draw a parry.

The defender attempts to parry in the inside guard.[503]

The attacker should redirect his cut, pulling the blade around to make cut 2 at the outside of the defender's arm.

---

[502] Charles Roworth, 1804. Pages 96-97.
[503] But sometimes, deliberately, should not parry, ensuring that the feint must be a real attack and not just a vague waving action.

The defender should parry in the outside guard, then riposte with cut 1 to the attacker's head.

The attacker should parry in the St. George's guard, then riposte with cut 3 to the inside of the defender's wrist.

The defender should parry with an inside guard. Then, maintaining blade contact, he should "thrust in carte" by turning his point towards the "inside of the upper part of the body, with the nails upward, and the edge of the sword turned rather upward to the left and well opposed towards your antagonist's weapon by keeping your pommel opposite your left temple at the time of longeing."[504]

The attacker should drop his hilt, lift his point, try to maintain blade contact, and slide his fort to the feeble of the defender's sword, carrying the defender's thrust safely to the side by way of an inside guard. He should then riposte with a swift vertical cut on the lunge at the defender's head.

The defender should slip back and parry with a high inside guard, then riposte with cut 2 at the attacker's head.

The attacker should parry with a St. George's guard, then riposte with a thrust in seconde. This should be performed by bringing your point towards the defender's body, "with your nails downward [the hand in pronation, the back of the hand facing upward], the edge of your sword turned to the right and opposed towards his blade."[505] The target for a thrust in seconde is below the opponent's sword arm; so the point needs to dip slightly, ready to be thrust home. The sword should be brought into the correct position, then the arm should be extended, and only then should the lunge be performed.

The defender should parry with an outside guard, then riposte with cut 1 to the attacker's head.

---

[504] Charles Roworth, 1804. Pages 69-70.
[505] Ibid. Page 70.

The attacker should slip back, parry in the St. George's guard again, then perform another thrust in seconde in exactly the same fashion as before.

The defender should parry with a hanging guard, then riposte with any descending cut to the attacker's head.

The attacker should slip back and make an appropriate parry, opposing fort to feeble, then make an appropriate riposte at the defender's head.

Observation: after making cut 3, the attacker may need to disengage his blade temporarily in order to form an inside guard. Depending on the relative sizes of the combatants, this may be an easier or more difficult action to perform. It is important to begin by withdrawing the leg and recovering backwards, giving some time and space for the disengagement and re-engagement in guard. If you begin with the arm motion and let the leg move last in this recovery, then the incoming thrust may well land before you manage to form your guard correctly.

Observation: when performing the thrusts in seconde, the attacker needs to control the engagement before he tries to thrust. If he simply shoves his point forward, without first opposing fort to feeble, then the thrust will probably go wide and will almost certainly not work. First things first: secure your safety with a good parry. Next, secure your continued safety by opposing fort to feeble. Discipline yourself and do not lunge just yet. Once your fort opposes the defender's feeble, then straighten your arm, extending your thrust towards his body. Then, and only then, you lunge.

Observation: the two occurrences of the thrust in seconde show that this action can be a parry and riposte against any descending cut. As long as the hilt of your sword is on your right side when you make your parry, you can bring your sword into the position ready for the thrust and then deliver the thrust with relative ease. The thrust in seconde becomes impossible when you parry with your hilt on the left side of your body, or if you make the parry with the feeble of your own sword – for example, if you parry in the hanging guard, and do not oppose fort to feeble correctly, then you will have difficulty transporting the opponent's blade into the right place for you to make your thrust in seconde. If you always catch the incoming attack on the fort of your blade, then you have the option of working with a thrust as a riposte.

Observation: this is not an easy sequence, so beginners should tackle it gradually, working on just two or three lines at a time. The emphasis should be on perfect execution throughout, with all the oppositions of fort to feeble in the right place and at the right time, and technical correctness is a must.

Lesson 10

> Cut at my head – Guard your face.
> Cut at my arm outside – Guard your belly.
> Cut at my face – Guard your head.
> Cut at my breast – Guard your arm outside.
> Cut at my belly – Guard your breast.[506]

This sequence is similar to lesson 7, in terms of performing several parries and ripostes in quick succession.

Both fencers stand in the outside guard.

The attacker makes cut 1 on the lunge at the defender's head.

The defender parries with the hanging guard and ripostes with cut 1 at the attacker's face.

The attacker parries with a high inside guard, then makes cut 4 at the underside and outside of the defender's elbow.

The defender slips back with an outside guard (opposing fort to feeble), and ripostes with cut 5 to the attacker's belly.

The attacker lifts his basket to shoulder height and pulls his point back towards him, turning his true edge to his left, parrying with

---

[506] Charles Roworth, 1804. Page 98.

an inside half hanger. He then lifts his point up and to the left, coming out of the guard with a cut 1 riposte to the defender's face.

The defender slips back and parries with a hanging guard, then ripostes with cut 1 to the attacker's head.

The attacker parries with a hanging guard and ripostes with cut 5 to the defender's breast.

The defender parries with an inside guard, then makes cut 4 to the underside and outside of the attacker's arm.

The attacker slips back and parries with an outside guard, the ripostes with another cut 5 to the defender's stomach.

The defender parries with an inside guard, then thrusts in carte at the attacker's breast.

The attacker slips back, maintaining blade contact, parrying with an inside guard to ensure his safety.

Observation: the defender's final action could also be a cut, but this would be awkward from the inside guard. If he parried the cut 5 to his stomach with an inside half hanger, then he would be able to whip his blade around and make a cut rather than a thrust. Both actions are equally acceptable ripostes, depending on the situation.

Observation: this lesson plays with different heights of attack on the torso: the top of the head, the face, the breast and the stomach. It is important to be precise with your targeting, so that your opponent has to place his parry correctly. This is an excellent exercise in precision in terms of parrying with your fort, rather than relying on your basket to defend your hand.

Comparing Angelo's and Taylor's Lessons

More detailed comparison of the lessons by Angelo (from the poster *The Guards and Lessons of the Highland Broadsword* in 1799) and Taylor shows that in general they are very similar. Four of the lessons are exactly the same, the rest have some differences.

In lesson 1, Taylor specifies a cut to the outside of the leg, whereas Angelo merely instructs a cut to the leg.

In lesson 4, Taylor specifies that the cut to the leg should be a feint.

In lesson 5, Taylor specifies a cut to the outside of the leg, whereas Angelo merely instructs a cut to the leg. Taylor adds an additional parry to the end of the sequence.

Taylor's lesson 6 begins in a similar fashion to Angelo's, but then develops completely differently. Either Taylor departed from the standard lesson, or Angelo modified the lesson over time.

Taylor's lesson 9 is quite different to Angelo's. Taylor modifies it heavily by adding several additional steps, including thrusts.

Taylor's lesson 10 is virtually the same as Angelo's, although he changes the order of attacking to the head and the belly.

It seems that Angelo provides more material describing and illustrating how to perform the lessons than Taylor. It may be most helpful to refer to Angelo's lessons first, and then to practise Taylor's variations upon them. Angelo was certainly the originator of these lessons; it is most likely that Taylor had to learn them when Angelo's method became the regulation method for broadsword, and that over time he modified how he taught them.

Regardless of whether you study Angelo's or Taylor's lessons, practising these sequences will be beneficial, as long as you bear in mind the advice and notes from earlier in this chapter.

5.6 Introducing Sparring

How do you introduce sparring to your students or to your fellow practitioners?

You could simply put on your masks and start fighting ... or you could do this intelligently, and make it a valuable part of your training.

First of all, what is sparring supposed to achieve? What is the point of sparring? A good answer is that sparring is supposed to give you the environment to put your skills to the test against an uncooperative opponent, without choreography or planning.

Sparring can be fun; it doesn't have to be a silent and serious affair. However, it should be working towards a goal rather than just playing at random. Furthermore, fencers should try to use techniques that they have learned within the system they have studied – if they branch out and incorporate other techniques and concepts, at least in the beginning, then they are no longer putting to the test what they have learned from this discipline. For example, if someone with copious experience in modern Olympic fencing uses the broadsword like a modern sabre when he begins sparring, then the exercise of sparring is pointless. Likewise, if someone who has studied MMA decides to close and grapple rather than remaining at appropriate cutting distance, then the sparring is a pointless exercise.

The instructor (or the individual appointed as coach) has a very important role during sparring: to keep an eye on what is happening and to ensure that it stays on track, that it remains sensible, helpful and safe. If at any point the sparring becomes unsafe, or becomes a waste of time, then the job of the coach is to stop the play and bring it back to being a safe and useful activity.

One problem that many people experience when they start sparring for the first time (regardless of martial art) is that they do not know what to do. They may only have taken a single lesson, so they may not have learned more than a handful of actions, and these can easily flee the mind when someone is put under pressure. Some people take to sparring like a duck takes to water, but not everyone has this natural affinity.

Instructors should therefore be prepared to ease more reluctant students into the exercise, and should not throw students in at the deep end. Even students who do take to sparring quite naturally should not be thrown in at the deep end, because what will sparring fast and hard without proper technique achieve, other than bad habits, poor results and copious bruising?

Another common problem is that people do not know what they are trying to achieve. Are they trying to score the most points? What is the objective in sparring?

Obviously, the objective should be not to receive any hits. If you can conduct a fight without receiving any hits, then you would be "still alive". Even if you cannot land any hits on your opponent, not receiving any hits is a much better result than scoring lots of touches and receiving lots of hits in return.

When someone is having difficulty understanding the objective of sparring, explain it to him, and take the opportunity to revisit the issue for yourself. You may find that such explanations encourage you to perform better yourself!

A useful exercise is sparring in slow motion, perhaps at half speed. Over time, as students become more familiar and happier with the idea of what they are trying to do, the speed can increase, until eventually people are moving at full speed.

When I run courses for beginners, I try to avoid sparring for the first couple of lessons, so that my students have time to learn a few basic strikes and guards. Then, I run slow motion sparring at half speed as the introduction to sparring, and over a period of weeks gradually increase the maximum speed at which I will let my students spar. It might be eight or nine weeks into a twelve-week course of study before I would let students spar at full speed. This is to ensure that my students are learning their basic techniques and fundamentals properly, without picking up bad habits from diving into sparring too fast, too hard, too soon.

Sparring is very beneficial. It is important to give students the opportunity to spar, and also to take the opportunity to do so yourself. Without sparring, you do not have the opportunity to test what you have learned against an uncooperative opponent. The best way to make sparring useful is to have a coach who can provide feedback to the two training partners who spar with each other, or for the training partners to coach each other if an external person cannot be found. Feedback is immensely important, and sparring for the sake of sparring without any meaningful feedback is a waste of time for everyone involved if there is no coaching to help students learn where they went wrong and how they can improve.

It might be worth choosing not to spar for some length of time if you are new to historical fencing, or if you have just recently begun to work with the broadsword. If you have put together a study group with some friends, then it might be a very good idea to work solely on the drills and exercises from Roworth's treatise to begin with, until you have some properly formed skills. Then,

316

once your fundamentals are in place, try some sparring to see how everything holds up (or falls apart) under pressure, then work with the drills and exercises again until you shore up your deficiencies.

Whenever you engage in sparring, you must wear the appropriate protective gear. A fencing mask is a must-have item; there is no sparring that should take place without one. Other items such as padded jackets, groin guards, etc. can be useful to acquire over time. The more protective gear you wear, the harder you can hit each other; the harder you hit each other, the better you have to structure and form your parries. Hitting hard is not a problem as long as everyone is equipped and trained to handle it – hitting hard for the sake of hurting your training partners is immature and irresponsible, and should be stopped instantly. Choosing to wear minimal protective gear and spar gently with people is always an option, although it limits some of the lessons you can learn. As with everything in martial arts, embracing one extreme point of view is usually detrimental to your development, whereas working with various approaches and points of view gives you the best chance to develop as a well-rounded and skilful individual.

Sometimes it may feel as if you have plateaued, that you used to be able to win against your training partners but now you always lose. Ed Rogers notes that there is an interesting link between speed and technical skill:

> When technique is equal between two opponents, they revert to speed. When speed is equal, they revert back to technique.[507]

So if you are no longer winning at sparring, maybe it means that your training partners have improved their technical skills, so you need to do something about your physical fitness and athleticism. Or alternatively, if your training partners have become faster, perhaps you need to go back to basics and improve your technical skills and fundamentals for a while. There is no shame in going back to basics, and indeed such practice should be encouraged on a regular basis!

---

[507] Ed Rogers, 2013. Page 10.

Finally, when you engage in sparring, try to conduct yourself in the style that you have studied. If you want to recreate Scottish broadsword, then do your best to fight in that style. You have so much fascinating material at your fingertips, so many sources and historical accounts, so many good examples to follow. It would be a shame to ignore all of this and fight in the method of another system.

5.7   General Training Advice

Whenever you train, make sure that you change partners. It may seem comfortable to spend a whole training session practising with the same partner – but you will sabotage your development if you do this. You need to have the opportunity to practise with people of different heights, speeds, strengths and experiences.[508]

By changing partners regularly during training, you gain several important benefits, and you avoid several problems. It is good to have the opportunity to practise with people who are better than you, but it is not fun to be stuck with a beginner for a whole session (or someone who wants to "win" every drill, or someone who resorts to strength rather than skill, etc.), when you need input from someone at your level or better in order to improve. By changing partners regularly, the best training partners have the opportunity to train with everyone, and no one is stuck for a whole lesson with bad training partners.

Work on your basics in every session. There is no point in moving forward to more advanced techniques or sequences when you struggle to remember which cut comes from which direction, or if you cannot recover swiftly from the lunge. Spend some time working on your basic skills, as rigorously and diligently as possible, and this will pay dividends.[509]

---

[508] Ben Kerr. "Changing Partners in Martial Training." *Encased in Steel*, 2012, accessed 1st October 2014. http://historical-academy.co.uk/ blog/2012/04/ 20/changing-partners-in-martial-training/

[509] Sean Hayes. "The Importance of Skill Progressions." Brian Price, 2005. Page 90.

This practice does not need to be boring – indeed, it should not be boring! The instructor should make it interesting and engaging, and it should be an enjoyable part of the practice. There are all kinds of methods to make reviewing the basics a fun activity while still paying attention to skill development. Games are always a good option. If you have difficulty thinking of games, drills or exercises, then you can always find examples and ideas on historical fencing forums online.[510]

Working with left-handed practitioners is always difficult. It can become even more difficult, if not impossible, when you start teaching Taylor's 10 lessons.[511] There are two options to deal with this problem, broadly speaking: the instructor must try to accommodate the left-hander, and modify every single drill or exercise; or the instructor must implement a rule that everyone practises right-handed.

The first option is the more inclusive, less offensive and generally softer option. A lot of instructors choose to do this and it is not necessarily wrong, but it is not necessarily the best option either. The instructor will need to have three versions of every action, sequence and exercise in his mind: right-hander with right-hander (normal), left-hander with left-hander (reversed), and right-hander with left-hander (different). This makes the instructor's life more difficult and may lead to less helpful training for the left-hander and his partners.

Choosing to implement the rule that all students must practise right-handed is harsher and less inclusive, but it allows everyone to learn the same material and work with the same drills. It makes the instructor's life significantly easier, so that he can spend more of his time, energy and expertise helping people develop their skills rather than trying to come up with variations of basic drills to deal with differently-handed training partners. It gives all practitioners the opportunity to train with everyone else without a problem. Finally, it gives the left-handers the best

---

[510] "Drills Drills Drills." *HEMA Alliance Forum*, 2010, accessed 2nd August 2014. http://hemaalliance.com/discussion/viewtopic.php?f=3&t=157
[511] Christopher Scott Thompson, 2010. Page 47.

opportunity to learn: they may learn the basics, techniques and sequences right-handed, so they may train with everyone and gain the best practice and learn theory most thoroughly; then when sparring, they can choose which hand to use, and either develop their right hand further, or learn to apply their lessons to their other hand.

It is important for the instructor to develop a policy with regard to handedness early, and then to apply it equally and strictly. It is not acceptable to let some people train with their left hand yet prevent others from doing so.

Sometimes, the best fencer does not always win. Sometimes, no matter how much training someone has, the best fencer in the club might be bested by a raw beginner.[512] It can be a very upsetting and humbling experience. It is important not to be discouraged when this sort of thing happens, but instead to learn lessons from the experience. For example, experienced fencers may be used to their opponent making a single attack on the lunge, followed by a retreat under guard, as described by the sources. However, a beginner may not be aware of this convention, and may advance with a flurry of attacks – the experienced fencer thus needs to learn to deal with people who fight "properly", but also must learn to handle people who fight "differently". The goal should always be to keep one's self safe, to receive as few hits as possible, and so working with beginners can be a valuable experience.

In a similar fashion, you may decide to participate in a competition after some length of time training. You may well find that the people who place well in tournaments do not subscribe to your point of view in terms of what is "good fencing". Rather than complaining about the situation, or swearing off competitions, this is an opportunity to realise that everyone always has a different point of view and a different approach to situations. You can then move forward and improve your own training and skills so that you can keep yourself safe against any opponent.

---

[512] Ben Kerr, 2010. Page 34.

Ultimately, when fencing, you are responsible for keeping yourself safe. If you allow your opponent to hit you, then this is your failing. It is not your opponent's problem if he can hit you. If someone beats you, even if they use a style of which you disapprove, then you must learn how to defend yourself better. Eventually, once you have been beaten often enough, you should be able to hold your own against all kinds of different approaches, styles and fighters – and maybe you will be able to demonstrate what you believe to be excellent historical technique even as you keep yourself safe.

5.8   Words of Wisdom from History

The concluding section of this chapter will present a few interesting words of wisdom from history that are good to bear in mind, and can be quite profound.

Sir William Hope concludes one of his essays in his *New Method of Fencing* with the following statement:

> I shall therefore conclude (...) with my Three Great Fundamentals, whereupon I erected The Sword-Man's Vade-Mecum, which are CALMNESS, VIGOUR and JUDGEMENT.[513]

If you conduct yourself with calmness, vigour and judgement, then you will mark yourself as a skilled and considerate fencer. Be calm, don't become angry or aggressive; be assertive and in control. Act with vigour by seizing your opportunities whenever they present themselves, be assertive, and make attacks with athleticism when it is the right time to go forward. Exercise good judgement and avoid putting yourself into silly and dangerous situations. Once you attain the right mental approach and attitude towards fencing, you will find that you enjoy the experience more, along with achieving greater success and taking fewer bruises or injuries.

---

[513] Mark Rector, 2001. Page 162.

In Cassell's *Complete Book of Sports and Pastimes*, the following advice is given about fencing practice, and especially about sparring:

> But mind this: fencing is the most stupid amusement in the world if it is not practised properly. Two fellows standing opposite, and poking at each other with foils, would soon get tired of the operation; or, if they did not, they might keep on at it for six hours a day all their lives, and never improve a little bit. Nay, they would probably incapacitate themselves from ever learning to fence at all, such bad habits would they acquire.
>
> The first steps in learning anything are bound to be tedious; a grammar book is never lively reading. But unless you will mug a bit at grammar you will never learn the language properly, and if you slur over the rudiments of fencing you will never do any good at it. And even after you have attained a certain proficiency, it is very necessary to be careful how you indulge in loose play, especially with opponents inferior to yourself, or your hand will soon lose its cunning, and it will take a strict course of longeing to get it back again.[514]

This contains some very good advice with regards to sparring. Too much of a good thing can often become a bad thing; it is better to undertake proper practice, learn the fundamentals, and develop your basic skills properly. Then you will be able to practise for longer, with greater understanding, and take more pleasure from the activity when you can do it properly.

The same book contains a very salient note about protective gear:

> We cannot too strongly urge you never to fence without any one who is not properly protected, with mask and jacket at any rate. In a school, indeed, it is seldom or ever that you will find any one inclined to neglect such a natural precaution, but sometimes, in a private room, or in the hall of a country house, you may meet one, a tyro most probably in the art, who will propose a bout at fencing, and simply pull his coat off.

---

[514] *Cassell's Complete Book*, 1896. Page 142.

> There is nothing more distressing than to inflict an injury on a friend while mutually engaged in sport; and indeed, when such accidents occur, the one who is injured may generally be considered to have the best of it.[515]

There is a common saying that "it's all fun and games until someone loses an eye." Well, this holds especially true for fencing. Don't be an idiot: wear your fencing mask whenever you are working with a sword, and wear protective gear appropriate for the activity that you undertake. It's not worth it to receive an injury that could so easily have been avoided, and it's also not worth it to be the person who has to live with causing such injury for the rest of your life.

To conclude this chapter, in 1805 Thomas Mathewson penned an excellent description of what we can achieve through careful and diligent study of fencing:

> It is the cultivation of this art that unfetters the body, strengthens it and makes it upright; it is it that gives a becoming deportment and an easy carriage, activity and agility, grace and dignity; it is it that opportunely awes petulance, softens and polishes savageness and rudeness, and animates proper confidence; it is it which in teaching us to conquer ourselves, that we may be able to conquer others, imprints respect, and gives true valour, good nature and politeness; in fine, which makes a man fit for society.[516]

---

[515] Ibid. Page 143.
[516] Paul Wagner and Mark Rector, 2004. Page 225.

Appendix A: Timeline of the House of Angelo

This appendix contains a brief timeline and some notes pertaining to each of the professional fencing instructors in the Angelo family, describing important dates and publications. The vast majority of this information has been drawn from Aylward's *The House of Angelo* and *The English Master of Arms*, although additional dates have been drawn from the *Descendants of Angelo Domenico Tremamondo* website,[517] and from Hutton's *The Sword and the Centuries*.

Some dates are unclear, and are represented by "????" in the notes. Sometimes this is because my reference books disagree on the date; sometimes it is because my books simply did not mention the dates at all. Since not every entry is complete, it is not a perfectly useful resource, and more work could be done to improve the timeline and its entries. However, for students looking for a bit more information about the Angelo family and their school, this appendix should provide a useful springboard for understanding and further study.

I have used my best judgement to resolve situations where more than one date is given for an event. Sometimes this will be based on a preference for a published author over an unpublished author; sometimes it will be based upon the date of publication. Since there are several resources, each giving slightly different dates for many of these events, putting together this timeline has been very reminiscent of piecing together a jigsaw.

The nomenclature (Angelo I, II, III, and IV) is Aylward's chosen method of reference. It simplifies the matter of referring to any particular member of the family, especially since Angelos II, III and IV were all named Henry Charles!

---

[517]Gio Angelo. "Descendants of Angelo Domenico Tremamondo." *Descendants of Angelo Domenico Tremamondo*, 10th October 2007, accessed 14th August 2014. http://angelo.gen.nz/

Domenico Angiolo Malevolti Tremamondo (Angelo I)

- born in 1717
- trained fencing under Andrea Gainfaldoni (an Italian master)
- trained fencing under Teillagory (a French master)
- came to London in 1754
- married Elizabeth Johnson in 1755
- first child (Henry Charles William) born in 1756
- changed his name to Angelo in 1758
- second child (Florella Sophia) born in 1759
- appointed riding and fencing master to George, Prince of Wales (and later George III) and Edward, Duke of York in 1759
- received premises in Leicester Square to conduct business in 1759
- appointed fencing master to the two younger brothers of the Prince of Wales, the Dukes of Gloucester and Cumberland, in 1759
- third child (Anne Caroline Eliza) born in 1763
- opened his fencing school at Carlisle House in 1763
- published *École des Armes* in 1763
- republished *École des Armes* in 1765
- fourth child (Catherine Elizabeth) born in 1766
- republished *École des Armes* in 1767
- fifth child (Elizabeth Tremamondo) born in 1768
- appointed fencing master to the Prince of Wales (later to become George IV) and Prince Frederick in 1771
- sixth child (George Xavier) born in 1773
- handed over the Carlisle House school to his son Harry in 1780[518]
- died in 1802

---

[518] According to Aylward's *The House of Angelo*, this was 1785; according to Aylward's *The English Master of Arms*, published three years later, this date was 1780.

John Xavier Tremamondo

(brother of Domenico Angelo)
- born in 1720
- joined Domenico in London in 1753
- married in 1763
- moved to Edinburgh in 1763
- became principal instructor of the Royal Academy of Exercises in Edinburgh in 1763
- died in 1805

Leonard Maria Tremamondo

(brother of Domenico Angelo)
- born in 1725
- joined Domenico in London by 1763
- became Superintendent at the Carlisle Street school by 1764
- attempted to emigrate to India in 1777
- died in ????

Henry (Harry) Charles William Angelo (Angelo II)

(son of Domenico Angelo)
- born in 1756
- attended Eton in 1764
- left Eton in 1772, went to Paris to study under Motet
- returned to London in 1775
- married Mary Bowman in 1778
- first child (George Frederick) born in 1779
- second child (Henry) born in 1780
- took over the Carlisle House school in 1780
- moved the school to Opera House in 1783[519]
- third child (Edward Anthony) born in 1787
- published The School of Fencing in 1787
- took over premises in the Guildhall Tavern, King Street, in 1788
- fourth child (Henry William) born in 1789
- Opera House destroyed by fire in 1789
- opened new school in 13 Bond Street in 1789
- took his second son Henry as partner in the Bond Street school in 1794
- broadsword & sabre method adopted for the British Army in 1796
- became Instructor in the Sword to the City of London Light Horse Volunteers when they formed in 1796[520]
- published Hungarian and Highland Broadsword in 1798
- published The Guards and Lessons of the Highland Broadsword in 1799
- moved from Guildhall Tavern to Paul's Head Tavern, Cateaton Street, in 1802
- City of London Light Horse Volunteers disbanded in 1806
- closed his school in Cateaton Street in 1806
- became fencing-instructor to Haileybury College in 1806
- retired as fencing-instructor to Haileybury College in 1813
- became Instructor in the Cutlass to the Royal Navy in 1813
- professional career ended by injury in 1820
- handed over the Bond Street school to his son in 1820
- remained Instructor in the Cutlass to the Royal Navy until at least 1828
- published Reminiscences of Henry Angelo, vol. I in 1828
- published Reminiscences of Henry Angelo, vol. II in 1830
- published Angelo's Pic Nic; or, Table Talk in 1834
- died in 1835

---

[519] The House of Angelo suggests that this happened in 1785, just after Harry took over from Domenico; however, The English Master of Arms suggests that it happened in 1783, three years after Harry took over the school.
[520] According to The House of Angelo, the regiment was formed in 1794 and Angelo was given the role in that same year; according to The English Master of Arms, the regiment was formed in 1796.

Henry Charles Angelo (Angelo III)

(son of Harry Angelo)
- born in 1780
- became partner in the Bond Street school in 1794
- took over general management of the Bond Street school in 1802
- published *Naval Cutlass Exercise* in 1813[521]
- published *Rules and Regulations for the Infantry Sword Exercise* in 1817
- took over ownership of the Bond Street school in 1820[522]
- moved the Bond Street school to 32 St. James Street in 1830
- married Mary Anne Heathcote in 1831
- became Superintendent of Sword Exercise to the Army in 1833
- published *Instructions for the Sword Exercise* in 1835
- published *Infantry Sword Exercise* in 1842
- republished *Infantry Sword Exercise* in 1845
- published *Angelo's Bayonet Exercise* in 1849
- died in 1852

Edward Anthony Angelo

(son of Harry Angelo, brother of Henry Angelo)
- born in 1787
- became Major in ????
- became Army Instructor in the Sword in ????
- became Colonel in ????
- published *Observations on Angelo's Military Exercises formed by (the late) Henry Angelo* in 1853
- died in 1869

---

[521] *The House of Angelo* suggests that Harry Angelo published this treatise in 1814, but Edward Anthony Angelo published a book in 1853 that said his brother Henry was the source of this system.

[522] According to *The House of Angelo*, this was 1817; according to *The English Master of Arms*, published three years later, this date was 1820.

William Henry Angelo

(son of Harry Angelo, brother of Henry Angelo)
- born in 1789
- opened a fencing school in Oxford in ????
- closed his fencing school in Oxford in ????
- returned to London, became manager at the St. James Street school in ????
- died in 1853

Henry Charles Angelo (Angelo IV)

(son of Henry Charles Angelo)
- born in ????
- married Elizabeth Mary Bungay in ????
- first child (Charles Heathcote Angelo) born in 1834
- second child (Arthur Angelo) born in 1836
- third child (Michael Angelo) born in 1838
- fourth child (Stewart Richard Angelo) born in 1841
- took over the St. James Street school in 1852
- published *The Bayonet Exercise* in 1853
- died in 1866

William McTurk

- born in 1818
- took over the Bond Street school in 1866
- closed the Bond Street school in 1887
- died in 1888[523]

---

[523] Aylward notes in *The English Master of Arms* that Henry Charles (Angelo IV) died in 1866, so the school was taken over by McTurk, who ran it until the lease lapsed in 1897 (p217). However, Alfred Hutton, writing in 1901, notes in *The Sword and the Centuries* that McTurk died in 1888 (p258). I have chosen to use Hutton's date, since his book was written was much closer to the time of McTurk's death, so it is more probably correct. Going by Aylward's note that the lease lapsed before McTurk died, it may well have been a typographical error to have written "1897", and so 1887 would be a more reasonable estimate for that event.

Appendix B: Timeline of Publications

This appendix outlines a skeleton timeline of publications about the Scottish broadsword, British regimental broadsword and sabre, singlestick, regimental bayonet, and some influential smallsword and foil treatises. There are doubtless other treatises that could be included in this timeline, but this should give students a frame of reference to understand where any source falls in the general development of the teaching and practice of these systems, and can be a handy timeline to which to refer.

The list has been compiled primarily from notes in Aylward's *The English Master of Arms* and *The House of Angelo*, along with the *Schola Gladiatoria* forum and other online and print resources.

The commentary in square brackets following a title is my note of what martial systems are described within that book.

1687   Sir William Hope (published as: W.H., Gent)
        The Scots Fencing Master
        [Scottish smallsword, inspired by the French method]

1691   Sir William Hope (published as: W.H., Gent)
        The Sword-Man's Vade-Mecum
        [Scottish smallsword, inspired by the French method]

1692   Sir William Hope (published as: W.H., Gent)
        The Compleat Fencing Master
        [Scottish smallsword, inspired by the French method]

1692   Sir William Hope (published as: W.H., Gent)
        The Fencing-Master's Advice to his Scholar
        [Scottish smallsword, inspired by the French method]

1694   Sir William Hope (published as: W.H., Gent)
        The Sword-Man's Vade-Mecum (2nd ed)
        [Scottish smallsword, inspired by the French method]

1705   Sir William Hope (published as: W.H., Gent)
        The Sword-Man's Vade-Mecum (3rd ed)
        [Scottish smallsword, inspired by the French method]

1705   Henry Blackwell
        The English Fencing Master
        [English smallsword, copied from Hope]

1707   Sir William Hope
        A New, Short, and Easy Method of Fencing
        [Scottish smallsword, inspired by the broadsword]

1711   Zachary Wylde
        English Master of Defence
        [traditional English backsword]

1714   Sir William Hope
        A New, Short, and Easy Method of Fencing (2nd ed)
        [Scottish smallsword, inspired by the broadsword]

1715   H.B. (perhaps Henry Blackwell, perhaps William Hope?)
        A Few Observations on the Gladiators' Stage-Fighting
        [commentary upon the fighting of the gladiators]

1724   Sir William Hope
        Vindication of the True Art of Self-Defence
        [Scottish smallsword, inspired by the broadsword]

1728   Donald McBane
        The Expert Sword-Man's Companion
        [Scottish smallsword and sheering sword]

1729   Sir William Hope
        Vindication of the True Art of Self-Defence (2nd ed)
        [Scottish smallsword, inspired by the broadsword]

1729   Monsieur Valdin
        Art of Fencing
        [French smallsword]

1730   Henry Blackwell
        The Gentleman's Tutor for the Small Sword
        [Enlish smallsword, inspired by Italian rapier]

1735   Captain John Godfrey
        Treatise on the Useful Art of Defence
        [traditional English backsword]

1737   Captain James Miller
        A Treatise of the Gladiatory Art of Defence
        [traditional English backsword]

1746   Thomas Page
        The Use of the Broad Sword
        [Highland broadsword, and broadsword & targe]

1747   Captain John Godfrey
        Treatise on the Useful Art of Defence (2nd ed)
        [traditional English backsword]

1763   Dominico Angelo (Angelo I)
        École des Armes
        [French smallsword]

1765   Dominico Angelo (Angelo I)
        École des Armes (2nd ed)
        [French smallsword]

1767   Dominico Angelo (Angelo I)
        École des Armes (3rd ed)
        [French smallsword]

1771   A. Lonnergan
        The Fencer's Guide
        [French smallsword(?), English broadsword, spadroon]

1771   Jean Olivier
        Fencing Familiarised
        [French smallsword]

1780   Jean Olivier
        Fencing Familiarised (2nd ed)
        [French smallsword]

1781   John McArthur
        Army & Navy Gentleman's Companion
        [French smallsword]

1784   John McArthur
        Army & Navy Gentleman's Companion (2nd ed)
        [French smallsword]

1787   Henry (Harry) Angelo (Angelo II)
        The School of Fencing
        [French smallsword]

1790   A Highland Officer (Captain G. Sinclair)
        Anti-Pugilism
        [regimental Scottish broadsword, with singlestick / cudgel]

1791   Archibald MacGregor
        Lecture on the Art of Defence
        [traditional Scottish broadsword]

1791   William Thomson
        Memoirs of the Old Highlander, Serjeant D. MacLeod
        [memoirs of a Highland warrior]

1791   William Thomson
        Memoirs of the Old Highlander, Serjeant D. MacLeod (2nd ed)
        [memoirs of a Highland warrior]

1791   William Thomson
        Memoirs of the Old Highlander, Serjeant D. MacLeod (3rd ed)
        [memoirs of a Highland warrior]

1796   John Gaspard le Marchant
        Rules and Regulations of the Sword Exercise of the Cavalry
        [British cavalry sabre]

1798   Charles Roworth
        The Art of Defence on Foot with Broad Sword and Sabre
        [British regimental broadsword / sabre]

1798   Henry (Harry) Angelo and Son (Angelo II and III)
        Hungarian & Highland Broadsword
        [British regimental broadsword / sabre]

1799   Thomas Rowlandson (under the guidance of H. Angelo & Son)
        The Guards and Lessons of the Highland Broadsword
        [British regimental broadsword / sabre]

1800   Captain G. Sinclair
        Cudgel-Playing Modernized and Improved
        [regimental Scottish broadsword, with singlestick / cudgel]

1804 Charles Roworth
The Art of Defence on Foot with Broad Sword and Sabre (2nd ed)
[British regimental broadsword / sabre / spadroon]

1805 Thomas Mathewson
Fencing Familiarized; a New Treatise on the Art of the Scotch Broad Sword
[British regimental broadsword / sabre]

1805 Major Anthony Gordon
A Treatise on the Science of Defence
[British regimental sabre / spadroon]

1809 Joseph Roland
The Amateur of Fencing
[French smallsword, British broadsword / spadroon]

1810 John McArthur
Army & Navy Gentleman's Companion (3rd ed)
[French smallsword]

1813 Henry Angelo (Angelo III)
Naval Cutlass Exercise
[British naval cutlass]

1817 Henry Angelo (Angelo III)
Rules and regulations for the infantry sword exercise
[British regimental broadsword / sabre]

1823 George Roland
A Treatise on the Theory and Practice of the Art of Fencing
[French smallsword]

1824 George Roland
A Treatise on the Theory and Practice of the Art of Fencing (2nd ed) [French smallsword]

1824 Charles Roworth
The Art of Defence on Foot with Broad Sword and Sabre (3rd ed)
[British regimental broadsword / sabre / spadroon]

1827 George Roland
An Introductory Course of Fencing
[French smallsword]

1828 Henry (Harry) Angelo (Angelo II)
Reminiscences of Henry Angelo, vol. I
[memoirs of an English fencing master]

1830 Henry (Harry) Angelo (Angelo II)
Reminiscences of Henry Angelo, vol. II
[memoirs of an English fencing master]

1830 Captain F. Ghersi
Traité sur l'Art de Faire les Armes
[French smallsword]

1835 Henry Angelo (Angelo III)
Instructions for the sword exercise
[British regimental broadsword / sabre]

1837 George Roland
An Introductory Course of Fencing (2nd ed)
[French smallsword]

1837 Donald Walker
Defensive Exercises
[wrestling, foil, broadsword, singlestick, etc.]

1842 Henry Angelo (Angelo III)
Infantry Sword Exercise
[British regimental sabre]

1845 Henry Angelo (Angelo III)
Infantry Sword Exercise (2nd ed)
[British regimental sabre]

1846 George Roland
An Introductory Course of Fencing (3rd ed)
[French smallsword]

1849 Henry Angelo (Angelo III)
Angelo's Bayonet Exercise
[British regimental bayonet]

1853 Henry Angelo (Angelo III)
Angelo's Bayonet Exercise (2nd ed)
[British regimental bayonet]

1853   Henry Charles Angelo (Angelo IV)
The Bayonet Exercise
[British regimental bayonet]

1853   Richard Burton
A Complete System of Bayonet Exercise
[British regimental bayonet]

1854   George Roland
Introduction to Fencing and Gymnastics
[French smallsword]

1857   Henry Angelo (Angelo III)
Angelo's Bayonet Exercise (3rd ed)
[British regimental bayonet]

1863   John Walsh and J.G. Wood
Archery, Fencing and Broadsword
[civilian foil and broadsword]

1863   Richard Burton
A New System of Sword Exercise for Infantry
[British regimental sabre]

1880   John Musgrave Waite
Lessons in Sabre, Singlestick, Sabre and Bayonet
[British regimental sabre / singlestick]

1882   Alfred Hutton
Bayonet Fencing and Sword Practice
[British regimental bayonet and sabre]

1889   Alfred Hutton
Cold Steel: a Practical Treatise on the Sabre
[British regimental sabre]

1889   Alfred Hutton
Fixed Bayonets
[British regimental bayonet]

1890   R.G. Allanson-Winn & C. Phillipps-Wolley
Broad-Sword and Single-Stick
[British regimental broadsword / sabre / singlestick, etc.]

1889   Alfred Hutton
        Old Sword Play
        [historical fencing weapons]

1898   R.G. Allanson-Winn & C. Phillipps-Wolley
        Broad-Sword and Single-Stick (2nd ed)
        [British regimental broadsword / sabre / singlestick, etc.]

1903   R.G. Allanson-Winn & C. Phillipps-Wolley
        Broad-Sword and Single-Stick (3rd ed)
        [British regimental broadsword / sabre / singlestick, etc.]

1905   R.G. Allanson-Winn & C. Phillipps-Wolley
        Broad-Sword and Single-Stick (4th ed)
        [British regimental broadsword / sabre / singlestick, etc.]

1911   R.G. Allanson-Winn & C. Phillipps-Wolley
        Broad-Sword and Single-Stick (5th ed)
        [British regimental broadsword / sabre / singlestick, etc.]

1920   R.G. Allanson-Winn & C. Phillipps-Wolley
        Broad-Sword and Single-Stick (6th ed)
        [British regimental broadsword / sabre / singlestick, etc.]

1925   Scouting Association
        Master-at-Arms Badge for Boy Scouts
        [singlestick, quarterstaff, foil, boxing, etc.]

1931   R.A. Hay
        Singlestick: The Calpe Method and Rules
        [British singlestick]

Appendix C: Suggested Reading List

For students who are eager to learn more about the discipline of the Scottish broadsword, the Academy of Historical Arts recommends the following sources for further study:

The Expert Sword-Man's Companion, by Donald McBane

This publication from 1728 does not give an awful lot of information about the use of the broadsword, but the story is highly entertaining and shows a lot of interesting contextual information about Highland swordsmanship and the British Army in the late 17th and early 18th centuries.

The Use of the Broad Sword, by Thomas Page

This treatise from 1746 provides a lot of interesting information and lessons about the use of the broadsword, and also the broadsword and targe. Roworth drew heavily on this source when writing his own book *The Art of Defence on Foot*, so it can be helpful to read the material upon which Roworth built his system.

Anti-Pugilism, by Captain G. Sinclair

This is a treatise from 1790, one of the earliest sources on the use of the Scottish broadsword, written by an officer in the Black Watch. It can be a little difficult to interpret the different lessons, but it provides excellent material to study.

Lecture on the Art of Defence, by Archibald MacGregor

This lecture from 1791 contains valuable information – not always set plays or sequences, but a lot of good ideas, principles and concepts. It is worth reading to help you understand the fencing theory of the period.

Memoirs of the Life and Gallant Exploits of the Old Highlander, Serjeant Donald Macleod, by William Thomson.

This book from 1791 is very similar to the story of Donald McBane, in that there is not a lot of helpful information about Scottish broadsword in particular, but there is a lot of good contextual information concealed within a very entertaining and engaging story!

The Art of Defence on Foot, with the Broad Sword and Sabre: adapted also for the Spadroon, or Cut and Thrust Sword. Improved, and Augmented with the Ten lessons of Mr. John Taylor, Late Broadsword Master to the Light Horse Volunteers of London and Westminster, by Charles Roworth

This 1804 edition of Roworth's treatise is the fencing source transcribed within this study guide. It is worth studying in detail because it contains many clear descriptions and good lessons to help a beginner learn how to fence with the broadsword.

Fencing Familiarized; or, A New Treatise on the Art of the Scotch Broad Sword, by Thomas Mathewson

This treatise from 1805 provides some good lessons on the use of the broadsword, as well as some excellent philosophy.

The English Master of Arms, by J.D. Aylward

This is an incredibly valuable scholarly work from 1956, discussing the various English masters and their treatises from the 12th to the 20th centuries. This book does a sterling job of putting a lot of material into context, and is an invaluable resource for anyone wanting to study the subject more deeply.

Highland Martial Culture, by Chris Thompson

This book from 2009 is a slim volume, but it provides some excellent research into the Highland martial culture that can help to put the more fencing-focused broadsword treatises into perspective.

Appendix D: Glossary of Terminology

Lines

Inside:	for a right handed fencer, everything to the left of your sword
Outside:	for a right handed fencer, everything to the right of your sword
Line of defence:	the straight line that runs directly between you and your opponent
Centre-line:	see *line of defence*

Cuts

Cut 1:	descending strike from the right
Cut 2:	descending strike from the left
Cut 3:	rising strike from the right
Cut 4:	rising strike from the left
Cut 5:	horizontal strike from the right
Cut 6:	horizontal strike from the left
Cut 7:	vertically descending cut (in some sources)

Guards

Prime:	hanging guard, point angled down to the left
Seconde:	hanging guard, point angled down to the right
Tierce:	outside guard
Carte:	inside guard
Parade / Parry:	a defensive, covering action

Thrusts

Seconde:	a thrust in the *seconde* position, targeted beneath the opponent's arm
Tierce:	a thrust in the *tierce* position, targeted above the opponent's arm
Carte:	a thrust in the *carte* position, targeted above the opponent's arm
Low Carte:	a thrust in the *carte* position, targeted below the opponent's arm

Footwork

Advance:	a controlled, short movement forwards
Longe:	see *lunge*
Lunge:	elongating your stance, so that the front foot extends forwards, carrying the body forwards in order to make an attack.
Retreat:	a controlled, short movement backwards
Slip:	withdrawing the front leg or the sword arm
Traverse:	movement forward or backward

Weapons

Backsword:	a single-edged basket-hilted sword
Broadsword:	a double-edged basket-hilted sword
Clamshellit sword:	the two handed sword with clamshell hilt
Claymore:	the basket-hilted broadsword
Dirk:	the long knife of the Highlanders
Lochaber axe:	a form of long, two-handed axe
Sabre:	a single-edged sword
Shearing sword:	similar to the spadroon
Smallsword:	a sword designed primarily for thrusting
Spadroon:	a sword designed both for cutting and thrusting
Targe:	the round shield of the Highlanders
Twa-handit sword:	the two-handed sword

Singlestick and Cudgel

Singlestick:	a country game, with a single stick
Cudgel:	a country game, often with two sticks

Appendix E: Where to Find Equipment

In the UK and within Europe, Corsair's Wares is our preferred retailer for training equipment, supplements and shiny things. Fallen Rook Publishing is the publishing division of Triquetra Services (Scotland), an educational charity, and Corsair's Wares is the retail division. All proceeds from purchases through Corsair's Wares go towards supporting the charitable activities of Triquetra Services (Scotland) and therefore supporting Fallen Rook Publishing and the Academy of Historical Arts.

For practitioners in North America, our colleagues at Purpleheart Armoury provide an excellent source of training tools (including singlesticks), protective equipment and assorted supplements:

Bibliography

Websites and Online Documents:

"A Brief History of Robert Dover's Games." *Robert Dover's Cotswold Olimpicks*, accessed 20th July 2014. http://www.olimpickgames.com/history/

"Altmark Incident." *Wikipedia*, accessed 21st July 2014. http://en.wikipedia.org/wiki/Altmark_Incident

"Ergrundung Ritterlicher Kunst der Fechterey (Andre Paurñfeyndt)." *Wiktenauer*, accessed 21st July 2014. http://wiktenauer.com/wiki/Ergrundung_Ritterlicher_Kunst_der_Fechterey_(Andre_Paurñfeyndt)

"Fencing at the 1904 Summer Olympics." *Wikipedia*, accessed 11th July 2014. http://en.wikipedia.org/wiki/Fencing_at_the_1904_Summer_Olympics

"Fencing at the 1904 Summer Olympics – Men's Singlestick." *Wikipedia*, accessed 11th July 2014. http://en.wikipedia.org/wiki/Fencing_at_the_1904_Summer_Olympics_–_Men%27s_singlestick

"Living Tradition ALIVE!" *Singlestick Yahoo Group*, 2003, accessed 21st July 2014. https://groups.yahoo.com/neo/groups/Singlestick/conversations/topics/964

"Master at Arms Activity Badge." *The Scouting Association*, accessed 11th July 2014. http://members.scouts.org.uk/supportresources/576/master-at-arms-activity-badge

"Singlestick." *Encyclopaedia Britannica*, accessed 20th July 2014. http://www.britannica.com/EBchecked/topic/546008/singlestick

"UK Singlestick 1900's to 2003." *Singlestick Yahoo Group*, 2003, accessed 21st July 2014. https://groups.yahoo.com/neo/groups/Singlestick/conversations/topics/997

Angelo, Gio. "Descendants of Angelo Domenico Tremamondo." *Descendants of Angelo Domenico Tremamondo*, 10th October 2007, accessed 14th August 2014. http://angelo.gen.nz/

Jenkins, Bethan. "Contextualising Western Martial Arts." *Linacre School of Defence*, January 2007, accessed 2nd August 2014. http://www.sirwilliamhope.org/Library/Articles/Jenkins/Contextualising.php

Thompson, Christopher Scott. "The Three Kingdoms Backsword Tradition and the Origins of the Highland Broadsword Manuals." *Cateran Society*, accessed 6th July 2014. http://www.cateransociety.com/The%20Three%20Kingdoms%20Backsword%20Tradition%20and%20the%20Origins%20of%20the%20Highland%20Broadsword%20Manuals.htm

Thompson, Christopher Scott. "A Brief History of Scottish Swordplay." *Cateran Society*, accessed 6th July 2014. http://www.cateransociety.com/A%20Brief%20History%20of%20Scottish%20Swordplay.htm

Tyler, Wat. "The Last Boarding Action of the Royal Navy." *WW2 People's War*, 6th November 2003, accessed 21st July 2014. http://www.bbc.co.uk/history/ww2peopleswar/stories/53/a1979553.shtml

Forum Threads:

"Differences between military and civilian saber styles?" *Schola Forum*, 2013, accessed 11th July 2014. http://www.fioredeiliberi.org/phpBB3/viewtopic.php?f=3&t=20644

"An article on Thomas Page and my views." *Schola Forum*, 2014, accessed 2nd August 2014. http://www.fioredeiliberi.org/phpBB3/viewtopic.php?f=3&t=20989

"Singlestick myths." *Schola Forum*, 2013, accessed 2nd August 2014. http://www.fioredeiliberi.org/phpBB3/viewtopic.php?f=31&t=20705

"Difference between 'singlestick' and 'cudgelling' (1832)." *Schola Forum*, 2013, accessed 2nd August 2014. http://www.fioredeiliberi.org/phpBB3/viewtopic.php?f=31&t=20465

"The house of Angelo and Highland swordsmanship." *Schola Forum*, 2013, accessed 2nd August 2014. http://www.fioredeiliberi.org/phpBB3/viewtopic.php?f=31&t=20130

"Roworth... or not?" *Schola Forum*, 2013, accessed 2nd August 2014. http://www.fioredeiliberi.org/phpBB3/viewtopic.php?f=31&t=20280

"Drills Drills Drills." *HEMA Alliance Forum*, 2010, accessed 2nd August 2014. http://hemaalliance.com/discussion/viewtopic.php?f=3&t=157

Facsimiles / Transcriptions / Translations:

Cassell's Complete Book of Sports and Pastimes: Being a Compendium of Out-Door and In-Door Amusements. London: Cassell and Company, 1896.

Master-at-Arms Badge for Boy Scouts. Glasgow: James Brown & Son, 1925.

The Mirror of Literature, Amusement, and Instruction: containing Original Essays. Vol. VII, London: J. Limbird, 1826.

The Mirror of Taste and Dramatic Censor. Vol. I, Philadelphia: Bradford and Inskeep, 1810.

The Mirror of Taste and Dramatic Censor. Vol. II, Philadelphia: Bradford and Inskeep, 1810.

Allanson-Winn, R.G. and C. Phillips-Wolley. *Broad-Sword and Single-Stick*. London: G. Bell and Sons, 1911.

Angelo, Henry. *Hungarian and Highland Broadsword, twenty-four plates designed by Thomas Rowlandson.* London: Henry Angelo, 1798.

Angelo, Henry. *Reminiscences of Henry Angelo, With Memoirs of his late Father and Friends, including numerous original Anecdotes and curious Traits of the most celebrated Characters that have flourished during the last Eighty Years*. Vol. II, London: Henry Colburn and Richard Bentley, 1830.

Hay, R.A. *Singlestick: The Calpe Method and Rules.* Gibraltar, January 1931.

Hone, William. *The Every-Day Book; or, Everlasting Calendar of Popular Amusements.* Vol. II, Part II, London: Hunt and Clarke, 1827.

Hone, William. *The Year Book of Daily Recreation and Information.* London: Thomas Tegg, 1832.

Hutton, Alfred. *Bayonet-Fencing and Sword-Practice.* London: William Clowes and Sons, 1882.

MacGregor, Archibald. *MacGregor's Lecture on the Art of Defence.* Paisley: J. Neilson, 1791.

Mathewson, Thomas. *Fencing Familiarized; or, A New Treatise on the Art of the Scotch Broad Sword: Shewing The Superiority of that Weapon, when opposed to an Enemy Armed with a Spear, Pike or Gun and Bayonet.* Salford, W. Cowdroy, 1805.

Page, Thomas. *The Use of the Broad Sword.* Norwich: M. Chase, 1746.

Peek, Hedley, and F.G. Aflalo. *The Encyclopaedia of Sport.* Vol. II, London: Lawrence and Bullen, 1898.

Rowlandson, Thomas. *The Guards and Lessons of the Highland Broadsword.* London: Henry Angelo, 1799.

Roworth, Charles. *The Art of Defence on Foot, with the Broad Sword and Sabre: uniting the Scotch and Austrian Methods into one Regular System.* London: T. Egerton, 1798.

Roworth, Charles. *The Art of Defence on Foot, with the Broad Sword and Sabre: adapted also for the Spadroon, or Cut and Thrust Sword. Improved, and Augmented with the Ten lessons of Mr. John Taylor, Late Broadsword Master to the Light Horse Volunteers of London and Westminster.* London: T. Egerton, 1804.

Roworth, Charles. *The Art of Defence on Foot, with the Broad Sword and Sabre: adapted also for the Spadroon, or Cut and Thrust Sword. Improved, and Augmented with the Ten lessons of Mr. John Taylor, Late Broadsword Master to the Light Horse Volunteers of London and Westminster.* New York: H. Durell, 1824.

Sinclair, George. *Anti-Pugilism or The Science of Defense Exemplified in Short and Easy Lessons for the Practice of the Broad Sword and Single Stick.* London: J. Aitkin, 1790.

Sinclair, George. *Cudgel-Playing Modernized and Improved; or, the Science of Defense, Exemplified in Short and Easy Lessons for the Practice of the Broad Sword and Single Stick, on Foot.* London: J. Bailey, 1800.

Somerville, William. *Hobbinol, or the Rural Games. A Burlesque Poem, in Blank Verse.* London: J. Stagg, 1740.

Waite, J.M. *Lessons in Sabre, Singlestick, Sabre & Bayonet, and Sword Feats.* London: Weldon and Co., 1880.

Walker, Donald. *Defensive Exercises; comprising Wrestling, as in Cumberland, Westmoreland, Cornwall, and Devonshire; Boxing, both in the usual mode and in a simpler one; Defence Against Brute Force, by various means; Fencing and Broad Sword, with simpler methods; the Gun and its Exercise; the Rifle, and its exercise; &c. &c. &c.* London: Thomas Hurst, 1840.

Books and Miscellaneous Documents:

Amberger, J. Christoph. *The Secret History of the Sword.* Orange, CA: Multimedia Books, 1999.

Aylward, J.D. *The House of Angelo.* London: The Batchworth Press, 1953.

Aylward, J.D. *The English Master of Arms.* London: Routledge & Kegan Paul, 1956.

Bezdek, Richard. *Swords and Sword Makers of England and Scotland.* Boulder: Paladin Press, 2003.

Browne, James. *History of the Highlands and of the Highland Clans.* Vol. II, part 1. Glasgow: A Fullarton & Co, 1834.

Cannan, Fergus. *Scottish Arms and Armour.* Oxford: Shire Publications, 2009.

Castle, Egerton. *Schools and Masters of Fencing.* Mineola, NY: Dover Publications, 2003.

Collins, Tony, John Martin and Wray Vamplew. *Encyclopedia of Traditional British Rural Sports*. Abingdon: Routledge, 2005.

Copinger, Walter Arthur. *The Law of Copyright, in Works of Literature and Art*. Clark, NJ: The Lawbook Exchange, 2012.

Crosnier, Roger. *Fencing with the Foil*. London: Faber and Faber, 1967.

Daeschner, J.R. *True Brits: A Tour of 21st Century Britain in All its Bog-Snorkelling, Gurning and Cheese-Rolling Glory*. London: Arrow, 2004.

Deazley, Ronan. *Rethinking Copyright: History, Theory, Language*. Cheltenham: Edward Elgar Publishing, 2006.

Farrell, Keith and Ben Kerr. *AHA Health and Safety Policy*. Academy of Historical Arts, 2012.

Farrell, Keith and Alex Bourdas. *German Longsword Study Guide*. Glasgow: Fallen Rook Publishing, 2013.

Fittis, Robert Scott. *Sports and Pastimes of Scotland*. Paisley: Alexander Gardner, 1891.

Gaunt, Peter. *Oliver Cromwell*. Oxford: Wiley-Blackwell, 1996.

Gibson, John. *Traditional Gaelic Bagpiping, 1745-1945*. Montreal: McGill-Queen's University Press, 1998.

Grant, James. *Legends of the Black Watch*. London: Routledge, Warne, and Routledge, 1859.

Grosart, Alexander. *Annalia Dubrensia, or Celebration of Captain Robert Dover's Cotswold Games*. Manchester: Charles E. Simms, 1877.

Harrington, Peter. *Culloden 1746: The Highland Clans' Last Charge*. London: Osprey, 1991.

Hughes, Thomas. *Tom Brown's School Days*. Cambridge: Macmillan and Co., 1857.

Hutton, Alfred. *The Sword and the Centuries*. London: Greenhill Books, 2003.

Johnson, Samuel. *A Journey to the Western Islands of Scotland*. London: W. Strahan, 1775.

Jones, James Rees. *Country and Court: England 1658–1714*. London: Edward Arnold, 1978.

Keltie, John. *History of the Scottish Highlands, Highland Clans and Scottish Regiments*. Vol. 1, Edinburgh: A. Fullerton, 1875.

Kirchner, Paul. *Dueling with the Sword and Pistol*. Boulder: Paladin Press, 2004.

Lawson, John Parker. *Historical Tales of the Wars of Scotland*. Vol. 1, Edinburgh: A. Fullerton, 1839.

Lawson, John Parker. *Historical Tales of the Wars of Scotland*. Vol. 2, Edinburgh: A. Fullerton, 1839.

Lawson, John Parker. *Historical Tales of the Wars of Scotland*. Vol. 3, Edinburgh: A. Fullerton, 1839.

Lawson, John Parker. *Historical Tales of the Wars of Scotland*. Vol. 4, Edinburgh: A. Fullerton, 1839.

Logan, James. *The Scottish Gael*. London: Smith, Elder and Co, 1831.

MacKechnie, John. *The Dewar Manuscripts. Volume 1: Scottish West Highland Folk Tales*. London: William MacClellan, 1963.

MacLean, J.P. *An Historical Account of the Settlements of Scotch Highlanders in America Prior to the Peace of 1783 together with notices of Highland Regiments and Biographical Sketches*. Glasgow: John MacKay, 1900.

Maugham, Robert. *A Treatise on the Laws of Literary Property*. Clark, NJ: The Lawbook Exchange, 2008.

Mazansky, Cyril. *British Basket-Hilted Swords*. Woodbridge: Boydell Press, 2005.

McLoughlin, Jim and David Gibb. *One True Enemy*. Kent Town: Wakefield Press, 2012.

Magnusson, Magnus. *Scotland: The Story of a Nation*. London: HarperCollins, 2000.

Melville, Herman. *White-Jacket: or the World in a Man-of-War*. New York: United States Book Company, 1892.

North, Charles Niven McIntyre. *The Book of the Club of True Highlanders. A record of the dress, arms, customs, arts and sciences of the Highlanders.* Vol. I, London: C.N. McIntyre North, 1880.

North, Charles Niven McIntyre. *The Book of the Club of True Highlanders. A record of the dress, arms, customs, arts and sciences of the Highlanders.* Vol. II, London: C.N. McIntyre North, 1881.

Oakeshott, Ewart. *European Weapons and Armour From the Renaissance to the Industrial Revolution*. Woodbridge: Boydell Press, 2012.

Oram, Richard. *The Kings and Queens of Scotland*. Stroud: Tempus Publishing, 2004.

Prebble, John. *The Darien Disaster*. New York: Holt, Rinehart and Winston, 1968.

Price, Brian. *Teaching & Interpreting Historical Swordsmanship*. Highland Village: Chivalry Bookshelf, 2005.

Rector, Mark. *Highland Swordsmanship: Techniques of the Scottish Swordmasters*. Union City: Chivalry Bookshelf, 2001.

Rogers, Ed. *Advanced Fencing Techniques: Discussions with Bert Bracewell*. Ramsbury: The Crowood Press, 2013.

Stewart, David. *Sketches of The Character, Manners and Present State of the Highlanders of Scotland; with details of The Military Service of the Highland Regiments*. Vol. 1, 3rd edition, Edinburgh: Archibald Constable and Co, 1825.

Taylor, William. *The Military Roads in Scotland*. Isle of Colonsay: House of Lochar, 1996.

Thompson, Christopher Scott. *Highland Martial Culture*. Boulder: Paladin Press, 2009.

Thompson, Christopher Scott. *Highland Broadsword: Lessons, Drills, and Practices*. Boulder: Paladin Press, 2010.

Thompson, Christopher Scott. *Broadsword Academy*. 1st edition, Lulu, 2012.

Thomson, William. *Memoirs of the Life and Gallant Exploits of the Old Highlander, Serjeant Donald Macleod*. 2nd edition, London: Peterborough-House Press, 1791.

Thomson, A.T. *Memoirs of the Jacobites of 1715 and 1745*. Vol. 1, London: R. Bentley, 1845.

Thomson, A.T. *Memoirs of the Jacobites of 1715 and 1745*. Vol. 2, London: R. Bentley, 1845.

Thomson, A.T. *Memoirs of the Jacobites of 1715 and 1745*. Vol. 3, London: R. Bentley, 1846.

Thorburn, W.A. *Uniform of the Scottish Infantry: 1740 to 1900*. Edinburgh: Scottish United Museum Service, 1970.

Timperley, Charles Henry. *A Dictionary of Printers and Printing*. London: H. Johnson, 1839.

Vivian, E. Charles. *With the Scottish Regiments at the Front*. London: Hodder and Stoughton, 1914.

Wagner, Paul and Mark Rector. *Highland Broadsword: Five Manuals of Scottish Regimental Swordsmanship*. Highland Village: Chivalry Bookshelf, 2004.

Wallace, John. *Scottish Swords and Dirks: An illustrated Reference Guide to Scottish Edged Weapons*. Harrisburg, PA: Stackpole Books, 1970.

Theses and Journal Articles:

"When were swords last used in combat by the British armed forces?" *Daily Mail*. 20th June 2003.

"Britain Orders Altmark Captured Off Norway." *The Evening Independent*. Vol. 33, no. 90, St. Petersburg, FL, 17th February 1940.

"Bravery of Men of Cossack." *The Straits Times*. Final edition, 19th February 1940.

Budgell, Eustace. *The Spectator* 161 (September 1711).

Czajkowski, Zbigniew. "Domenico Angelo – A Great Fencing Master of the 18th Century and Champion of the Sport of Fencing." *Studies in Physical Culture and Tourism* 17(4) (2010): 323-334.

Darling, Anthony. "The Earliest Scottish Basket-Hilted Swords." *Man at Arms* (July/August 1979): 18-23.

Hay, R.A. "Singlestick – I. History." *The Sword* (Winter 1949): 150-153.

Hay, R.A. "Singlestick – II. History." *The Sword* (Spring 1950): 37-40.

Kerr, Ben. "A Comparison of the Training and Application of Techniques Between War and the Formal Duel in Scotland from 1690 to 1740." MLitt Thesis, University of Glasgow, September 2010.

Madden, Locker. "Cudgels & Singlestick." 1986.

Blog Articles:

Bober, David. "'The Navy's here!' HMS Cossack frees prisoners from the Altmark, 16 February 1940." *Naval Matters*, 16th February 2014, accessed 21st July 2014.
http://navalmatters.wordpress.com/2014/02/16/the-navys-here-hms-cossack-frees-prisoners-from-the-altmark-16-february-1940/

Bourdas, Alex. "Muscular imbalances in the hip, part 1." *Encased in Steel*, 2013, accessed 2nd October 2014. http://historical-academy.co.uk/blog/2013/07/05/muscular-imbalances-in-the-hip-part-1/

Bourdas, Alex. "Muscular imbalances in the hip, part 2." *Encased in Steel*, 2013, accessed 2nd October 2014. http://historical-academy.co.uk/blog/2013/07/12/muscular-imbalances-in-the-hip-part-2/

Bourdas, Alex. "Upper Crossed Syndrome." *Encased in Steel*, 2013, accessed 2nd October 2014. http://historical-academy.co.uk/blog/2013/08/02/upper-crossed-syndrome/

Chouinard, Maxime. "Singlestick... Or is it? Stick sports in America, an investigation." *I Don't Do Longsword*, 23rd December 2013, accessed 20th July 2014. http://hemamisfits.wordpress.com/2013/12/23/singlestick-or-is-it-stick-sports-in-america-an-investigation/

Farrell, Keith. "Analysing Historical Sources." *Encased in Steel*, 2011, accessed 1st October 2014. http://historical-academy.co.uk/blog/2011/09/17/analysing-historical-sources/

Gordon, Jonathan. "Henry Angelo's Ten Lessons of Highland Broadsword (Part 1)." *The HEMAists*, 9th August 2014, accessed 1st October 2014. http://thehemaists.com/2014/08/09/henry-angelos-ten-lessons-of-highland-broadsword-part-1/

Kerr, Ben. "Changing Partners in Martial Training." *Encased in Steel*, 2012, accessed 1st October 2014. http://historical-academy.co.uk/blog/2012/04/20/changing-partners-in-martial-training/